About the Author

John Warwick Montgomery

John Warwick Montgomery is Professor-at-Large at the Institute for Theology & Law in Irvine, California and Strasbourg, France. He holds eight earned degrees besides the LL.B.: the A.B. with distinction in philosophy (Cornell University; Phi Beta Kappa), B.L.S. and M.A. (University of California at Berkeley), B.D. and S.T.M. (Wittenberg University, Springfield, Ohio), M.Phil. in Law (University of Essex, England), Ph.D. (University of Chicago), and the Doctorat d'Université from Strasbourg, France. He is author of over one hundred scholarly journal articles and more than thirty-five books in English, French, Spanish, and German. He is internationally regarded both as a theologian (his debates with the late Bishop James Pike, death-of-God advocate Thomas Altizer, and situation-ethicist Joseph Fletcher are historic) and as a lawyer (barrister-at-law of the Middle Temple and Lincoln's Inn, England; member of the California, Virginia, and District of Columbia Bars and the Bar of the Supreme Court of the United States). He is one of only a few persons to have received the Diploma of the International Institute of Human Rights *cum laude*, and was the Institute's Director of Studies from 1979 to 1981. From 1980 to 1983 he served on the Human Rights Committee of the California Bar Association. He is honored by inclusion in *American Law, The Directory of American Scholars, Contemporary Authors, Who's Who in France, Who's Who in Europe, International Scholars Directory* (editor-in-chief), and *Who's Who in the World.*

Human Rights and Human Dignity

John Warwick Montgomery

Distributed by Word Publishing
Dallas London Sydney Singapore

Second Printing (with revisions)

Library of Congress Cataloging in Publication Data

Montgomery, John Warwick.
Human rights and human dignity.

Bibliography: p.
Includes indexes
I. Civil rights—Religious aspects—Christianity
2. Man (Christian theology). 3. Apologetics—
20th century. I. Title.
BT738.15M65 1986 241'.62 86—4057

ISBN 0-945241-02-X

Place of Printing *Printed in the United States of America*

Editor Steven W. Webb, Probe Books

Designer Louise Bauer

Cover Hanlon & Associates

What Is Probe?

Probe Ministries is a nonprofit corporation whose mission is to help reclaim the primacy of Christian thought and values in Western culture through media, education, and literature. In seeking to accomplish this mission, Probe provides perspective on the integration of the academic disciplines and historic Christianity. The members and associates of the Probe team are actively engaged in research as well as lecturing and interacting with students and faculty in thousands of university classrooms throughout the United States and Canada on topics and issues vital to the university student.

Probe Books should be ordered from WORD PUBLISHING: Dallas, London, Sydney, Singapore; 1-800-433-3340 or in Texas at 1-800-792-3270. Further information about Probe's materials and ministries may be obtained by writing to Probe Ministries, International, P.O. Box 801046, Dallas, Texas 75204.

To
the memory of

ARTHUR HENRY ROBERTSON

of the Middle Temple, Barrister
Professeur Associé,
University of Paris
Secretary-General,
International Institute of Human Rights

and—most important—Friend.

Contents

List of Illustrations

Book Abstract

In his address, "Human Rights: An Appeal to Philosophers" (1952), jurist Felix Cohen declared: "Today the peoples of the world ask for philosophical vision in meeting the practical question: What rights, if any, can a man claim of me not because he is my brother or my neighbor or my colleague or co-religionist or fellow-citizen, but just because he's human?" One could hardly imagine a more important question, and this book attempts to answer it.

The order of discussion (though not the conclusions) follows Huber and Tödt's programmatic in their *Menschenrechte—Perspecktiven einer menschlichen Welt* (1977): "We must first of all consider the legal character of human rights and then turn to the ethical problems. When we have done that we shall be able to engage in theological reflection." Theological reflection will in fact turn out to be the only route by which the dilemmas of human rights can be resolved.

From a survey of existing human rights protections in international and domestic law and the labors of governmental and nongovernmental organizations in the field, we tackle the philosophical problems of defining and justifying human rights. The inadequacies of philosophical solutions will point the way to a transcendent answer, which, however, will not be found either in several major religious alternatives or in religious natural rights theory. Biblical revelation, examined in the light of accepted canons of legal evidence, will provide the needed foundation for human rights, and the closing chapters expound its transcendent vision of human dignity.

chapter one

Human Rights: The Need

Human rights stands revealed as an idea that polarizes, encouraging uncritical support and also extreme reaction from both secularists and religionists. But the stark reality of man's inhumanity to man in our time compels us to take the human rights movement with the utmost seriousness.

Today the term *human rights* is part of everyone's vocabulary. It has become essential coin of the realm for the statesman, the journalist, and the man on the street. Philosopher R. G. Frey does not exaggerate when he writes:

> There is a tendency today to clothe virtually all moral and social issues in the language of rights, in order to be able to demand one's due. Thus, issues about the treatment of children have given way to children's rights, about the demands of (some) women to women's rights, about the despoliation of forests to the rights of trees or of the environment generally, about abortion to the rights of the foetus

and the rights of the mother, and about the farming and treatment of animals to animal rights.

Declarations of human rights have come into their own, and an increasing number of things—from emigration to a minimum income, housing, a job, old age insurance, and medical assistance—are now simply ceded us as of right. Some groups derive further sustenance from such declarations: some homosexuals, for example, now maintain that certain (proposed) pieces of legislation infringe their human right to freedom of sexual expression. What we should do about the poor of the Third World is increasingly transformed into an issue of the poor having a moral right to subsistence (in its various facets) against us and our incomes and food supplies. Political liberals in the United States have swept up human rights into their ideologies, and governments around the world are taken to task on their treatment of their citizens.

So far as I can see, our alleged moral rights have proliferated to such an extent that they now run to every corner of our lives, and only someone completely out of touch with American social and political reality today would find surprising a friend's claim that we have a moral right to a society free of nuclear power plants and free of the terrible noises of modern contraptions, or Alan Gewirth's claim that we have a moral right not to have cancer inflicted upon us.

Moral rights have become the fashionable terms of contemporary moral debate, and one interest group after another has moved to formulate its position in terms of them. The reason is obvious: to fail to cast its wants in terms of rights and so to fail to place itself in a position to demand its due is to disadvantage itself in this debate *vis-à-vis* other groups which show no such reluctance. And what group is prepared to do that?[1]

No One Is Against Human Rights

Not only has the vocabulary of human rights become universalized: the concept seemed until very recently to have everyone's approbation. During my tenure as Director of Studies at the International Institute of Human Rights in Strasbourg, France, I observed that—whatever the severe political and ideological differences among faculty, staff, and students from some sixty countries, including Iron Curtain and Third World nations—everyone without exception favored human rights! To have opposed human rights would have been *lèse majesté:* the equivalent of an American's opposing apple pie, motherhood, or the flag.

. . . Or *Almost* No One

But the use of human rights as a shibboleth and a political football has devalued its coinage. Former President Carter spoke much about human rights, yet left a yawning chasm between aspirations and reality. The U.S.S.R., while roundly condemning American interference in Vietnam's inherent right to national self-determination, invaded Afghanistan. The French-Spanish political cartoonist Puig Rosado cynically pictures naked modern man about to eat the cheese of human rights, blithely unaware that it is the bait of a mouse- (in fact, man-) trap (see figure 1).[2]

Figure 1
"Droits de l'homme" by Puig Rosado

Rights Can Be Dangerous

That the dangers of rights theory are not purely theoretical can be seen in the animal rights movement—one of the more recent spin-offs of human rights activism. Here is a recent article from *The [London] Times*[3]:

Wolf released by rights group kills two sheep

A wolf was among animals released from the Palace Rigg country park near Cumbernauld in central Scotland early yesterday by intruders. It killed two sheep before it was tranquillized and returned to captivity.

A man claiming to represent the Animal Liberation Army telephoned the BBC.

Eighteen pens and cages were thought to have been forced open and it was believed last night that five foxes, two wild cats and, possibly some mink and polecats were still at large.

And animal rights advocate John Aspinall, speaking on "Man's Place in Nature," unabashedly declares:

> I must say that I am among that group of people who, to borrow an expression from Teddy Goldsmith, would regard a demo-catastrophe as an eco-bonanza. In other words, I would be very happy to see 3½ billion humans wiped from the face of the earth within the next 150 or 200 years and I am quite prepared to go myself with this majority. Most of you sitting here are redundant in every possible sense of the word. Even though you may be the vanguard of the youth politik of the "rights of animals", you are as redundant and as unnecessary as are most other human beings, when you come to it.

I would just remind you of Professor Revie's famous article in the *Scientific American*, in which he described the increase of man's population from one million years ago, when he estimated the world population of human beings at 100,000 (which is a third of the population of Nottingham) to a time after the discovery of fire, when the figures started to soar to today's four billion. If that is not redundancy, if that is not a burden of unnecessary bio-mass, then I don't know what is!

Let us all look forward to the day when the catastrophe strikes us down! With what resounding applause would the rest of nature greet *our* demise![4]

Here Rosado's "man-trap" of rights does not seem so farfetched.

Theologians Raise Their Critical Voices

Extremism among rights movement activists together with growing cynicism vis-à-vis human rights has afforded traditionalist critics of the movement an opportunity to express their ideological opposition. Thus, neo-Thomist French philosopher Michel Villey finds the earliest definition of "human rights" in atheist Thomas Hobbes' *Leviathan* and identifies four consequences of human rights theory: individualistic anarchy, collectivistic totalitarianism, the economic triumph of bourgeois capitalism, and the political triumph of dictatorial socialism.[5] Among American Evangelicals, T. Robert Ingram writes a volume characteristically titled *What's Wrong with Human Rights*,[6] and lawyer John W. Whitehead tells us that "from a biblical perspective, 'rights' as such do not exist."[7] Even responsible theologians desiring to integrate Christian faith and human rights now point up those aspects of the human rights movement apparently deserving of Christian critique. Professor Marc Lienhard of the University of Strasbourg declares, for example, that

The Christian theologian, and particularly the Protestant theologian, will have a number of reservations to make about this vision of things. He will contrast the optimistic conception, which sees man endowed with reason and capable of fulfilling his potentialities and achieving a just social order, with the biblical message of the subjection of man and the reality of sin. He will also question an over-individualistic interpretation of the traditional conception of human rights. If the prime consideration is to preserve the right of the individual in relation to society and the State, does this not overlook the social status of man whom Aristotle defined as a «political animal»? Is there not a temptation to lapse into egotism or abstraction? It will also be pointed out that the Bible contains no irrefutable evidence of the idea that man, by the mere fact of his existence, is entitled to make a number of fundamental demands or claims on other members of society. There are admittedly commandments which tie in with human rights (e.g. Matthew 7:12; Romans 13:7), though rather than rights or demands written into man's nature as such, what is involved is an attitude towards one's neighbour, not of inherent rights but of responsibility and service due to him. The Christian ethic is, on principle, directed towards others because it reposes on love.[8]

But is this all that need be said? Does cynicism on the part of the disenchanted secularist or ideological critiques by Christians offer an adequate response to the contemporary human rights movement? I sincerely doubt it. Too much is at stake, and just how much is at stake can be seen from an understanding of the movement's origins and the context in which it operates today.

How the Modern Human Rights Movement Began

Contemporary concern for human rights grew directly in reaction to man's inhumanity to man during the Second World War. Axis atrocities, especially the wanton destruction of six million Jews, other religious minorities, and political dissidents, impelled the Allies to conduct War Crimes Trials at Nuremberg and in the Eastern theater of war. These trials were specifically designed to punish violations of human dignity. This is how Associate Justice Robert H. Jackson of the U.S. Supreme Court, who served as Chief Counsel for the United States at Nuremberg, put it in his closing address:

> It is common to think of our own time as standing at the apex of civilization, from which the deficiencies of preceding ages may patronizingly be viewed in the light of what is assumed to be "progress." The reality is that in the long perspective of history the present century will not hold an admirable position, unless its second half is to redeem its first. These two-score years in this twentieth century will be recorded in the book of years as one of the most bloody in all annals. Two World Wars have left a legacy of dead which number more than all the armies engaged in any war that made ancient or medieval history. No half-century ever witnessed slaughter on such a scale, such cruelties and inhumanities, such wholesale deportations of peoples into slavery, such annihilations of minorities. The terror of Torquemada pales before the Nazi inquisition. These deeds are the over-shadowing historical facts by which generations to come will remember this decade. If we cannot eliminate the causes and prevent the repetition of these barbaric events, it is not an irresponsible prophecy to say that this twentieth century may yet succeed in bringing the doom of civilization.
>
> Goaded by these facts, we have moved to redress the blight on the record of our era.[9]

Efforts to "redress the blight" led to the drafting of the United Nations' *Universal Declaration of Human Rights* and covenants on civil and political as well as economic, social, and cultural rights, and also to the creation of the European Convention on Human Rights and the legal machinery for its implementation. The late A. H. Robertson, one of the founding fathers of the European system of human rights protection, wrote:

> The same factors which led the United Nations to concern itself with the protection of human rights

produced a similar result, but to a more marked degree, in Europe.

The first of these factors was a natural reaction against the Nazi and Fascist systems which had provoked the Second World War and wreaked such havoc on the rights of millions during the course of that conflict. The denial of human rights was not merely an incidental result of their machinations; it was a deliberate instrument of policy and even a pre-condition of their establishment. If the dictators had built their empires by suppressing individual freedoms, then an effective system for the protection of human rights would constitute a bulwark against the recrudescence of dictatorship.

Secondly, during the immediate post-war years, it soon became evident that the democratic systems of Western Europe needed protection not only against a possible revival of the pre-war dictatorships but also against another kind of regime which had established its hold on half the continent. The principles championed by the French Revolution, some of which had already been enshrined in the Bill of Rights and even in Magna Carta, were menaced by a new political philosophy in which the dictatorship of the proletariat gave all power to the state and reduced the individual to a cypher. The preservation of democracy and the maintenance of the rule of law necessitated foundations, in the words of Robert Schuman, "on which to base the defence of human personality against all tyrannies and against all forms of totalitarianism." Those foundations were the effective protection of the rights of man and fundamental freedoms.[10]

Inhumanities of the Right and of the Left

As Professor Robertson stresses, the end of World War II by no means wrote the last line to the catalog of twentieth-century "cruelties and inhumanities" described by Justice Jackson at Nuremberg. If anything, human rights violations since the end of the Second World War have multiplied geographically and ideologically. National Socialism represented the extreme right politically—one of its most indefatigable enemies being Marxist Communism, at the far left of the political spectrum. Yet the U.S.S.R. and other Marxist states have produced one of the worst human rights records of modern times. I have set forth that record elsewhere; here I shall merely repeat the categories of established violations: repression of political and ideological dissent; disregard of religious freedoms; class discrimination and the persecution of minorities, especially Jews; unjustifiable emigration controls; and inhuman punishments.[11]

Human Rights Violations Are Universal

The Uganda of Idi Amin Dada demonstrated that the Third World was fully capable of modern barbarism. Apartheid policy in the Union of South Africa has been universally condemned[12]—and South African scholars have countered with a massive publication showing the extent of human rights violations in the very countries condemning South Africa.[13] Responsible organizations such as the International Commission of Jurists and Amnesty International have recorded the appalling extent and universality of contemporary man's inhumanity toward his fellows. Thus—to take but one example—Amnesty International has just published a report evidencing the practice of torture or ill-treatment of prisoners in nearly one hundred countries; the report leaves no doubt that in the past four years prisoners have been tortured or cruelly treated in at least one out of every three countries in the world.[14]

Human Rights Are Too Important to Be Dismissed

Inescapably one is forced to the conclusion that whatever the deficiencies of human rights thinking, the movement draws attention to a global problem of overwhelming significance. The area of human rights is not merely a forum for academic or theological critique; it is (or should be) a battleground in which human dignity is at stake and the enemy is no less than barbarism. Joel Feinberg is surely correct when he maintains that human rights are indispensably valuable possessions. A world without [them], no matter how full of benevolence and devotion to duty, would suffer an immense moral impoverishment. Persons would no longer hope for decent treatment from others on the ground of desert or rightful claim. Indeed, they would come to think of themselves as having no special claim to kindness or consideration from others, so that whenever even minimally decent treatment is forthcoming they would think themselves lucky rather than inherently deserving, and their benefactors extraordinarily virtuous and worthy of great gratitude.

Rights, on the other hand, are not mere gifts or favors, motivated by love or pity, for which gratitude is the sole fitting response. A right is something a man can *stand* on, something that can be demanded or insisted upon without embarrassment or shame. . . . A world with claim-rights is one in which all persons, as actual or potential claimants, are dignified objects of respect, both in their own eyes and in the view of others. No amount of love and compassion, or obedience to higher authority, or *noblesse oblige,* can substitute for those values.[15]

The Task

The task, therefore, is twofold: to establish a system of effective human rights protection (the practical task), entailing the satisfactory identification and justification of human rights (the theoretical task). Logically, to be sure, the second precedes the first, but—as we shall quickly see—the human rights field affords an illustration of the adage that life is bigger than logic: human rights activity goes on with considerable vitality and positive results in spite of the most serious theoretical shortcomings. We shall consequently begin with an overview of the juridical and other means currently available for the protection of human rights internationally and nationally, and endeavor to see how well they work. Then we will face the underlying issue of what properly constitutes—and may ultimately be capable of justifying—human dignity.

chapter two

Human Rights: Existing Protections*

The critics of human rights activity generally do not know what they are talking about. That is to say, they are woefully ignorant of the scope and depth of international and domestic mechanisms for the protection of human rights. This chapter is devoted to an overview of existing protections on the international, regional, and national level, and not only includes a survey of the developed international and comparative law of human rights but also touches on international humanitarianism law, the work of nongovernmental organizations in the field, and the contributions of Christian groups to the promotion and protection of human dignity.

---

*If you are already acquainted with the existing systems of human rights protection, or are primarily interested in the philosophical and theological analysis of human rights questions, you may wish to proceed immediately to chapters 3 through 8. Some readers may prefer to use chapter 2 for reference purposes—to refresh the memory on certain unfamiliar aspects of the current human rights scene.

A Challenge to the Reader

Few fields of endeavor make as extensive demands on the student as does the field of human rights. One must be prepared to face, *inter alia,* the most detailed practical questions of international and comparative law, as well as the most fundamental problems of philosophy and theology. Though (as noted at the end of chapter 1) the philosophical issues of defining and justifying human rights ought strictly to precede matters of human rights practice, we shall take up the latter first. This will have the advantage of providing an overview of existing human rights protections—thereby eliminating at the outset the notion that the field consists of "sound and fury, signifying nothing." But at the same time it will immerse the nonlegally trained reader in an unfamiliar environment of treaties and international juridical machinery. Professor Claude of the University of Maryland does not exaggerate: "The intricacies of declarations, conventions, committees, commissions, and covenants can easily stagger the imagination of human rights scholars, delight the international bureaucrats, and bedevil human rights victims."[16] I shall do my best to smooth the reader's way, and frequent bibliographic citations will offer collateral help where desired.[17]

Three Generations of Rights

Though I postpone until the next chapter a thoroughgoing discussion of the proper meaning of the expression "human rights," one can obtain a satisfactory denotative, working definition of the term by the use of French jurist Karel Vasak's categorization of "three generations" of human rights. Vasak, who assisted Nobel Prize winner René Cassin in the founding of the International Institute of Human Rights, Strasbourg, and later served as Director of Human Rights for UNESCO, employs the three watchwords of the French Revolution—*liberté, égalité, fraternité*—to categorize human rights protections and aspirations.

Civil and Political Rights

The "first generation" of human rights, suggested by the concept of "liberty," embraces the civil and political freedoms that were so central to the eighteenth-century French and American revolutions. Citizens of the United States are particularly well-acquainted with "first-generation" human rights, for they are given constitutional status in the first ten amendments to the Federal Constitution and are also enshrined in the constitutions of all the States of the Union (in contrast with France, where the Declaration of the Rights of Man, though possessing great moral force, has no legal status). These "civil liberties," as they are generally termed on the national or domestic level, are extensively incorporated into the Universal Declaration of Human Rights (Articles 2–21), and are largely of a *negative* rather than positive nature (freedom *from* the abuse and misuse of political authority). Indeed, these rights epitomize the Western liberal-political ideal of individual freedom over against the encroaching power of the state. In a very real sense, they are the concrete recognition of the truth of Christian historian Lord Acton's aphorism, "Power corrupts, and absolute power corrupts absolutely."[18]

Economic, Social, and Cultural Rights

"Second-generation" human rights refer to economic, social, and cultural rights. Underlying them is the concept of social equality. They take their modern origin particularly from the socialist traditions of the early nineteenth century (what Engels called "utopian socialism, an infantile disorder") and from the Marxian socialism of the latter part of that same century. Articles 22–27 of the Universal Declaration of Human Rights catalog many of these rights: the right to work, to rest, and to leisure (paid holidays), and the right to social security, to education, and to the protection of one's inventions and literary achievements. These second-generation rights are often regarded as more *positive* than negative in nature, not in the sense of their having a higher value, but in that their realization is difficult (in some cases virtually impossible) without affirmative state action. Thus they entail a more positive role for the state and have been especially emphasized (at least in theory) by Eastern-bloc nations.

Solidarity Rights

The "third generation" of human rights—so-called "solidarity" rights—are more recent, nebulous, and controversial. Emphasis on them has come about in the last ten years as individuals and nations, particularly under the impetus of the Third World, have become aware of the essentiality of global cooperation for survival. These rights are an expanding category which at least include national self-determination, the right to economic and social development, the right to benefit from the "common heritage of mankind" (sharing of the earth's resources and wealth—as embodied in the recent United Nations Law of the Sea Treaty[19]), the right to a healthy environment, the right to peace, and the right to humanitarian disaster relief.[20] Third-generation rights have received the criticism that owing to their vagueness and lack of effective legal status, emphasis upon them can water down the more well-established first and second-generation rights—to the detriment of the entire field of human rights;[21] and there is little doubt that they are being used as a political agenda by Third World and Marxist states for achieving propaganda advantages and doubtful redistributions of wealth. But surely at minimum the third-generation rights point to the truth that our world has become a global village in which, as Christian poet and preacher John Donne classically put it, every man's death diminishes every other man: "Never send to know for whom the bell tolls; it tolls for thee."[22]

In sum, the content of human rights today reflects the deepest values and concerns of the three most influential interest groups on the face of the planet: the politically individualistic West (first-generation rights), the socially orientated, collectivistic East (second-generation rights), and the developing Third World (third-generation rights). Predictably, each interest group tends to regard its own favored category of rights as self-evident and the others as suspect! In this book I hope to present a more balanced perspective.

Human Rights Not Pie in the Sky

Are the human rights to which attention has just been given no more than expressions of the ideals of interest groups? Do they have any legal teeth in them? Are they in any realistic sense *enforceable*? One receives the impression that many believe human rights to be nothing but a pious hope. True, the effectiveness of legal enforcement varies with the category of the human right in question: Third-generation rights have relatively little enforceability, second-generation rights possess rather more legal strength, and first-generation rights have the greatest legal sanctions behind them. But taken as a whole, the human rights field can offer an impressive array of juridical, political, and sociological machinery to buttress its claims. We shall now survey that machinery—necessarily in a cursory fashion—beginning with the universal protections offered in the United Nations system, proceeding to regional systems of human rights protection, internal (domestic) state protection, and finally nongovernmental machinery such as the humanitarian law activity of the International Committee of the Red Cross and the work of Christian organizations.

The UN System

As indicated in chapter 1, the inhumanities of World War II led both to the Nuremberg War

Crimes Trials and to the formation of the United Nations. It was only natural that the protection of human rights should have been a major concern among the UN's founding fathers. We shall briefly note the following areas of the UN system that pertain to human rights: (1) the Universal Declaration, (2) the Covenants, (3) the Commission, (4) the Conventions, and (5) UNESCO, the ILO, and the High Commissioner for Refugees.

(1) The Universal Declaration

The Universal Declaration of Human Rights, whose major author, René Cassin, locates its ideological roots in the Ten Commandments,[23] is a comprehensive enumeration of first- and second-generation human rights, with a foreshadowing of third-generation rights in Article 28. Since, however, the Universal Declaration is not a treaty, but constitutes only a proclamation of the General Assembly, it is generally regarded as having no legal force. Over against this viewpoint, the argument has been vigorously advanced by Professor John P. Humphrey, former Director of the UN Division of Human Rights, that the emergence of a juridical consensus evidenced by state practice subsequent to its original proclamation has made the Declaration binding as part of the law of nations. Humphrey's case is worth quoting *in extenso:*

> The conventional wisdom of certain jurists is to say that, while the Declaration may have great moral and political authority, it is merely, as its preamble says, "a common standard of achievement" and has no binding legal force; the Covenants on the other hand are binding on all states that ratify them. It is unlikely, however, that the Covenants will ever be universally ratified; but if, by the development of a new rule of customary international law, the Declaration has become an authentic interpretation of the human rights provisions of the Charter, then its provisions, like those of the Charter itself, bind all member states. If, in addition to becoming an

authentic interpretation of the Charter the Declaration has become part of the customary law irrespective of the Charter, it is also binding on all states whether they are members of the United Nations or not. This would mean amongst other things, that if, for example, a country were expelled from the Organization under article six of the Charter, that country would nevertheless continue to be bound by the Declaration. In countries, moreover, in which the customary law of nations is part of the law of the land, the Declaration could be invoked before and applied by national courts.

The question of the juridical character of the Universal Declaration is not, therefore, an idle academic exercise. If the thesis set forth in this essay that it has become part of the customary law of nations is correct then its adoption by the United Nations on 10 December, 1948, was a far greater achievement than its authors could ever have imagined.[24]

(2) The Covenants

Whether Humphrey's argument can be sustained or not—and in any case one must never underestimate the important influence on world public opinion exercised by General Assembly resolutions and other "political" (as compared with legal *in stricto sensu*) activities of the UN[25]—the two UN human rights Covenants, the International Covenant on Civil and Political Rights and the International Covenant on Economic, Social, and Cultural Rights, *are* treaties and are binding under international law on all those states that have ratified them.[26]

To be sure, a nonratifying state is not legally bound by the provisions of a treaty it has not ratified; the United States, for example, which has ratified neither Covenant, is not bound by them. Here we encounter a sad fact that will be met with repeatedly: the U.S., owing to a combination of misplaced pride in its own Bill of Rights, chauvinism, and not a little nationalistic isolationism, has one of the worst nonratification records where international human rights treaties are concerned. Of course, one can reply that, in line with Jesus' parable of the two sons in Matthew 21, it is better not to ratify human rights treaties but nonetheless observe human rights, rather than—like the U.S.S.R.—to ratify them and then not observe them. Surely, however, the ideal is *both* to ratify *and* to support the human rights and fundamental freedoms that these treaties embody!

What sanctions exist against violations of the Covenants? It should be emphasized that individual redress is possible only in a single instance: where the violating state is not merely a state-party to the Covenant on Civil and Political Rights but has also ratified its Optional Protocol; in this single case an individual subject to the jurisdiction of the state in question can lodge a complaint against it. The UN Human Rights Committee deals with these complaints. For fairly obvious ideological and practical reasons, the U.S.S.R. and its satellites have not ratified the Optional Protocol. Considering the few years which have gone by since the Optional Protocol entered into force in 1976, Professor Sohn is doubtless correct in his judgment that "it is too early to comment on the system established by the Optional Protocol."[27]

Besides the Optional Protocol procedure, a reporting system exists under the Civil and Political Covenant: the states-parties to that Covenant undertake to submit to the Human Rights Committee reports on the difficulties faced in their implementation of the Covenant. Moreover, states-parties may specifically recognize the competence of the Human Rights Committee to hear interstate complaints under Article 41—but since this offers the possibility that the state in question will find itself in the posture of a defendant, Eastern-bloc states such as the U.S.S.R. have not done so.

For sanctions relating to the Covenant on Economic, Social, and Cultural Rights, an Optional Protocol procedure for individual redress does not exist, doubtless because of the impracticality of dealing in that way with rights such as adequate education and leisure time, which can seldom be attained overnight. Instead, the Economic and Social Council (ECOSOC) set up an independent biennial reporting system, whereby states-parties report how they are implementing human rights. A state will first report on Articles 6–9, then two years later on Articles 10–12, and two years after that on Articles 13–15—so that every six years each state-party will have made a full report of its endeavors to improve the level of economic, social, and cultural rights among its people.

(3)
The Commission

But reporting systems have obvious inadequacies: states prefer to report the good, not the bad; reports can disappear into the mass of UN documentation; reports seldom lead to concerted action.[28] The Human Rights Commission (totally distinct from the Human Rights *Committee* referred to above) and its related Sub-Commission go well beyond the reportorial function. The Commission is the UN's central policy organ in the human rights field. Though its members act as representatives of their states, not in an individual capacity (and thus are politically orientated), their activity has transcended the political, especially in the *ad hoc working groups and committees* formed to investigate human rights conditions in particular countries (e.g., Chile, El Salvador, Guatemala, Bolivia, South Africa, Namibia). The specialists in these working groups examine and evaluate information submitted to them, conduct interviews, and even make on-site visits (though only with the consent of the governments concerned).[29]

The Sub-Commission on Prevention of Discrimination and Protection of Minorities consists of persons serving only in their individual capacities, not as representatives of their particular countries. Under the important procedure that was established in 1970 by *ECOSOC Resolution 1503*, the Sub-Commission and its working groups deal with "consistent patterns of gross and reliably attested violations of human rights." No remedies are available for individuals per se, but numerous communications alleging individual violations are often the best proof that gross and massive violations of human rights are indeed occurring in a given country. Moreover, *any* state that is a UN member can be the subject of investigation, since ECOSOC 1503 is a resolution of the Council, not a treaty provision only applicable to those who ratify it.

The effectiveness of the procedure is illustrated by its success in bringing about the release of some five hundred Greek political prisoners during the reign of the colonels. At first there was reticence to publicize the details of violations, but since 1980 the powerful weapon of public opinion has been used to correct abuses. Thus, the Commission, following Resolution 1503 procedure, recommended that ECOSOC declare that Malawi failed "to co-operate with the Commission on Human Rights in the examination of a situation said to have deprived thousands of Jehovah's Witnesses in Malawi of their basic human rights and fundamental freedoms between 1972 and 1975, which failure constrains the Economic and Social Council to publicize the matter."[30]

(4) The Conventions

Besides the Covenants on Civil and Political, and on Economic, Social, and Cultural Rights, other important UN treaties have advanced the cause of human rights. Particularly deserving of mention are the Convention on the Prevention and Punishment of the Crime of Genocide, the International Convention on the Elimination of All Forms of Racial Discrimination, and the International Convention on the Suppression and Punishment of the Crime of Apartheid. The United States, incredibly, has ratified only the first of these treaties, and its ratification of the Genocide treaty in February 1986 occurred after thirty-six years of Senate opposition.[31] The Genocide Convention expressly refers disputes between the parties relating to its construction, application, or fulfillment to the International Court of Justice at The Hague. The Racial Discrimination Convention utilizes an attractive procedure for fact-finding and conciliation and benefits from a permanent UN Committee on the Elimination of Racial Discrimination.[32] There is an investigatory group on apartheid established by the General Assembly, and the Assembly, by a similar exercise of power deriving inherently from the UN Charter, has also created an investigatory group on the Israeli-occupied territories, where numerous allegations of discrimination have arisen.

(5) UNESCO, the ILO, and the UNHCR

UNESCO has recently come under severe and deserved criticism for financial irresponsibility and for the anti-Western bias of its current Secretary-General, Senegalese Muslim Amadou Mahtar M'Bow. The United States withdrew its membership on 31 December 1984, and Britain, after putting UNESCO on notice that it was likely to follow suit unless radical changes took place in UNESCO's orientation and finances, did in fact pull out of the organization a year later (31 December 1985).

But the present crisis must not obscure UNESCO's valuable long-term contributions to international human rights. UNESCO publications, especially in promoting the teaching of human rights, are indispensable. As an independent specialized UN body acting under its own charter, UNESCO deals with human rights primarily from a moral rather than a legal standpoint, and it is limited to its spheres of expertise (education, information, science, culture). At the same time, the UNESCO Convention against Discrimination in Education is a legal instrument, whose construction or application, when in dispute, is subject to the judgment of the International Court of Justice. A Protocol to that Convention establishes a Conciliation and Good Offices Commission to seek amicable settlement of disputes pertaining to discrimination in education.[33] Indeed, some twenty-five other conventions, most of which concern human rights, have been adopted by UNESCO, and these are implemented by a reporting system (not, however, one allowing for individual complaints or petitions). In 1978 a complaint procedure available to individuals and nongovernmental organizations came into operation, but its "confidential nature . . . , the emphasis on friendly settlement, and the lack of strong implementation or oversight mechanisms suggest that the procedure is rather weaker than some of those established by the ILO or regional organizations."[34]

The International Labor Organization (ILO) has also received much bad press for its politicizings of activity within its sphere. In 1977 the United States withdrew from the organization—but rejoined in 1980 on the ground that ILO officials had returned the organization to its original purposes. As with UNESCO, legitimate criticism should not blind us to the importance of the ILO's human rights contributions. The ILO adopts and implements international labor standards by way of conventions and recommendations dealing with such vital matters as freedom of association and the right to organize labor unions, collective bargaining, the abolition of forced labor and discrimination in employment, child labor, women in the labor market, on-the-job safety, social security, and migrant workers. The ILO supervises ratified conventions, evaluating both "representations" (Article 24 of the ILO Constitution) and "complaints" (Article 26) against states-parties for nonobservance of the 156 ILO conventions. Apart from these sophisticated contentious procedures, which have been resorted to more and more in recent years, the ILO's Committee of Experts and Conference Committee have long engaged in noncontentious supervisory activity. From 1968 to 1978,

> direct contacts took place in 28 countries (15 in Latin America, 7 in Africa, 4 in Asia, and 2 in Europe). They involved discussion of some 222 cases of shortcomings in the application of ratified conventions. In 115 cases, affecting 23 countries, the Committee of Experts subsequently noted improvements. Other results have included improved compliance with various constitutional obligations and additional ratifications.[35]

The office of UN High Commissioner for Refugees, located in Geneva, Switzerland, was established early in 1951 by the General Assembly; it has received two Nobel Peace Prizes. Its present incumbent is Poul Hartling, a Danish Lutheran pastor[36]—which should not appear strange, since the Book of Exodus tells us that Moses, in obedience to God's command, established cities of refuge; also, "Constantine made all Christian churches places of asylum, and the concept of general asylum emerged from the Benedictine Order of Cluny in the tenth century when the 'Peace of God' was invoked during combat for church environs and their inhabitants."[37]

The year 1951 also marked the appearance of the Convention Relating to the Status of Refugees, whose definition of refugee was expanded by a Protocol in 1967. Uncommonly, the United

States has ratified this Convention (strictly speaking, the U.S. ratified the Protocol only, but the Protocol incorporates the Convention by reference). The Convention does not expressly require a state to admit refugees to its territory, but it does offer substantial protections to those who have in fact entered as refugees. Thus, for example, Article 31 exempts refugees from normal immigration procedures when they have escaped at the peril of their lives or personal freedom; and Article 33 sets forth the basic principle of *nonrefoulement*—that a state shall not "expel or return" a refugee to a territory "where his life or freedom would be threatened on account of his race, religion, nationality, membership of a particular social group or political opinion." Exceptions are made for those who would endanger the receiving country's security or those convicted of serious crime, and, in general, the Convention excludes from the ambit of its protections war criminals or those who have committed crimes against humanity (as defined in the international agreements underlying the War Crimes Trials at the end of World War II).

Evaluation of the UN System

The not inconsiderable human rights accomplishments of United Nations agencies and organizations demonstrate that ideological differences are no absolute bar to successful work in the field—as long as pragmatic overlap exists between ideological opponents. We might diagram the point as shown in figure 2, using the U.S. and the U.S.S.R. as examples.

But it also follows that the greater the real or imagined ideological differences, the less the achievement; and one should be aware that in such cases achievements may exist on paper only, disguised by the semantic ambiguities of the treaty, convention, or agreement. Moreover, when a state is committed, as are Socialist bloc states, to a philosophy of policy-orientated legal instrumentalism (the end justifies the means), signing an agreement does not necessarily mean what it purports to mean.[38] The Helsinki Final Act (though admittedly not a treaty) is a good illustration: citizens of the U.S.S.R. who have attempted to rely on their government's signature to it as a basis for emigration have received a rude awakening. Marxist states are also gun-shy of what they view as international interference in their domestic affairs, and prefer to stress the "promotion" rather than the "protection" of human rights. Socialist opposition has been the chief roadblock to creating a centralized UN High Commissioner for Human Rights, analogous to the exceedingly effective UN High Commissioner for Refugees.[39]

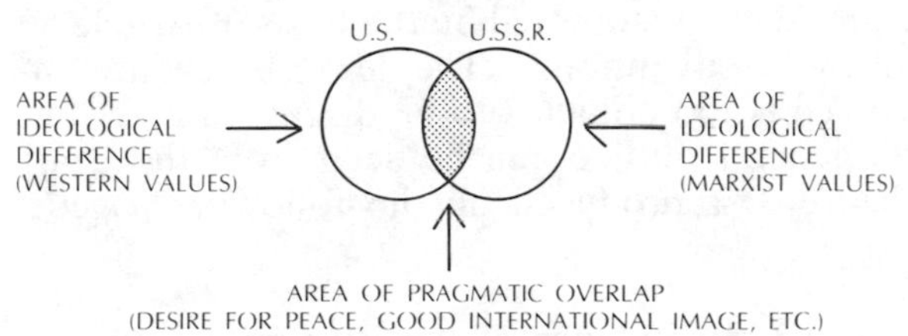

Figure 2
Ideological Differences & Pragmatic Overlap in the UN Human Rights System

Moving now from global to regional systems of human rights protection, we find—as would be expected—that where the ideological common ground is the most extensive, there the human rights protections are the most effective.

The European System

By all odds, the most sophisticated system of human rights protection in the world today is the European system, centering in Strasbourg, France. This system arose, as did the UN system, in reaction to the inhumanities of the Second World War, but unlike the UN system, it provides a tribunal (a kind of supreme court of human rights) before which cases can be brought for legal resolution and judgment. Those states that have ratified the European Convention on Human Rights (1950)[40] are bound to implement the tribunal's judgments. If (as in seventeen of the twenty-one member states) the state-party to the Convention has also made a specific declaration under Article 25 that it accepts the right of individual petition, then that state can be brought before the European Commission and the European Court of Human Rights by "any person, nongovernmental organisation or group of individuals claiming to be the victim of a violation by one of the High Contracting Parties of the rights set forth in this Convention." Compensation for material and even nonmaterial damage can be ordered on the basis of Article 50 of the Convention.[41] The legal procedure involved is too complex to be discussed here, but its general outline can be seen from the chart (figure 3) reproduced on the following page.[42]

The Thalidomide Case

The jurisprudence of the European Commission and Court of Human Rights now spans three decades, with decisions and judgments bearing on the whole range of civil liberties guaranteed in the European Convention. A particularly striking example of the workings of the system is the well-known London *Sunday Times* thalidomide case: when the House of Lords refused, while the original thalidomide case was under review, to permit the *Sunday Times,* on pain of contempt, to publish an article detailing the negligence of the defendant company who sold thalidomide to the victims of that

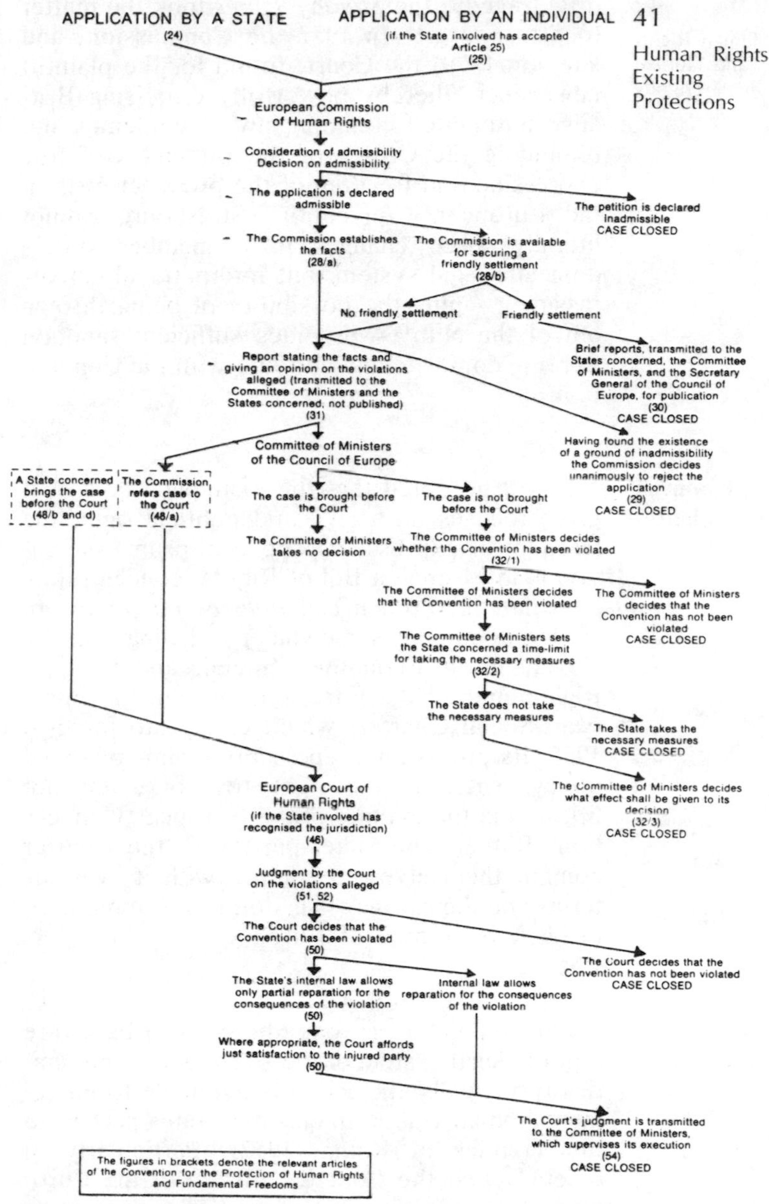

Figure 3
Procedural Flow-chart of the European Human Rights System

drug tragedy, the *Sunday Times* took the matter to Strasbourg.[43] In 1977 the Commission, and later (in 1979) the Court, found for the plaintiff newspaper, thereby powerfully criticizing Britain's antiquated common law of contempt and reminding the Crown of the principles of free expression and freedom of the press set forth in the European Convention. Strasbourg cannot literally force changes in a member state's domestic legal system, but international embarrassment—plus the possibility of being thrown out of the club[44]—provides sufficient sanction to bring domestic law into line with the Convention.

The European Social Charter

It will be noted that the example I have just given focuses on a civil and political right, the freedom of expression. The European Convention is in essence a Bill of Rights, concentrating on what the French call *libertés publiques*. In 1961 a document somewhat paralleling the UN Covenant on Economic, Social, and Cultural Rights entered the European system: the European Social Charter, which came into force in 1965. Its provisions, representing aims of social policy, such as the right to work, are not litigated in the manner of the European Convention. Rather, the states-parties to the Charter commit themselves to comply with its various terms and their progress in doing so is monitored inside the Council of Europe.[45]

EEC Protections

For completeness, one should also be aware that the legal system of the European Communities (principally the EEC) is available to implement human rights among the states-parties to the Treaties of Rome (1957). Particularly in recent years, the Court of Justice of the European Communities in Luxembourg has been willing to apply the "general principles of law"—as reflected particularly in the European Convention on Human Rights—to human rights issues brought before it.[46] The significance of this avenue in European human rights protection lies especially in the fact that the Treaties of Rome formed a supra-national quasi-federal entity, in which decisions of the Luxembourg Court (unlike those of the Strasbourg Court) automatically become binding on the domestic courts of the member states.[47]

The Critics Answered

The European human rights system has received some harsh criticisms from diverse quarters. Marxists and such responsible Western human rights authorities as Frank C. Newman have noted the relatively small number of complaints that are ever declared admissible before the European Commission.[48] American Evangelicals, taking their lead from pop eschatologist Hal Lindsey, frequently assert that the European Economic Community, with its ten members, represents the ten toes of the great image in the Book of Daniel and thus is a vehicle of the antichristic end times.[49]

To the observation that but a small number of complaints survive the admissibility tests, I reply that one should stress quality, not merely quantity: the positive human rights value of those cases that have survived must never be underestimated. And more complaints are declared admissible all the time, as litigants and their legal advisors become more sophisticated in the jurisprudence of the Commission and the Court.

Hal Lindsey's Apocalypticism

As for the Hal Lindsey apocalyptic, aside from my noting that EEC membership hardly remains at a stable ten (Greenland is in the process of withdrawal, while Spain and Portugal became members on 1 January 1986, raising the membership to twelve) and that the states-parties to the European Convention on Human Rights number no less than twenty-one, I must point to the severe biblical strictures against the unpardonable sin of attributing the work of God to Beelzebub (Matt. 12:24–33; Mark 3:22–30; Luke 11:15–20). If, as Jesus says here, "the tree is known by its fruit" (Matt. 12:33), then the European machinery by which fundamental advances in human rights have come about can be regarded as even potentially antichristic only at the critic's extreme spiritual peril.

The Secret of Success: Shared Values

In sum, as Professor A. H. Robertson has well observed, although "it is simply not possible in this imperfect world to devise any system which will be perfect and complete," nevertheless "the European system for the protection of human rights is the best yet established by any international organization."[50] Doubtless the underlying reason for this success is the shared values of the European states—all of them deriving their legal systems ultimately from the Classical-Christian Code of Justinian or biblically informed common law, and their moral orientation from the Holy Scriptures. Even though for many post-Christian Europeans such values now represent inherited capital rather than a contemporary commitment, the common European value system offers human rights advantages not available in the diversified UN atmosphere.

The American System

A further illustration of the high correlation between shared values and a sophisticated mechanism of human rights protection is afforded by the inter-American regional system. Here matters become somewhat more complicated than in the European sphere, because two formal statements of rights (not just a single Convention) must be taken into account.

Its "Convention-Based Regime"

We begin with a word about the American Convention on Human Rights, which was much influenced by the European Convention (indeed, such founding fathers of the European Convention as A. H. Robertson advised the framers of the American Convention). The American Convention, which entered into force on 18 July 1978 and which remains unratified by the United States, created a mechanism for human rights protection paralleling in a number of ways the European structure (thus, for example, a Commission and Court exist in both).

But there are interesting differences, the most striking being that in the European system, complaints by states-parties are normative, while individual complaints are possible only if a state-party has accepted Article 25 of the European Convention, whereas in the American system it is just the reverse: as soon as a state has ratified the American Convention, the Inter-American Commission on Human Rights has jurisdiction to deal with complaints by individuals against that state, but interstate complaints require not only that the two or more states in question have ratified the Convention but also that they have expressly recognized the right of the Commission to hear interstate complaints. Perhaps in the individualistic Americas the idea of individual complaints against government is less threatening than the idea (commonplace in a Europe of mutually critical national states) of one state being called to task by another! In any case, individuals are the ultimate victims of all human rights violations, so the American system shows admirable sensitivity in the approach it takes.

Procedural Mechanisms

Robert E. Norris thus describes the current procedural mechanisms relating to complaints under the American system:

As a result of the entry into force of the American Convention on Human Rights in 1978, the Inter-American Commission on Human Rights (IACHR) was reorganized in 1979 under a new Statute, which establishes separate petition procedures for complaints against member states of the Organization of American States (OAS) that are parties to the Convention as well as those that have not ratified. Parties to the Convention are subject to the petition procedure set forth in article 19(a) of the Statute, pursuant to articles 44–51 of the Convention, while other member states continue to be subject to the former procedure of the IACHR, preserved in its basic form in article 20 of the Statute.

The essential aspects of the two procedures have been harmonized by the Commission's new Regulations. The prerequisites for admissibility of the petition, the stages of processing, and methods of fact-finding and reporting or publication of findings are essentially the same under both procedures. In either case, an admissible petition initiates an inquiry that may result in a decision on the merits of the complaint and in specific recommendations to the government of the state concerned. Although the Commission's recommendations are not binding, its inquiry and final report may have a salutary effect by focusing attention upon the alleged violation or situation of the victim. The Commission is explicity [*sic*] authorized to work toward a friendly settlement under the procedure provided for state parties to the Convention, and it is not precluded from seeking this type of remedy in the case of states that are not parties. The principal difference between the remedies available under either procedure is that petitions brought against state parties may eventually be referred to the Inter-American Court of Human Rights for a binding decision, if the state concerned has accepted the Court's jurisdiction.[51]

The American Declaration and the "Charter-Based Regime"

Norris speaks in passing of OAS member states that have not ratified the American Convention. Clearly they are not bound by it. What, then, are their human rights obligations? The answer is that they are morally—if not legally—

obligated to the provisions of another instrument, the American Declaration of the Rights and Duties of Man (1948). That Declaration, strictly speaking, has not entered into force, since it lacks the minimum number of necessary ratifications. However, the revised OAS Charter—amended by way of the so-called "Protocol of Buenos Aires" (1970)—transformed the Commission from an ambiguous "autonomous entity" of the OAS into one of its principal organs and in effect incorporated the Statute of the Commission by reference. Professor Thomas Buergenthal—so renowned an authority on the American system that, even though his country has not ratified the American Convention, he has been appointed to the bench of the Inter-American Court of Human Rights—reasons as follows from these juridical premises:

> Article 2 of the Statute [of the Commission] provides that "for purposes of this Statute, human rights are understood to be those set forth" in the American Declaration. This provision must be read together with Article 150 of the OAS Charter which requires the Commission to "keep vigilance over the observance of human rights." The OAS Charter does not, however, define "human rights." Therefore, since Article 150 incorporates the provisions of the Statute by reference, "human rights" within the meaning of Article 150 are those "set forth" in the American Declaration. The human rights provisions of the American Declaration can today consequently be deemed to derive their normative character from the OAS Charter itself.[52]

The importance of this argumentation becomes particularly clear when the fact is noted that only seventeen of the twenty-seven members of the OAS have ratified the American Convention (and among the nonratifiers are the Central and South American countries having the worst human rights records in the hemisphere).[53] Since 1970 the nonratifiers have found themselves, by virtue of their OAS membership alone, under intensified pressure from the American Declaration as invigilated by the same Commission that enforces the American Convention.

The Convention and Declaration Compared

How do the Convention and the Declaration differ? A comparison of the two texts will show that each has certain advantages over the other.[54] The Declaration is less specific in its definitions of civil and political rights than the Convention, but includes a much broader range of economic, social, and cultural rights. Also, the Declaration presents a commendable balance between rights and *duties* by the inclusion of a chapter specifically devoted to duties. Oddly enough, such an emphasis on duties is rare in Western-bloc human rights instruments, though normative in Eastern-bloc constitutions.[55] A prime motivation of Socialist states to emphasize duties is doubtless their desire to inculcate subservience to political authority. The American Declaration of the Rights and Duties of Man can be seen, on the contrary, to stress the biblical theme of man's duty to his fellows based on universal brotherhood (see the language of the Declaration's preamble).

Right to Life and *Roe v. Wade*

The American Convention, modeled as to general structure on the European Convention, does very little with economic and social rights (in these categories it protects only property and family rights). Its strength lies in the area of civil and political liberties. Though the enumerated civil and political rights do not differ greatly from what one finds in the American Declaration, these rights are defined with much more specificity. One important example will be mentioned. The Declaration states the right to life in the following general terms (Article 1): "Every human being has the right to life, liberty and the security of his person." The Convention, however, adds a vital defining element as to when such protection shall commence (Article 4[1]) and goes into detail on the death penalty and capital punishment (Article 4[2–6]). Article 4[1] reads: "Every person has the right to have his life respected. This right shall be protected by law and, in general, from the moment of conception. No one shall be arbitrarily deprived of his life." As I have written elsewhere:

> The United States has not ratified the American Convention, and the strong wording of this right-to-life article has worried more than a few congressmen: might not the United States, after ratification, find itself a defendant before the Inter-American Court of Human Rights because of *Roe v. Wade*?
>
> Whether such a worry is realistic or not (and the U.S.—if it does ratify the Convention—may well take the coward's way out by qualifying its ratification of Article 4 by a "reservation" or "statement of understanding"), the American Convention sharply illustrates the tension between *Roe v. Wade* and the powerful trend toward maximizing human rights on the international scene.[56]

The wording of the American Convention on the right to life directly reflects Catholic-Christian influence from South and Central America, and leads to the sobering thought that international human rights protections and ideals may exceed the level of civil rights in our own highly secularized "land of the free and home of the brave."

What of the Future?

The American regional human rights system is in its infancy. The Inter-American Court of Human Rights could only be constituted after the American Convention came into force in 1978, and it has thus not yet had the opportunity to produce a case-law tradition.[57] Professor Buergenthal warns that "the political instability of the region, whose causes are many and which is reflected in cyclical and often violent vacillations between representative democracy and military dictatorship, makes it hazardous to predict the future effectiveness of the inter-

American human rights system."[58] But if the thirty-year history of the European regional system, on which so much of the American system is modeled, can serve as a predictor, one may not unrealistically expect the American system to achieve much in the promotion and protection of human dignity in the Western Hemisphere.[59]

Asia

Not a great deal can be said about the regional protection of human rights in areas other than Europe and the Americas. Asia is entirely lacking in such a system. Professor Riad Daoudi of the Law Faculty of Damascus University, in a lecture series on "Human Rights in Africa and Asia" delivered at the July 1984 study session of the International Institute of Human Rights, asserted that "the inexistence in Asia of a regional convention or of an institutionalized system of human rights is the consequence of the absence of a regional political structure." Certainly that is a significant explanatory factor, but even more important may well be—as I shall stress in chapter 5—the absence of clear commitment to absolute ethical ideals of human worth in the Asian religions that create the *Weltanschauungen* in that part of the globe.

Africa

As for Africa, the most impressive practical advance has been in the area of refugee protection. A Convention Governing the Specific Aspects of Refugee Problems in Africa was adopted by the Organization of African Unity (OAU) in 1969. The basic principle of *nonrefoulement* is stressed, but the Convention goes much further: for the first time in any international agreement it declares that signatory states must not only protect refugees already within their jurisdictions but also "use their best endeavors consistent with their respective legislations to receive refugees" (Article 2[1]). Moreover, "for reasons of security, countries of asylum shall, as far as possible, settle refugees at a reasonable distance from the frontier of their country of origin" (Article 2[6]).

In 1981, the OAU adopted an African Charter on Human and Peoples' Rights, whose chief author was the distinguished Muslim Keba M'Baye, a judge of the International Court of Justice. The Charter establishes an African Commission on Human and Peoples' Rights, and "reflects a strong preference for mediation, conciliation, and consensus as opposed to confrontational or adversarial procedures"[60]—doubtless reflecting the drafters' background of African tribal and customary dispute resolution. It would be premature to detail the content or structure of this fledgling African system, since "it is unlikely that the Charter will enter into force in the near future."[61] Moreover, the seriousness with which at least some African states may eventually treat their obligations under the Charter is placed in doubt by the enthusiastic reception Idi Amin of Uganda received at OAU sessions while he was in power: evidently anti-colonial strength was more impressive than human rights to many influential African statesmen.

The "Full-Belly" Thesis

A central theme in African human rights discussion requires a word here. It is frequently argued that in the developing countries of the world, civil and political liberties must take a back seat to economic and social rights and to "third-generation" solidarity rights. Are not political freedoms a luxury that poverty-stricken African states, long subjected to colonial domination, can ill-afford? Should not all human rights efforts in such a context be directed toward economic, social, and educational advance?

In a word, No! The very idea of justifying the sacrificing one set of rights for another is the sure destruction of human rights in general. Indeed, since "man does not live by bread alone," were total economic success to occur within a framework of, say, totalitarian injustice, life would be hopelessly impoverished anyway—as George Orwell's cacotopian novel, *1984*, so well demonstrates. Rhoda Howard has made this point with consummate effectiveness in her essay "The Full-Belly Thesis: Should Economic Rights Take Priority over Civil and Political Rights? Evidence from Sub-Saharan Africa."[62] After arguing that both civil and political rights are (1) necessary for economic development and redistribution of wealth, (2) necessary to preserve social order and social and cultural rights, and (3) necessary in and of themselves, she concludes: "The 'full belly' may not always precede moral integrity, the right to community, or political freedom in the value system of an individual."

Internal State Protections

In our examination of international and regional systems that protect human rights we must not forget the more familiar protections under national law. The greatest single instrument to protect human rights on the national level is a written and entrenched constitution.

The U.S.

Though the United States has a sorry record in that it has seldom ratified international human rights treaties, "American constitutional rights in fact satisfy international requirements as regards the bulk of civil and political rights, and these have the special character and protection enjoyed by supreme law."[63]

West Germany (BRD)

The right-to-life provision of the German Basic Law (the German federal constitution) gave the Federal Constitutional Court of West Germany the opportunity in 1975 to strike down a relaxed abortion provision of the Federal Diet's penal code reform law.[64]

Written Constitutions Not Enough

But written constitutions are no guarantee that human rights will be enforced: the U.S. Supreme Court, in *Roe v. Wade*, influenced by the secular climate of opinion in contemporary America and by a pragmatic, instrumentalist jurisprudence, reached a decision exactly opposite to that of West Germany's Federal Constitutional Court. Why? The current president of the Federal Constitutional Court, Dr. W. Zeidler, told me in personal conversation on 18 July 1984 in Karlsruhe that in his opinion it was the Christian religious convictions of the Court that had motivated its judgment; certainly that was the last thing the Blackmun Court was concerned with in *Roe v. Wade*.[65]

Socialist States

An even stronger illustration of the same point—that a written constitution will only guarantee human rights if the legal climate surrounding it is infused by the right value system—is provided by the U.S.S.R. and other Socialist states. These nations invariably have written constitutions, and they are often models of human rights rhetoric, both in the civil-political and (especially, as one might expect) in the economic-social areas; and they commonly include not only statements of rights but also well-expressed catalogues of citizens' duties. But they often function more in the breach than in the observance—and, what is worse, their effectiveness is unpredictably dependent on a relativistic Marxist ethic in which the end justifies the means and on the vagaries of Party policy.[66]

The U.K.

The other side of the coin is that a written constitution is not a *sine qua non* for the adequate protection of human rights as long as the proper value system informs the national and legal life of the country. *In the last analysis a nation's deepest convictions as to human worth will be far more important than its particular constitutional mechanisms*. The United Kingdom is a classic example. The English Constitution is unwritten, but is no less real for all that. It consists of a heritage of rights and freedoms going back to the Magna Charta (and behind that to the biblical principles on which it rests), extended and fleshed out through common-law judicial decisions across the centuries by a host of predominately Christian jurisprudents such as Sir Matthew Hale and Sir William Blackstone.[67] The written constitutions not only of the United States but also of Commonwealth and former Commonwealth countries testify to the depth and power of this unwritten tradition.[68]

At the End of the Day, a Nation's Value System Makes the Difference

True, there is much agitation today in English legal circles for a written—and preferably entrenched—bill of rights.[69] This is due, quite understandably, to a realization that with increased secularization and the changing nature of English society through massive immigration, Parliament may have a progressively more difficult time keeping a clear eye on the unwritten verities of the English Constitution. The United Kingdom has been the most popular respondent before the European Commission and Court of Human Rights, suggesting that the time for a written and entrenched Bill of Rights may well have come. Lord Scarman, among others, would like to see the problem solved by the direct incorporation and entrenchment of the European Convention on Human Rights into English law. On balance, unrestrained parliamentary sovereignty is a dangerous political theory in a secular society, and a written constitution to which the legislature is subject has decided advantages for human rights—but the factor of utmost importance will be the conception of human dignity that informs the nation, its legislators, and its judges.

The NGOs

Discussion to this point may have give the false impression that the promotion and protection of human rights depend solely on governments—operating domestically, regionally, or internationally. In point of fact, nongovernmental organizations (NGOs) are a powerful factor on the human rights scene.

International Humanitarian Law and the ICRC

Heading the list of NGOs is the International Committee of the Red Cross (ICRC). Its sphere of concentration is the field of humanitarian law, sometimes regarded as part of the international and comparative law of human rights, sometimes as an independent domain.[70] The ICRC originated in the work of Henry Dunant, who witnessed the incredible carnage at the battle of Solferino (1859) and determined to do something to reduce the unnecessary sufferings of war. The name "Red Cross" has reference to the sacrificial death of Christ on the cross for the sins of the world and the biblical admonition: "Even hereunto were ye called: because Christ also suffered for us, leaving us an example, that ye should follow his steps" (1 Peter 2:21). So clear is this Christian connection that Muslims, disturbed by the symbol, have formed parallel "Red Crescent" societies; "Red Lion" and "Red Sun" organizations now exist respectively in Israel and the Far East. The ICRC coordinates the work of some 130 national societies on all five continents.

The Law of Geneva and the Law of The Hague

Dunant's labors also resulted in the Geneva Convention of 1864—the first modern multilateral convention expressing humanitarian objectives as legal provisions. It focused on protecting war victims by establishing a neutral status for medical personnel (the use of the famed Red Cross emblem). The original Geneva Convention was enlarged in 1906, and by way of The Hague Conventions of 1899 and 1907 its principles were extended to the regulation of the conduct of warfare and the protection of victims of maritime conflict. By 1929 these developments led to a Convention specifically protecting prisoners of war. After World War II, the four current Geneva Conventions were drawn up (12 August 1949); 154 states have ratified them. These cover (1) wounded and sick combatants in the field, (2) combatants who have been wounded at sea or shipwrecked, (3) prisoners of war, and (4) civilians in time of war.

Two Additional Protocols (8 June 1977) have been ratified by 32 and 26 states respectively; they endeavor to speak to the newer problems of modern warfare (mercenaries, wars of liberation, etc.). Protocol I sets forth fundamental rules applicable to international armed conflicts, while Protocol II deals—rather weakly—with internal conflicts such as civil wars (narrowing the scope of common Article 3 of the four Geneva Conventions, which also treats noninternational conflicts, but augmenting the previously afforded protections to victims of internal wars). In effect, the Protocols seek to combine the so-called "Law of The Hague" (conduct of hostilities) with the "Law of Geneva" (protection of victims) in a world where these lines are increasingly blurred.

Humanitarian Law in a Nutshell

Here is a summary of the main points of the some six hundred articles of international humanitarian law today, as drawn up by lawyers of the ICRC; it is not a legal instrument, but it well surveys the vital field of operation of the ICRC:[71]

FUNDAMENTAL RULES OF INTERNATIONAL HUMANITARIAN LAW APPLICABLE IN ARMED CONFLICTS

1. Persons *hors de combat* and those who do not take a direct part in hostilities are entitled to

respect for their lives and physical and moral integrity. They shall in all circumstances be protected and treated humanely without any adverse distinction.

2. It is forbidden to kill or injure an enemy who surrenders or who is *hors de combat*.
3. The wounded and sick shall be collected and cared for by the party to the conflict which has them in its power. Protection also covers medical personnel, establishments, transports and *matériel*. The emblem of the red cross (red crescent, red lion and sun) is the sign of such protection and must be respected.
4. Captured combatants and civilians under the authority of an adverse party are entitled to respect for their lives, dignity, personal rights and convictions. They shall be protected against all acts of violence and reprisals. They shall have the right to correspond with their families and to receive relief.
5. Everyone shall be entitled to benefit from fundamental judicial guarantees. No one shall be held responsible for an act he has not committed. No one shall be subjected to physical or mental torture, corporal punishment or cruel or degrading treatment.
6. Parties to a conflict and members of their armed forces do not have an unlimited choice of methods and means of warfare. It is prohibited to employ weapons or methods of warfare of a nature to cause unnecessary losses or excessive suffering.
7. Parties to a conflict shall at all times distinguish between the civilian population and combatants in order to spare civilian population and property. Neither the civilian population as such nor civilian persons shall be the object of attack. Attacks shall be directed solely against military objectives.

Implementation

What is done to insure that these humanitarian principles are in fact observed? War is hell, and the built-in tension between humanitarianism and warfare keeps the ideal from ever being fulfilled perfectly in practice. But a common provision of four Geneva Conventions and Protocol I establishes a mechanism of Protecting Powers, whereby (with the consent of all the governments concerned) a neutral country can act to protect the interests of any party to the conflict and its nationals. Suppose, however—as is often the case—that no Protecting Power can be agreed upon: then, under the Conventions and Protocol I, the ICRC itself may enter the picture and carry out numerous specific humanitarian functions. For instance, "whether or not there is a Protecting Power, ICRC delegates are allowed to visit all places in which there are prisoners of war, including places of internment, imprisonment, and labour, and to interview the prisoners without witnesses."[72]

Amnesty International and Private Monitoring Groups

Aside from the International Committee of the Red Cross, doubtless the best-known NGO in the human rights field is the London-based Amnesty International, with forty national sections all over the world.[73] Amnesty was the product of the vision of Peter Benenson, a Catholic lawyer. During its twenty-year history it has proven again and again the central importance of publicity in rectifying human rights violations. By publishing innumerable reports on violations in particular countries (and Amnesty studiously avoids political bias: a violation is a violation, whether committed by the Left or by the Right), pressure is brought heavily to bear on the violators. Intense letter-writing campaigns concerning particular victims have again and again led to the release of prisoners. Even the most repressive governments generally do not want to be the focus of negative world public opinion, and they often consider it politically expedient to release the victim rather than court massive disapproval in the forum of nations.

Similar in approach to Amnesty are the small, private, often heavily persecuted monitoring groups, especially in (but not limited to) Eastern-bloc countries. They endeavor to publicize the deviations of the state from its international or domestic human rights commitments, so as to pressure the state into fulfilling the obligations it has taken upon itself. Examples of such groups are those monitoring observance of the Helsinki Final Act, and the recently formed KOPP groups in Poland, focusing on police brutality in the wake of the murder of Father Popieluszko.[74]

The ICJ & the Lawyers Committee for Human Rights

A specialized NGO is the International Commission of Jurists, based in Geneva. It regularly publishes reports on the extent of law observance, due process, and natural justice throughout the globe. One of its especially effective techniques is the sending of legally trained observers to trials of dissidents, and the wide dissemination of the resulting reports. The presence of ICJ observers has unquestionably made the political kangaroo court more difficult to conduct and justify.[75] In the United States, a similar NGO is the prestigious, New York-based Lawyers Committee for Human Rights, whose director, Michael H. Posner, has carried the legal battle for international human rights to Uganda and Haiti and is credited with nudging the Reagan administration away from supporting ex-President Ferdinand Marcos of the Philippines, a notorious human rights violator.

Christianity

One of the most powerful forces in today's human rights struggle is the Christian church. We have already encountered numerous illustrations of direct and indirect biblical influence on the modern human rights movement—from René Cassin's assertion that the Universal Declaration has its source in the Ten Commandments to the symbolic focus of the ICRC on the

Cross of Christ. More will be said about such ideological influences in the final chapters. Here, I wish only to point up some of the practical efforts made by Christians in the contemporary domain of human rights.

RCs and Ecumenical Organizations

Among "mainline" churches, Roman Catholicism has shown a commendable concern to relate Christian faith to human rights.[76] In his famous encyclical, *Pacem in Terris* (1963), Pope John XXIII dealt at length with human rights and interrelated human duties, and specifically (paras. 143–45) called on the United Nations to go much further than it had gone in implementing the ideals of the Universal Declaration. The 1975 Pontifical Commission document *Justicia et Pax* is a handsome assertion of man's worth as a child of God, and it does not hesitate to tie human rights to the Incarnation: "The mystery of the Incarnation—the Son of God assuming our human nature—adds new light to the traditional and global vision of man and his dignity." Two important books have been devoted solely to the work of Pope John Paul II in the promotion of human rights.[77]

Protestant ecumenical organizations (the World Council of Churches, the Lutheran World Federation, the World Alliance of Reformed Churches, the Reformed Ecumenical Synod, etc.) have also issued a variety of declarations and working-papers in the human rights area.[78] Unfortunately, the theological weaknesses of some of these groups have tended to reduce their pronouncements to the level of the platitudinous, and their attempts at activism (particularly within the WCC) have not infrequently made them the dupes of Marxist and revolutionary movements.

Fundamentalists

As already noted, some Evangelicals, particularly those enmeshed in sociological Fundamentalism, look with great suspicion on the human rights movement. They do so on the basis of one or a combination of the following beliefs: (1) international organizations are inherently unspiritual and may be the vehicles of centralized antichristic power at the end of time; (2) the United States is "God's country" and thus requires no improvement in human rights; (3) human rights is a manifestation of the "social gospel" rather than of the true biblical gospel of salvation; (4) the Christian must separate from unbelievers and not cooperate with those who do not fully agree with him doctrinally. Those who hold to the full panoply of these opinions may not inaccurately be regarded as "so narrow-minded that they can see through a keyhole with both eyes simultaneously." They contribute little or nothing to the promotion and preservation of human dignity, in spite of their commendably high view of biblical authority. Ironically, they have the biblical answer to man's inhumanity to man, but they seal themselves off hermetically from those who so desperately need that message.[79]

Evangelicals

Fortunately, most Evangelicals do not suffer from these Fundamentalist blindspots. Their activities nationally and internationally in behalf of human rights are impressive. Examples—by no means exhaustive—include Michael Bourdeaux's Keston College in England (with its focus on ameliorating the state of persecuted Christians in Eastern Europe and the Soviet Union), the French ACAT organization (Christian Action for the Abolition of Torture), Christian Solidarity International (a kind of Christian equivalent of Amnesty), and the concerted efforts by American Evangelicals (such as Dr. Harold O. J. Brown, U.S. Surgeon General C. Everett Koop, the late Francis Schaeffer, and the present writer) to oppose present-day abortion practices in the United States and reverse *Roe v. Wade* through a right-to-life Amendment to the Federal Constitution.[80]

A Closing Word to the Optimist

At the close of this bewildering survey of existing mechanisms of human rights protection, what advice can be given to the concerned reader? If he is an activistic optimist, he must be warned that the key to productive human rights action lies in the effective choice of strategies. An examination of appendix 5 ("Checklist to Help Select the Most Appropriate Forum") will underscore the need for specific training in this complex field—particularly graduate education in the international and comparative law of human rights. A warm heart and a soft head are particularly dangerous in this field of endeavor.

. . . And to the Pessimist

If, however, the reader inclines toward quietistic pessimism, observing that, with all the mechanisms we have discussed, human rights violations still seem to occur with impunity to the Right and to the Left, I remind him that, nonetheless—as Professor Bassiouni has so well put it—because of all these efforts "the veneer of civilization thickens."[81] Granted, it is only a veneer, but on its thickness depends the life and well-being of countless persons across the globe. The Christian especially should be exercising his or her best efforts to increase the depth of the human rights layer, for, as we shall see in subsequent chapters, if the Christian does not provide a justification for human dignity and worth, no one else will.

chapter three

The Dilemma, Part One: Defining Human Rights

In one of Arthur Train's delightful Tutt and Mr. Tutt *lawyer stories, we are introduced to Cephas McFee: "The mainspring of Mr. Cephas McFee's life was his instinct for acquisition, for getting things and holding on to them. He called it 'having his rights.'" What, in fact, are rights? In this chapter, we enter the domain of philosophical analysis, discovering that human rights are neither entities, nor mere prescriptions, nor wants, needs, choices, or claims. Human rights are found to be* entitlements, *and the source of the title will ultimately require an appeal to the transcendent.*

Human Rights Law Goes Only So Far

Our survey of existing human rights protections has hopefully achieved its purpose: to lay to rest the ghost that human rights activity is but "sound and fury, signifying nothing." Yet only the most uncritical reader will be entirely satisfied with the picture that has emerged. Eberhard Welty has listed four "defects and dangers" related to an exclusively juridical, treaty-orientated approach to human rights:

i. It is to be deplored that mankind is no longer prepared to acknowledge God as the author and guarantor of right, as fundamental rights are thereby deprived of their only true sanction. Opinions, power, and the will of men are substituted for God; the sanctity and effectivness [*sic*] of right are surrendered.

ii. Important rights are all too easily overlooked (either from want of discernment or purposely for "tactical" reasons) and not included in the declaration (because of self-interest; out of consideration for the views of one or the other world-power; or because the defeated nations did not participate).

iii. Here human agreement cannot guarantee that the rights which have been declared to be such are in reality genuine fundamental human rights; it cannot guarantee that liberty has not been falsely restricted, or that a false tolerance has not been practised (for example, certain "concessions" and exceptions may be made in favour of totalitarian states).

iv. Fundamental human rights established in this positivist manner remain valid only as long as the partners to the contract abide by their agreement and are prepared to carry it out. When new agreements are being drawn up some very unfortunate and disturbing changes may take place.[82]

Philosophical Analysis Is Unavoidable

Clearly we must go beyond the purely descriptive and endeavor to understand human rights at the normative level. This will require doing philosophy—first, to shed light on the very meaning of the concept of human rights, and then to determine whether such a conceptualization is justifiable. Though of immense importance, the task before us in the present chapter and the one following is not especially popular:

"the role of philosophy in the twentieth-century human rights dialogue has been virtually overshadowed by the widely publicized contributions from the realms of diplomacy and politics."[83] But having subjected nonlawyers to the rigors of the preceding chapter, we have no qualms about immersing the philosophically untrained in the deep waters of epistemology.

Even where the water is the shallowest, philosophical analysis is valuable. Felix Cohen, in his delightful essay, "Human Rights: An Appeal to Philosophers," asks us to

> consider, for example, a completely Machiavellian cynic who views the discussion of human rights as a process of noise-making by which rival diplomats seek to put their adversaries in corners and bid against each other for the support of the wretched of the earth. May not such an amoralist teach us something about the motivations and significant conditions of assertions about human rights, and thus help us to understand what goes on in the heart and nerve centers of the world?[84]

To be sure, such minimalism will not for a moment satisfy the quest for an in-depth understanding of human rights. To do that, one must attack the fundamental definitional question.

Rights neither Entities nor Capable of Reduction

Alan White, Ferens Professor of Philosophy in the University of Hull—who will offer us considerable assistance in this chapter—provides a useful starting point by stressing that, whatever else a "right" may be, it is not an entity and it cannot be reductionalistically explained away by reference to other, associated concepts.

> Clearly "right" (like "duty" etc.) does not denote any entity, whether physical, mental, or fictional. Having a right is neither like having a ring nor is it like having an idea. Nor is denying the existence of certain rights like denying the existence of centaurs or of El Dorado. . . .

The notion of *a right* cannot, I have argued, be explained either as referring to or denoting any kind of entity—though statements about rights can be true or false and because of this, be factual—or as being equivalent to or mutually implicative with any of the notions with which it commonly keeps company, such as *duty* or *obligation, ought, liberty, power, privilege,* or *claim.* Nor can it be reduced to the notions of *right* or *wrong*. This is not to say that the notion of a right cannot be explained or understood by reference to these other notions. On the contrary, this, I have argued, is the only way to understand it. But the notion of a right is, I contend, as primitive as any of these other notions and cannot, therefore, be reduced to or made equivalent to any one or any set of them. Nor can it be explained as being a complex or system of these. To interpret the nonconceptual relations between a right and a liberty, a power, a privilege, a duty, etc. as part of the notion of a right is to make the same sort of mistake as it would be to interpret the relations between right, good, ought, duty, obligation, as parts of any one of these notions.[85]

Aiken's Prescriptivism

If a right is not an entity, does this mean that it is necessarily only *prescriptive*? Henry Aiken has proposed that human rights are no more (and no less) than prescriptions for taking "primary moral responsibility for all other persons."[86] But one is certainly not obliged to go this route of ethical noncognitivism (noncognitivism is always an epistemological last resort). And even if Aiken were correct, his approach to human rights is a classic begging-of-the-question, for it leaves unsolved the root problem of the nature and content of "moral responsibility" (What is truly moral? What action is truly responsible action?).

Rights ≠ "Wants"

To determine what rights *are,* it is essential to know what they *are not*. Rights are most often confused with *wants* or with *needs*. Confusion between rights and *wants* is endemic in today's climate: individuals and social groups readily transmute their agendas, in fact based on desire (to receive fifty cents more per hour, to vacation in Tahiti), into alleged rights. Such confusion is a mark of immaturity. One must arrive at the point where other people, the government, and, indeed, the Supreme Being, are no longer seen as a Santa Claus obligated to slake one's desires. It is the central thesis of one of the most valuable contemporary schools of clinical psychology, Albert Ellis's Rational-Emotive Therapy, that the universe and one's fellows do not owe one the satisfaction of one's desires.[87] Queries Felix Cohen: "Does not civilized society rest in large part upon the distinction that most of us learn in childhood between wanting something and recognizing the right of another to grant or withhold that which is desired?"[88]

Nor Do Rights = "Needs"

The faulty identification of right with *need* is more subtle. The classic expression of this view is Hobbes' *Leviathan,* where need is presented as a fully sufficient basis to establish rights. Modernly, it is Joel Feinberg who endeavors to found valid moral claims on primary human needs. The result, he argues, is to establish commitments "to the conception of a right which is an entitlement *to* some good, but not a valid claim *against* any particular individual."[89] Freeman has termed this approach the "manifesto" sense of right, and illustrates it with Principle 4 of the United Nations Declaration of the Rights of the Child (1959): "The child shall have the right to adequate nutrition, housing, recreation and medical services." He asks pointedly: "But who in Bangladesh or Uganda is to bear the duty of providing these services?"[90]

> Though those who hold this view are not very careful in their expression of it, they obviously wish to restrict the relation of rights and needs to a small class of the latter, sometimes called "basic" or "crying" needs. But even here there is a good deal of ambiguity about the position. Sometimes it takes

the extreme, but clearly mistaken, form of equating rights with such needs, either directly or via the equation of both with claims. Clearly, however, a need of food and shelter is not the same as a claim to these; and we shall see later that the very common equation of a claim to something, such as food or shelter, with a right to it is equally mistaken. More usually, it is argued that a right is "based on" or "arises out of" a (basic) need. Here again this is sometimes taken as a direct connection between the two, but more commonly as mediated by a connection of both to a claim. The first alternative gains whatever plausibility it has by emphasizing that the connection holds only because the need is for something valuable, such as food, shelter, life, or freedom. In other words, the right is really based not on the need itself, but on the worth of what it is a need for. That is, it is argued that one has a right to what is good for one.[91]

In reality, a need constitutes neither a necessary nor a sufficient condition to establish a right, and it is surely not the case logically that because *x* is good for me, I have a right to it. (Such would follow, not so incidentally, only if a benevolent Creator were to promise me, in terms like Romans 8:28—"all things work together for good to them that love God"—that He would meet my genuine needs; then I could claim that promise and assert a right to what was good for me.) As against the equation of rights with needs, it has further been pointed out that "apparent conflicts in the human personality itself (noted by Freud and others) raise the question of a basic incompatibility among the various human rights that are linked to conflicting elements in the human personality."[92] In other words, people often do not know what they really need, so any attempt to found a theory of fundamental human rights on expressions of need will be a shaky business.

Hohfeldian Analysis

If rights cannot be explained by wants or needs, what exactly are they? Perhaps the most useful clarification in the entire literature of the subject was provided by Stanford law professor Wesley Hohfeld, who observed the ambiguities in the use of the term "right" in legal literature: "The term 'rights' tends to be used indiscriminately to cover what in a given case may be a privilege, a power, or an immunity, rather than a right in the strictest sense."[93] The strict sense of the term, in Hohfeld's analysis, involves a right-holder who is entitled to something; here there will be a correlative duty in another. The importance of such analysis becomes plain when one begins to look at particular human rights more closely; for example,

> the International Covenant on Civil and Political Rights does not permit a state to derogate from the right set forth in article 8 not to be held in slavery or servitude. The same article also prohibits a state from requiring an individual to perform forced labour; yet, that right is subject to derogation in time of public emergency under article 4. Is the right not to be enslaved an *immunity* or an *absolute right,* and the right not to perform forced labour merely a *privilege,* since there are times when the latter right is not available?[94]

First- and Second-Generation Rights Clarified

It is fairly widely recognized that the "first-generation" rights (civil and political liberties) fall either into Hohfeld's strict category of right as entitlement, with correlative duties, or—at the very least—function as immunity rights. The object of "first-generation" rights is primarily to restrain government from encroaching on the liberties of the subject. In contrast, "second-generation" rights (economic and social rights) require positive government action and seem to identify rights with needs. Conflicts between the two generations of rights are not uncommon:

> The dilemma has surfaced, for example, in this form. Access to adequate health care is a human right in a welfare state and is based on legislative enactments. Although the justiciability of this right

is limited, a government will be under strong pressure to act if there is a serious failure of the health system. One cause of failure may be the geographically or socially skewed distribution of doctors or dentists; a remedial act might be to introduce compulsory service for doctors in medically backward areas. However, doctors who have been ordered to serve under such schemes have felt this to be an infringement of their professional "freedom rights." Some such cases have ended up in the European Court of Human Rights.[95]

Should We Expel Second-Generation Rights From the Club?

Can such tensions be dismissed—in theory, though of course not in practice—simply by arguing that second-generation rights do not deserve to be called rights? We have already seen that needs per se are not equivalent to rights, so economic and social needs cannot be elevated to the status of rights merely by recognizing their existence as needs. The limitation of true human rights to the first generation is the approach taken by Maurice Cranston,[96] by "libertarian capitalist" Robert Nozick,[97] by atheistic philosopher of political conservativism Antony Flew,[98] and by R. S. Downie. Downie, for example, maintains—employing much the same reasoning as Richard Wasserstrom—that nothing can be a true human right that is enforceable at the expense of other rights.[99]

Why Second-Generation Rights Deserve to Retain Their Status

But even the most sacred civil and political liberties (the nonderogable rights) may have to be sacrificed *in extremis* on the ground of lesser-of-evils necessity (torturing the anarchist to force him to tell where he has hidden the bomb capable of killing thousands of innocent people). If first-generation rights do not cease to be genuine rights under these circumstances, neither do second-generation rights. Alan Gewirth is surely correct that even though economic and social rights do not quite meet Cranston's three tests of an authentic human right (universality, practicability, paramount importance), they come close enough to warrant inclusion.[100] Indeed, the case can be made stronger yet. David Watson has shown that any use of Cranston's tests to deny status to second-generation rights will result in the parallel elimination of first-generation rights.[101] Moreover,

> in support of socioeconomic rights as human rights, Melvin Rader criticizes certain liberals for their failure to interpret freedom in both its negative and positive senses. Rader insists that negative freedom (translated as civil or First Amendment liberties) is often too narrowly construed as the absence of *governmental restraint* on the individual. When power differentials among social classes interfere with the negative freedom of the weaker class, then governmental restraints on the unduly powerful can actually facilitate negative freedom. Rader cautions that although civil liberties are necessary, they are not sufficient for a free society. To guarantee any measure of positive liberty, human beings must have the "instruments" with which to make free choices. For the most part, these instruments are expressed as the basic socioeconomic rights satisfying the needs for food, clothing, shelter, health, education, among others. Civil rights cannot be guaranteed if socioeconomic rights are lacking; thus both, in this view, are to be counted as human rights in that both are necessary conditions for freedom.[102]

Pace Hohfeld, a Unitary Right Underlies the Diversity of Rights

Hohfeld's analysis of the semantic spread of the concept of right can thus aid us in clarifying what we mean or should mean when we talk of particular human rights. The danger of Hohfeldian analysis is that one may lose track of any underlying, unified concept of right. "Despite Hohfeld, there is no doubt that 'right' is a unitary concept."[103] White argues the point in the following terms:

> Though there are important differences between a legal and a moral right or between an institutional and a logical right to something, just as there are

differences between a right to act and a right to receive, such differences, I have argued, are not differences in the concept of *right* as such, which has the same logical characteristics wherever it occurs, but are due to the ways the right is qualified, just as the important differences between, for example, what is morally, legally, and logically right or between what is morally, legally, and logically obligatory are not due to differences in the notions of *right* and *obligatory*, but to differences in their qualifiers.[104]

But What Is This Underlying Idea? Will or Interest?

But if among the Many rights there is indeed a One, what is it? Here the debate rages between the so-called "will" theorists and the "interest" theorists. We shall first consider the *will theory*.

"Choice" Is Not the Answer

The will theory stresses the place of *choice* or of *claims* in the nature of all genuine rights. H. L. A. Hart—by far the most distinguished contemporary advocate of will theory—asserts that in "the strict usage of most modern English jurists following Austin," a person who has a right is a person who "may at his option demand the execution of the duty [owed him] or waive it."[105] A right, therefore, is in essence a legally protected choice. However, as White well argues:

> To this it may be objected, first, that some rights, such as the judge's right to pass sentence on a convicted criminal, a parent's right to punish his children, or my right to assume something or to criticize somebody, as well as my right to help or heal somebody, have . . . no correlative duties and, therefore, none that could be demanded or waived.[106]

Also,

> If young children, babies, imbeciles, the comatose, etc., can have rights, these would be rights which in fact could not carry any power of waiver; and if animals, foetuses, and, *a fortiori*, inanimate objects

could have rights, these would be rights which logically could not carry a power of waiver. This is not, of course, to deny that there are rights which allow me to waive any duties they may involve, as when I can exempt you from your duty not to deprive me of the property in which I have a right not to be deprived or to assault me in a boxing contest or a surgical operation, though I have a right not to be assaulted.[107]

Nor Are "Claims"

Hohfeld's approach is sometimes said to reduce to the notion that rights in the strict sense are merely claims. Whether or not this does justice to Hohfeld, the viewpoint is certainly a common expression of will theory. Thus, Antony Flew proposes that "rights be attributed only to those capable of—or, to allow for infants, capable of becoming capable of—themselves claiming rights for themselves, and in and by that claim undertaking the reciprocal obligation to respect the rights of others."[108]

A somewhat more sophisticated variation of the same approach is offered by Martin Golding, who distinguishes claims from *acts of claiming:* a person may—even though he personally makes no claim—possess a genuine right as long as the right is predicated on *another's* act of claiming.[109] It will be noted that although in what we might term "The Golding Variation" no particular claimant need be specified for a genuine right to exist, true rights still depend on the recognition of them. Unhappily, neither Flew's nor Golding's identification of rights with claims holds up under criticism.

Clearly, there is no logical connection between making a claim, whether indicative or subjunctive (or imperative), and having a right to that which is claimed. For first, one may have a right to something which one has not claimed, either indicatively or subjunctively (or imperatively), at all. I may have a right to some money or a right to know a name, though I don't indicatively claim the money or to know the name, either because I don't think I have the money or the knowledge or because I know I haven't. Or I may have a right to be given something, whether money, protection, or freedom, for which I make no subjunctive (or imperative) claim because I have no desire for it. Secondly, one may claim something, either indicatively or subjunctively, to which one has no right. Thus, I may claim to have some money or to be surprised. Or I may claim that I (should) be given some protection, immunity or goods which I have no right to have. Indeed, my claim that I have or do so and so may be proved and my claim that I (should) have or be given such and such may be granted, without its being proved or granted that I have or be given rights in respect to so and so and such and such. To uphold my claim to be the long-lost heir gives me a right to the estate. To admit my claim to the authorship of the document is not to admit any supposed right to be the author. And granting my claim, like granting my request or demand, to be given protection or immunity is granting that I (should) be given them, not that I (should) be given a right to them. Not even rightly claiming, much less merely claiming, something gives one a right to it. Hence, taken at their face value, common philosophical and juristic analyses of *rights* as "legally enforceable claims", as "recognised" (Ritchie), "inviolable" (Catholic writers quoted by McCloskey), "strong" (Wasserstrom), or "valid" (Feinberg) claims, are confusions between "rightly claiming" something and "having a right" to it. It is simply a mistake to assert that "we mean by a right something that can be justly claimed". . . .

. . . .

I conclude that having a right to something and having a claim to it are not mutually implicative nor, therefore, equivalent notions. Much less are rights and claims themselves—even true or justified claims—the same.[110]

Interest Theory Preferable to Will Theory

The most distinguished representative of the contrasting *interest theory* of rights—and a formidable critic of will theory—is Neil MacCormick, Regius Professor of Public Law and the Law of Nature and Nations at Edinburgh University. It will perhaps have been noted in passing that Antony Flew qualified his will theory by including among legitimate possessors of rights those "capable of becoming capable of claiming rights for themselves" (i.e., infants). MacCormick effectively argues that the rights of children constitute a death-blow for will theory, since both law and morality endeavor to protect the child's interests by attributing rights to him or her (the right to life, to property, to inheritance, etc.) without any correlative duties actual or potential.[111] Having a right, then, means simply having one's interests as a human being protected by the imposition of normative constraints.

But What Can Interest Theory Do With Animal and Environmental Rights?

Here, however, a door is opened through which more than children can enter. If the interest theory is correct, and human beings—whether they are capable of claiming rights or not—nonetheless have rights by virtue of the fact alone that they are human, then why are such species-rights limited to mankind? Cannot interest theory likewise embrace the animal kingdom and, indeed, all of nature? One recalls how Albert Schweitzer's philosophy of "reverence for life" made it very difficult for him to kill flies in his operating theater at Lambaréné. Christopher Stone, in his well-known work *Should Trees Have Standing?* speaks of a kind of universal consciousness inhabiting things, and sees this as justification for granting legal rights to natural objects.[112] But on the basis of the interest theory of rights (as opposed to the will theory), consciousness is not even needed!

Interest Theory Trivialized

Where, then, is the line to be drawn? R. G. Frey notes that "if you go into a forest, you see a good many trees that are not only not flourishing but also appear altogether mediocre specimens beside others," and queries: "Do even these mediocre trees have inherent value?"[113] Environmentalist application of interest theory, "if applied rigorously, for instance, to trees, dirt, and land mass, might prevent us from building anything which brings economic gains to people."[114] And there is no reason why one must stop with "natural" as opposed to "artificial" objects. In critiquing an essay by environmentalist Tom Regan, Frey well shows the conclusions to which such reasoning can lead:

> Nothing in Regan's paper, and nothing I have said so far, precludes Rolls Royces having inherent value. Indeed, I should have thought that they fit Regan's demands perfectly. For consider: someone who all his life has been condemned to a Ford is, if he acquires a Rolls Royce, very likely, in view of its quality, to have an attitude of admiring respect towards it. He talks of it as environmentalists talk of natural objects: he speaks of his awe, amazement, and wonder at the car and its performance; he raves about its beauty; he tells his friends of its controlled fury, its power and force, its response to the touch, its sleekness; he marvels at the extraordinary harmony and functioning in its parts. And if Regan had not given up his earlier view of inherent value, our car owner would have said his car satisfied that view precisely; for if to have inherent value is for a thing to be good of its kind, then most definitely, Rolls Royces have inherent value. If, however, they have inherent value, then we have *prima facie* no reason to exclude them from the theory of value being developed for an environmental ethic.
>
> Those distressed to find that their ethic encompasses automobiles require criteria for including natural objects but not cars within the class of things which have inherent value. It is easy to see how some possible attempts to exclude cars—to deny that they are sentient or conscious or possessed of some psychological state or living, for instance—will be prejudicial in the extreme to (many or all) natural objects.[115]

In the face of these formidable difficulties, Australian philosopher Michael Tooley goes to the opposite extreme, arguing that "basic moral principles should involve neither terms referring to particular biological species, nor the general concept of membership in a biological species"—from which he draws the appalling conclusion: "It follows that the fact that abortion and infanticide result in the destruction of innocent human beings cannot, in itself, be a reason for viewing such actions as wrong."[116] Species membership thus becomes no ground for attributing rights or for the necessary application of interest theory.

Human Rights Debilitated

Professor Melden tries to get around this impasse by establishing human value socially: "All persons are alike in being members of the moral community; and morally flawed as any person may be, he is, as a member of that community, the responsible object of the moral interest of everyone else."[117] But, of course, this praiseworthy ideal leaves completely unanswered the fundamental question as to why one should attribute rights to humans at all—flawed or unflawed—any more than to rocks, rats, or the Rolls Royce.

Transcendence the Key to Defining Human Rights

The interest theory of rights is surely to be preferred to the will theory, for rights do not logically depend on the extent to which they are recognized or claimed. "A right, it would be safe to say, is obviously a form of entitlement arising out of moral, social, political, or legal rules."[118] But in order for the interest theory not to collapse upon itself, inherent human value and entitlement to rights—over against the natural and animal worlds—must be established. Melden, without being aware of it, touches on the only possible means of successfully doing so when he writes:

> Even if the origin of natural or human rights is to be ascribed to the agency of God, this would be intelligible only if in endowing men with rights God also endowed men with a nature suitable to the possession of those rights. For we do not ascribe rights to animals unless we attribute human characteristics to them.[119]

Were there a transcendent Source of human rights—a God who both declared to what rights human beings are entitled *qua* human beings, and who created human beings in His own image so that these rights are entailed by God's very nature—*then,* and only then, could there be a satisfactory interest-orientated definition of human rights. But this is just another way of saying that the problem of defining human rights leads inexorably to the deeper question of justifying the rights one is at pains to define.

Rights as Entitlements

In the last analysis, rights are *titles*. White puts it this way:

> To have the right to V is to have something more positive than simply the liberty to V or even a claim to V, but it is not something so constraining as the duty or obligation to V, so enabling as the power to V or so selective as the privilege of Ving. Liberty opens something to me, duty or obligation closes something, power makes me capable of it, whereas a right gives me a title to it.
>
> Whoever has a right has a title, something which entitles him, which gives him a sort of ticket of justification to do or be given so and so, to be or to feel such and such. Though the possession of this does not entail the rightness or wrongness of certain behaviour, either by him or by others, nor entail certain duties or obligations on them, it provides a strong reason, moral, legal, or otherwise, for or against such behaviour, where it would be appropriate. His right gives him immunity from at least certain sorts of criticism for what he does even when his doing this in other circumstances or somebody else's doing it in these circumstances would be open to criticism on grounds which are

> prima facie applicable to what he does within his rights. Moreover, his possession of a right can expose them to possible criticism for interfering or even for not helping where such interference or help is relevant. A right to V is normally linked either to some rule about Ving, for example a right to bring a guest into the club, to take a resit examination, to unemployment benefit, or to some explicitly or implicitly accepted convention, whether legal, moral, institutional, logical, etc., about Ving, for example a right to damages, to free speech, to vote, to assume so and so, or to feel proud of such and such, which the holder of a right can appeal to in order to justify his Ving. Such a rule or convention gives him a right to V by allowing his Ving a measure of exemption from criticism, objection, interference, etc. It allows him this because he or his situation falls into a certain class for which Ving is appropriate or proper or has a particular point, as when, for example, a parent, student, or driver or someone who has worked hard, has been provoked or has achieved something has a right to such and such.[120]

Titles Are Relational: The Transcendent Again

On reflection, it will be observed that the concept of "title" or "entitlement" is *relational:* it always implies a source or justification of the title in question. White sees this clearly:

> To have a right is necessarily to have it in virtue of something, either of some feature of one's situation or of having been given it by someone who had the right, authority or power to give it. In the latter case we can ask "Who gave you the right to V?"; in the former, "What gives you the right to V?". I shall call this second question a request for the "ground" of the right, though writers on this topic have in fact used a battery of phrases, including "based on", "at the root of", "give rise to", "springs from", "resulting out of", etc.[121]

Thus, whether we consider the relational nature of rights as entitlements or analyze the necessary implications of interest theory, the conclusions are the same: human rights logically require an identification of human value and pose the question of "someone"—Someone!—who has "the right, authority or power" to give them. And the quest to *define* rights cannot be separated from the need to *justify* them. To that task of justification we now direct our attention.

chapter four

The Dilemma, Part Two: Justifying Human Rights

Now to an analysis and critique of the most influential contemporary philosophies of human rights. Seven moral theories warrant our attention: Benthamite utilitarianism, legal positivism or realism (represented by H. L. A. Hart, Hans Kelsen, and Ronald Dworkin), John Finnis's revived natural law theory, sociological jurisprudence (Roscoe Pound and Julius Stone), neo-Kantian moral philosophy (John Rawls and Alan Gewirth), Marxism, and the McDougal-Lasswell-Chen policy-orientated philosophy of human rights. To each we ask the $64,000 question: can you justify human dignity?

Our study of existing human rights practice led to a preliminary conceptual dilemma: What does one really mean when one talks about human rights? And our analysis of this basic definitional issue has brought us to an even more puzzling question: how can human rights, properly understood, be legitimated? Here we shall need to examine the most influential modern and contemporary philosophies of human rights to see if any of them is capable of justifying human dignity.

Positivism and Relativism

One of the products of the general secularization of life and thought in the nineteenth century was the rise of scientific positivism, or scientism: science was supposed to be value-free and capable of handling all human difficulties. Auguste Comte and his followers—such as Ruth Benedict in the twentieth century—developed a relativistic sociology and anthropology according to which each culture operates in terms of its own values and no single value system could or should be imposed upon all.[122] From this secular, relativistic soil grew the political philosophies of utilitarianism and legal positivism or realism.[123]

Bentham, the Well-Stuffed Utilitarian

The great name in utilitarian legal philosophy is that of Jeremy Bentham. As a humanitarian reformer he deserves high praise (he was, for example, largely responsible for the 1834 Hilary Rules, a precursor of the 1873 Judicature Act which cleaned up many of the grossest features of English civil procedure immortalized by Charles Dickens). Bentham was also an archetypal eccentric: he favored, *inter alia,* mummifying the dead and using them as utilitarian, decorative art objects. Bentham himself, appropriately stuffed, may still be seen in a glass case at University College, London.

Bentham wrote a book-length critique of Blackstone's *Commentaries* (1765–70), in which the first professor of English common law at Oxford founded human laws on the law of nature and scriptural revelation.[124] For Bentham, "natural and imprescriptable rights'' were nothing more than ''nonsense upon stilts.'' He declared that ''from the law of nature come imaginary rights—a bastard brood of monsters.''[125] In Bentham's view, which greatly influenced the father of legal positivism, John Austin, law is but a species of command, and the only true rights are the rights given by the positive law of the state.[126] These rights should be created on the principle of utility: to achieve the greatest good for the greatest number. But in advocating ''utility,'' Bentham naively and uncritically assumed the validity of his own conservative English morality and social values. His utilitarianism leaves entirely unanswered the root question, ''Useful for *what?*''

H. L. A. Hart, Analytical Realist

The most influential contemporary representative of legal positivism or realism is H. L. A. Hart, a thinker schooled in the best traditions of the analytical philosophy movement. Hart has raised to a level of considerable sophistication the rather simplistic nineteenth-century view that law and rights are no more than products of the commands of a sovereign (John Austin) or the results of judicial decision (John Chipman Gray). In Hart's view, law requires a social dimension (rules have an ''internal aspect'') and can only function by way of ''shared morality.'' There is always a ''union of primary and secondary rules'' (not just rules imposing duties but also rules of recognition, change, and adjudication by which law comes to function as such).[127] Since for Hart, as much as for Bentham or Austin, human rights are the product of positive law and not natural morality, they make sense only through successful appeals to a sense of community.[128]

But, as Rosenbaum well observes, Hart's ''community'' approach to rights does not tell us ''how to obtain universal agreement on the essentials of a community" or "how it is possible to experience the sense of community when the competing views around the world on the nature of community seem to thwart the development of a unified concept of human rights."[129] The force of these criticisms becomes particularly evident when we note that for Hart the ultimate "rule of recognition" on which any given legal system (and, therefore, any system of human rights protection) is founded is *unjustifiable* outside of the system itself.

> We only need the word 'validity', and commonly only use it, to answer questions which arise *within* a system of rules where the status of a rule as a member of the system depends on its satisfying certain criteria provided by the rule of recognition. No such question can arise as to the validity of the very rule of recognition which provides the criteria; it can neither be valid nor invalid but is simply accepted as appropriate for use in this way. To express this simple fact by saying darkly that its validity is "assumed but cannot be demonstrated", is like saying that we assume, but can never demonstrate, that the standard metre bar in Paris which is the ultimate test of the correctness of all measurements in metres, is itself correct.[130]

We are thus left—as in the case of sociological and anthropological relativism—with no single, unified, justifiable conception of human dignity.

Hans Kelsen, Continental Positivist

The same deficiency is equally plain in the legal philosophy of Hans Kelsen, the most prominent twentieth-century representative of continental legal positivism. Kelsen's interest in human rights is plain from his book, *The Law of the United Nations*.[131] But, characteristically, he can only consider human rights from the standpoint of an actual or potential structure of positive legal protections, since in his "pure theory of law" legal norms are no more than hypothetical statements stipulating that a given sanction ought to be executed under certain conditions.[132] Legal systems are hierarchical in structure (*Stufenbau*), grounded in a basic norm (*Grundnorm*)—and, as with Hart, there is no possibility of establishing the ultimate validity of one such norm (and thus of any one legal system or view of human rights) over against another.

> It is of the greatest importance to be aware of the fact that there is not only one moral or political system, but at different times and within different societies several very different moral and political systems are considered to be valid by the men living under these normative systems. These systems actually came into existence by custom, or by commands of outstanding personalities like Moses, Jesus or Mohammed. If men believe that these personalities are inspired by a transcendental, supernatural—that is a divine authority—the moral or political system has a religious character. It is especially in this case when the moral or political system is supposed to be of divine origin that the values constituted by it are considered to be absolute. If, however, the fact is taken into consideration that there are, there were and probably always will be several different moral and political systems actually presupposed to be valid within different societies, the values constituted by these systems can be considered to be only of a relative character; then the judgment that a definite government or a difinite [*sic*] legal order is just can be pronounced only with reference to one of the several different political and moral systems, and then the same behavior or the same governmental activity or the same legal order may with reference to another moral or political system be considered as morally bad or as politically unjust.[133]

Taking Ronald Dworkin Seriously

Ronald Dworkin, H. L. A. Hart's American successor at Oxford, is attempting to carry legal realism well beyond the levels of either Kelsen or Hart. In understanding the nature of legal systems, one cannot stop, as does Hart, even with the sophisticated distinction between primary and secondary rules. Beyond the secondary rules lie "principles, policies, and other sorts of standards,"[134] for "the 'law' includes principles as well as rules."[135] How far we have now traveled from the rigidity and simplicity of Benthamite utilitarian positivism (which Dworkin attacks in no uncertain terms)! But Dworkin's "principles" are no more justifiable ultimately than Kelsen's *Grundnorm* or Hart's rule of recognition, for Dworkin refuses to derive them from or test them by a natural or "higher" law.

Dworkin's human rights theory focuses on what he regards as the absolutely fundamental moral right of every person to equal concern and respect. This right must be "taken seriously" in the political and moral spheres and must be seen to underlie (not result from) legislation, adjudication, social practices, or community decisions. And how does Dworkin justify his assertion that everyone has the fundamental right to equal concern and respect? Answer: he doesn't. He calls the principle "axiomatic" and states that "our intuitions about justice presuppose . . . this most fundamental of rights."[136] But one man's presupposition may be—and through history often has been—another man's poison.[137]

Moreover, the reduction of human rights to "equal concern and respect" does not sufficiently take into account the range and complexity of the entitlements involved when legal and moral rights are asserted.

> A man in the United States who asserts a moral right on behalf of his child to sing Christmas carols in school (court decisions there have upheld a bar on singing carols in the public schools) is neither overtly nor in some subtle way arguing that his child is being shown a degree of concern and respect drastically at odds with that being shown to his neighbour's children; indeed, unless these terms are construed exceedingly broadly, he is not arguing about concern and respect at all. Rather, he is arguing, as he sees it, about the legitimate extent of

a court's power to interfere with his child's freedom, in circumstances where he and a good many others cannot make out the clear and present danger necessary in order to justify such a limitation of freedom. Likewise, when the National Rifle Association in the United States asserts on behalf of its members a moral (and legal) right to bear arms, its claim is neither directly nor indirectly grounded in some demand for concern and respect, equal or otherwise, but in some demand to show the clear and present danger necessary in order to impose limits on its members' freedom. Of course, it is using a claim to a right in order perhaps to elicit a measure of concern and respect for its members' views, but that is not the same thing as saying that its claim is about concern and respect.[138]

Legal Realism Frighteningly Unrealistic

The single gravest problem with all forms of legal realism or positivism is their limitation of rights to the confines of particular legal systems or jurisprudential orientations. No overriding, justifiable standard of human dignity is brought to bear on the human situation. As the great Belgian philosopher of law Ch. Perelman succinctly puts it,

> This conception of juridical positivism collapses before the abuses of Hitlerism, like any scientific theory irreconcilable with the facts. The universal reaction to the Nazi crimes forced the Allied chiefs of state to institute the Nuremberg trials and to interpret the adage *nullum crimen sine lege* in a nonpositivistic sense because the law violated in the case did not derive from a system of positive law but from the conscience of all civilized men. The conviction that it was impossible to leave these horrible crimes unpunished, although they fell outside a system of positive law, has prevailed over the positivistic conception of the grounding of the law.[139]

An Oscillation of Ideas

In the nineteenth century, legal positivism or realism replaced a much older juridical philosophy, the theory of natural law. In chapter 5 we shall examine the historic, theological version of this philosophy and learn why it fell upon evil days and was replaced at stage center by positivism during our modern secular era. Here we merely note that the overwhelming difficulties with all varieties of realism (as we just observed them) are producing still another pendulum-swing in the history of ideas—a swing back to natural law thinking.[140] But the most influential representatives of the current natural law revival do not operate theologically; rather, they attempt philosophically to establish a ground within human nature for absolute human rights, a ground allegedly surpassing positive law and cultural relativity.

John Finnis and Natural Law

The most impressive contemporary effort to rehabilitate natural law as the basis of human rights is provided by John Finnis, fellow of University College, Oxford. Finnis is Roman Catholic and much concerned with the interpretation of Thomas Aquinas vis-à-vis the arguments he presents, but Finnis's great work, *Natural Law and Natural Rights,* is not disguised theologizing. He is thoroughly trained in analytical philosophy and attempts to show in the most general sense that "practical reasonableness" in ordering human affairs requires an approach to the state, law, and human rights that will preserve and extend human goods (specifically: life, knowledge, play, esthetic experience, friendship or sociability, religion, etc.). "There are human goods," he writes, "that can be secured only through the institutions of human law, and requirements of practical reasonableness that only those institutions can satisfy."[141]

> What Finnis is trying to show is how any common enterprise of human beings, aims at achieving a common good, and hence demands something which can only be called political or governmental

authority. Nor is the function of such authority to be understood exclusively, or even primarily, in terms of any mere exercise of coercive force. No, it is rather for the necessary and indispensable coordination of the efforts of the different agents of the community that the authority is instituted in the first place; and it is only through the exercise of such a directing and coordinating authority have [*sic*] the common good of the community can even be concretely determined, much less achieved. And as for law—human law or positive law—it is nothing if not the indispensable instrument of such a public or governmental authority, aimed at the attainment of the good of the community. Moreover, since the good of the community is not literally collective good, or even an additive good, but simply the well-being of each and all of the members of the community individually, the law needs to be so constituted as to respect the rights of the individual members of the community. And here again, in his discussion of the rights, i.e. the natural rights, of citizens, Finnis is very careful to construe such rights—e.g. common law rights, such as the right to property, to a fair trial, to protection against self-incrimination, to safeguards against viol [*sic*]—not as absolute rights, in the way in which this term is so often understood now-days, but rather as rights that are justified in terms of the natural needs and requirements of the individual, if he is ever to be able to live the life of a truly moral and autonomous human person.[142]

Finnis's commendable attempt to establish human rights in terms of practical reasonableness and the common good of the community suffers from great difficulties, however. Bankowski has pointed out that, of the several "human goods" Finnis sets forth, only "knowledge" is effectively justified by his retortive argument that one cannot argue against it without cutting the ground out beneath one's own feet. And even in the case of knowledge the vital question is still left open: "what items of knowledge we should seek."[143] Indeed, Finnis "is better at showing how law needs to be grounded in ethics, than he is at showing how the principles of ethics are discoverable right in the very facts of nature and reality."[144]

What *Is* Natural?

Like every natural law thinker, Finnis must solve the problem of defining what man's nature really is. True, man frequently desires knowledge, life, and friendship; but it is equally the case empirically that human beings have often sought to deceive, kill, and subjugate their fellows. After all, Hobbes—and Machiavelli before him—built his totalitarian social theory strictly on the natural law basis that human life is "nasty, brutish, and short"! A successful natural law theory must be able to say whether the good or the bad in human life is truly "natural" and to what degree—for otherwise no one can determine what rights are properly to be protected in society.

The Problem of "Doin' What Comes Naturally"

The Naturalistic Fallacy

And this dilemma connects with the related quandary for natural law thinkers as to how, even if we know what human nature actually consists of, we can justify deriving an "ought" from the "is." The great analytical ethicist G. E. Moore termed this difficulty the "naturalistic fallacy": the false idea that once you know what is natural you will have justified it as a positive value.[145] In reality, even as the natural fact of murder or torture doesn't justify killing or inhuman punishment, so the natural fact of self-preservation or truth-seeking doesn't in itself vindicate the alleged right to life or civil liberties.

Roscoe Pound's Sociological Jurisprudence

The weight of the naturalistic fallacy presses even more heavily on the labors of American sociological jurisprudent Roscoe Pound, who in his later years moved in the direction of natural law thinking.[146] Pound's guiding principle was "social engineering," by which he meant the political and legal ordering of human relations to maximize all interests with the least sacrifice of the totality of interests. Interests for him fell into three categories: individual (civil rights, domestic relations, freedom of contract, property ownership, etc.), public (interests of state), and social (security, general morality, social resources, etc.).[147]

On the positive side, "his identification of the interests involved takes into account the realities of the social process; he shows us how to focus on rights in terms of what people are concerned about and what they want."[148] But, as I was at pains to show in the preceding chapter, needs do not per se constitute rights. To assume that one can automatically move from the sociological description of interests to a normative philosophy of human rights is to commit the naturalistic fallacy with a vengeance. Not for nothing is the naturalistic fallacy often termed the sociologist's fallacy!

The Quasi-Absolutes of Julius Stone

Pound's Australian disciple Julius Stone critiqued his mentor's list of interests,[149] and ultimately offered a scheme of his own. But Stone did not really advance the search for a solid philosophy of human rights by his list of "ideals which may be regarded as quasi-absolute precepts of material justice in our own time and place."[150] One does not avoid the naturalistic fallacy by calling one's normative principles "quasi-absolute—absolute so far as it is given to us, to our generation of humans, to know and act by absolutes." The very notion of a qualified absolute is self-contradictory (if it is less than absolute, it *isn't* absolute). More important, in the face of Dachau, the Gulag, and similar examples of twentieth-century inhumanities of man toward man, human rights principles must be able to be established as absolute *without qualification:* quasi-absolutes never offer satisfactory resistance to demonic evil.

Two highly influential contemporary philosophies of social ethics have been built on a neo-Kantian base: John Rawls' "theory of justice" and Alan Gewirth's vindication of human rights.[151]

> Both Rawls and Gewirth have given expression to treating persons as equals in terms of variant interpretations of Kantian universalizability. Gewirth has followed Kant more literally: he has argued that ethical reasoning, as such, is marked by a certain phenomenology—namely, in reasoning ethically, an agent abstracts from her or his particular ends, and thinks in terms of what general requirements for rational autonomy the agent would demand for the self (so idealized) on the condition that the requirements be consistently extended to all other agents alike. Rawls's argument is more abstract but to similar effect: we start not from the particular agent, but from the concept of rational persons who must unanimously agree upon, while under a veil of ignorance as to who they are, the general critical standards in terms of which their personal relations will be governed. For Rawls, the veil of ignorance performs the same function as Gewirth's abstraction of the agent from her or his ends (in thinking ethically, one respects higher-order capacities of personhood, not lower-ends which happen to be pursued); and, the contractual agreement is the functional equivalent of Gewirth's universalization (what all persons would agree to comes to the same thing as what any person, suitably idealized, would demand for one's self on the condition that it be extended to all alike). Now, importantly, both these theories appeal to consequences in arguing that certain substantive principles would be universalized (Gewirth) or agreed to (Rawls). Thus, Gewirth has argued that the universalizing agent would assess the necessary substantive or material conditions for rational autonomy and would univeralize [*sic*] those conditions; the consequences of universalization thus importantly determine what would be universalized. Correspondingly, Rawls's contractors consider the consequences of agreeing to certain standards of conduct as part of their deliberations.[152]

Rawls and Gewirth heroically endeavor to bypass the naturalistic fallacy through Kantian "practical reason." Though "oughts" may not be able to be established as metaphysical absolutes, it can, by starting from a point of moral neutrality, be shown that everyone is committed to "prudential rights" by virtue of the desire to further one's own self-interest and achieve one's own goals. From Kant's categorical imperative (so act that your action may become a universal rule) one arrives at Gewirth's principle of generic consistency (PGC): act in accord with the generic rights of your recipients as well as of yourself.[153] How successful is such neo-Kantian reasoning?

Rawls

Looking first at Rawls, we find ourselves in the presence of the single most influential moral philosophy of this generation, but a theory nonetheless replete with difficulties.[154] Even without going into the considerable technicalities of Rawls' system, several overall points of critique warrant our reflection. (1) It has been pointed out that Rawls' economic models and extensive use of Von Neumann's utilitarian game theory exhibit a concern with "distribution to the exclusion of production," that "by employing those models of analysis, Rawls buys into their underlying psychological presuppositions," and that his Western-liberal welfare economics is "the pure theory of the cargo cult."[155] In other words, Rawls' theory of justice is irredeemably *Western:*

Too Western?

> In spite of its admirable comprehensiveness, the concealed sociological assumptions and ideological leanings of Rawls' theory, when disclosed, make its application very restrictive and its claim to generality spurious. . . . In spite of Rawls' protestations to the contrary, it is clear that his concept of the ideal of a person is a priori. . . . Rawls substitutes for the real individual of flesh and blood an ideal, Kantian-type person. . . . The Rawlsian scheme of social

cooperation in the pursuit of justice is still unworkable in many parts of the world. . . . Rawls' principles of justice and the priority rules are basically *conservative* in their inspiration, designed to conserve the existing liberties of the groups and at the same time to reflect an awareness of the necessity for a just redistribution of the primary goods.[156]

Not Western Enough?

(2) Yet Rawls' approach to equal distribution is also seen, by politically conservative critics, to reflect a hopeless betrayal of Western values. Antony Flew writes:

> Having . . . hung up the Veil of Ignorance, Rawls puts the basic question to his hypothetical contracting parties. After the endearing frankness of his confession that "We want to define the original position so that we get the desired solution," it comes as no surprise that they cannot but "acknowledge as the first principle of justice one requiring an equal distribution. Indeed, this principle is so obvious that we would expect it to occur to anyone immediately." Given that the zombies have deliberately been rendered ignorant of all those particularities of actual, flesh and blood, historically situated, humanly related, individuals upon which possibly unequal claims might be grounded: to them it must indeed seem obvious. . . .
>
> From the beginning . . . the entire Rawls contractual project tacitly presupposes that all tangible or intangible goods—whether already at hand or to be produced or discovered later—all goods of every kind arising within the artificially unknown state borders of the artificially unknown territories being or to be inhabited by his thought-experimental group, everything is collective property, available for distribution or redistribution at the absolute discretion of the group.[157]

And Robert Nozick offers a disquieting example:

> An application of the principle of maximizing the position of those worse off might well involve forceable redistribution of bodily parts ("You've

been sighted for all these years; now one—or even both—of your eyes is to be transplanted to others''), or killing some people early to use their bodies in order to provide material necessary to save the lives of those who otherwise would die young. To bring up such cases is to sound slightly hysterical. But we are driven to such extreme examples in examining Rawls.[158]

Certainly Aprioristic

(3) No time will be spent arbitrating the question as to whether Rawls is too conservative or too liberal politically (and the two extremes are not by any means mutually exclusive!). What is of immediate interest is that *both* criticisms have stressed the unprovable, aprioristic nature of Rawls' method (''concealed sociological assumptions''—''a priori''—''the entire project tacitly presupposes . . .''). D. J. Bentley of Christ Church, Oxford, writes: ''How does Rawls know that this is how rational beings would behave in the 'original position'? I think the answer must be that Rawls has loaded the odds fairly heavily against any other choice.''[159] Princeton philosophy professor Thomas Scanlon speaks of the ''residual indeterminacy'' of Rawls' theory of justice and holds that ''in the end the adoption of an alternative view is not wholly precluded.''[160] And Robert Paul Wolff, author of the most thorough book-length examination of Rawls' philosophy, puts his finger on the central weakness of this entire presuppositionalistic social ethic when he observes:

> Even if Rawls's theorem can be established, the self-interested moral skeptic may still decline to make a once-and-for-all commitment, even to a principle chosen from self-interest. Fidelity to principle is not, after all, deducible from bare formal rationality, at least not without some rather powerful metaphysical assumptions about the timeless character of the moral agent (*qua noumenon*, in Kant's language).[161]

And Internationally Irrelevant

The application of this criticism to Rawls' theory vis-à-vis international human rights is particularly devastating. Anthony D'Amato has argued that Rawlsian philosophy actually "may impede the spread of human rights," for it has no necessary impact internationally—beyond the boundaries of the individual societal models Rawls treats.

> Why couldn't one person, or a group of people, choose not to participate in the original-position negotiations? Can we not imagine a group of people saying the following: "Exclude us from your negotiations. If you set up a society, we may deal with you, if we choose, and you may choose to deal with us or to avoid us. If you produce goods that we want, we may offer to exchange them for surplus goods that we have produced which you may want. But we do not want to be part of your society."[162]

Gewirth

Gewirth's variation on Kantian moral theory also lacks necessitarian character.

> This approach to justifying basic human rights, which Gewirth calls "the dialectically necessary method," certainly can be questioned. For example, it does not seem obvious to me that Gewirth's account of action and its conditions is morally neutral, as he claims it is; much like Rawls' original position, it seems as much a disguised philosophical anthropology as anything else. Furthermore, why the actor must obey the principle of noncontradiction is not entirely clear to me. . . .
>
> Likewise, many individual steps in the argument are extremely controversial, even if we accept the method. For example, the move from "Freedom and well-being are necessary goods for A" to "A has and claims rights to freedom and well-being" seems to me insufficiently justified and based on a dubious account of the correlation of rights and duties. Furthermore, I am not convinced that the principle of universalizability, by which Gewirth moves from individual prudential rights to human rights, is morally neutral, as it must be according to the dialectically necessary method.[163]

Thumbing One's Nose at Universalization

Putting it concretely, when Gewirth declares that one must logically act in accord with the generic rights of the recipient (as when Kant asserts categorically that one must act so that one's action could become a universal rule), the reply of the thoroughly self-centered person, the fanatic, the revolutionary, or the anarchist may well be: "I'll act without regard for others (or the other side) if I can get away with it." Experientially, we all know that others do not or cannot always give the actor tit for tat, so in the absence of a final accounting (a Last Judgment) the unprincipled person may well choose to disregard the rights of others when he has the power to get away with it. The condottieri of Machiavelli's time, Burckhardt tells us, enjoyed the game of rolling boulders from their castles down onto their peasants working in the fields; since they feared neither God nor man, they did what pleased them, in total disregard of any principle of universalization. Human rights violations of our day have the same shape, and the violators continue to say, "So what?"

Kantianism, a Blind Alley

Gewirth's difficulties, like Rawls', are at root those of his mentor Kant. Though Kant never traveled physically more than fifty kilometers from his Königsberg birthplace, the dubious influence of his critical philosophy has circled the globe.

> In the end, we must conclude that Kant failed to discover a way to deduce objective, obligatory ends from the mere analysis of what it is to be a rational agent. He was therefore unable also to establish the unconditionally universal validity of any substantive principles of practical reason. My own view is that his failure was inevitable, because there are no such principles, but in any event, I am convinced that Kant's arguments do not work.[164]

The existence of "substantive principles of practical reason" is hardly foreclosed by our preceding discussion (and human rights would be groundless without them), but it is painfully clear that their discovery or vindication is not to be found in the neo-Kantian labors of Rawls and Gewirth.

Marxism

Marxist human rights theory, with one of the world's two greatest superpowers standing politically behind it, has unparalleled impact. Having treated the Marxist philosophy of human rights *in extenso* elsewhere,[165] I shall do no more here than to list its salient characteristics and the fundamental objections the system calls down upon itself. The Marxist view of human rights entails commitment to the following basic doctrines: (1) human rights depend on social and economic factors, (2) private property is detrimental per se to human rights, (3) the state creates whatever human rights in fact exist, (4) international organizations, governments, and individual interest groups have no business interfering in the domestic affairs of a state on the pretense of correcting alleged human rights violations (the "noninterference principle"), (5) the individual is not a proper subject of international law or international human rights protection.

These principles, to be sure, do not arise out of nothing. They derive from the monolithic, architectonic Marxist world view, characterized by a materialistic metaphysic, the materialistic-economic reinterpretation of Hegel's dialectic, an ethic of the end justifying the means, and an apocalyptic view of history in which class struggle will inevitably pass through the phase of a temporary dictatorship of the proletariat to a classless society in which both the state and law will have withered away, being no longer necessary.

The Failings of Marxist Theory

The Marxist philosophy of human rights is clearly an uneasy mix of legal positivism (the state determines rights) and secular natural law thinking (true social justice is realizable only when man's nature can develop free of economic inequities). Thus, Marxism suffers from the already discussed failings of both of these viewpoints.

In particular, as to human nature, Marxism claims that the ultimate source of all violations of human dignity lies in the bad economic conditions to which mankind is subject; yet obviously it is man himself who has created these conditions! Absent a doctrine of personal redemption (to which an atheistic system can hardly appeal), Marxism is left with no assurance that manipulations or revolutionary alterations in man's external economic environment will ever bring in a millennium of human dignity.

Bad Theory Leads to Bad Practice

And Marxist statism, combined with acceptance of the gross ethical fallacy that the end justifies the means, leads to a relativistic approach to human rights. Party policy determines the content of human rights on an ad hoc basis, with the result that human rights are continually subordinated to political goals and sheer expediency. In spite of the genuine concern of many Marxist thinkers and activists for a more just society, and their laudable stress on furthering the social and economic rights of the disenfranchised, Socialist states have—predictably—built up one of the very worst records of human rights violations in the modern world.

Policy-Orientated Human Rights

Policy-orientation in human rights is by no means limited to Marxism, however. The most ambitious Western attempt to date to set forth a philosophy of human rights operates from a "policy-oriented approach . . . which is contextual, problem-solving and multi-method," allegedly offering "a comprehensive map of what is meant by human rights in terms of the shaping and sharing of all values."[166] This philosophy—which has affinities with Pound's sociological jurisprudence—was developed, primarily at Yale, by Professor Myres McDougal and the late Professor Harold Lasswell. These authors, together with Professor Lung-chu Chen of the New York Law School, editor of the American Bar Association's journal, *Human Rights,* published in 1980 a massive tome entitled, *Human Rights and World Public Order: The Basic Policies of an International Law of Human Dignity.*[167]

McDougal, Lasswell, and Chen proceed on the premise that demands for human rights are demands for wide sharing in all the values upon which human rights depend and for effective participation in all community value processes. The interdependent values they specify are the demands relating to (1) respect, (2) power, (3) enlightenment, (4) well-being, (5) wealth, (6) skill, (7) affection, and (8) rectitude. They assemble a huge catalogue of the demands which satisfy those eight values as well as all of the ways in which they are denigrated.

McDougal, Lasswell, and Chen find a great disparity between the rising common demands of people for human dignity values and the achievement of them. This disparity is due to "environment" factors, such as population, resources, and institutional arrangements, and also to "predispositional factors", *i.e.,* special interests seeking "short term payoffs" in defiance of the common interests that would further human rights values. The ultimate goal, as they see it, is a world community in which a democratic distribution of values is encouraged and promoted; all available resources are utilized to the maximum; and the protection of human dignity is regarded as a paramount objective of social policy. While they call their approach a policy-oriented perspective, their choice of *human dignity* as the "super-value" in the shaping and sharing of all other values has a natural right ring to it.[168]

The Pros and Cons

The McDougal, Lasswell, and Chen theory has received high praise. Unlike most of the approaches we have dealt with in this chapter, it is not merely a social or political ethic with potential application to human rights, but a philosophy specifically geared to human rights—genuinely "attentive to international legal standards."[169] At the same time, it has serious defects. There is "the difficulty in making use of their system. Their list of demands is huge; . . . both trivial and serious claims are intertwined; and the whole is presented in a complex prose that is sometimes impenetrable."[170] More significant (indeed, fatal) is the absence of any sufficient underlying justification for the values propounded by the system.

Fifty Million Frenchmen

Chen declares that "the comprehensive set of public order goals we recommend for postulation, clarification and implementation are those which today are commonly characterized as the basic values of human dignity, or of a free society. This is not an idiosyncratic or arbitrary choice but a product of many heritages."[171] But the fact alone that "many heritages" agree on goals or policy doesn't necessarily make them right. The naturalistic fallacy again raises its ugly head. Fifty million Frenchmen can *still* be wrong!

A Personal Anecdote

My external examiner for the M.Phil. degree in law at the University of Essex was Dr. Rosalyn Higgins of the London School of Economics, who had studied at Yale and accepts the policy-orientated approach to human rights.[172] She naturally did not feel comfortable with my criticism of Marxist human rights theory for its policy orientation. When I asked her (she is of Jewish background) how she would have been able to oppose in principle the Nazi racism of the 1930s and 1940s when the Third Reich was simply carrying out consistently its own national and juridical policies, she admitted that policy-orientated human rights theory had not solved that problem. But if a human rights philosophy cannot deal with *that* problem, it has surely been weighed in the balance and found wanting.

Neglecting the Human Heart

While claiming that human rights policies are justified contextually, Chen himself has to admit the widespread "failure . . . of not recognizing the fundamental importance of respect, when appraised among all values in human motivation and impact."[173] But why does this occur? Why do human beings not respect each other? Why do they so readily disregard each other's human dignity? Chen suggests that human rights violations are essentially "monuments to sheer intellectual failure."[174] We respectfully disagree. Even the most intellectually sophisticated catalogue of human rights policies and goals offers no guarantee whatever that people or governments will follow them. The depths of human motivation sadly continue to be untouched by the policy-orientated philosophy of human rights—yet it is ultimately the human heart that holds the key to respect for others.

The End of the Road

And so our guided tour of the most influential contemporary philosophies of human rights comes to a close. With all the good will in the world, I must nonetheless agree with Professor White:

> None of the answers commonly suggested to the question "What gives one the right to so and so?", that is, none of the grounds suggested for any of the rights which it is maintained we either have or ought to have, shows . . . any strictly logical connection between the right in question and the basis suggested for it. All that it is possible to argue is that the suggested basis gives a non-deductive, evaluative reason for possession of the right, a

> reason which is, of course, often supported by common sense, our shared moral values, the apparatus of the law, some institutionalized system of regulations or conventions, etc.[175]

As has so often been the case in the history of thought, the philosophers have shown themselves to be long on the questions and short on the answers. But the cruciality of preserving human rights in today's human jungle will not permit us the luxury of stopping at such a point. A qualitatively different route must be found to justify human dignity.

chapter five

The Essentiality of Transcendence and the Failure of Religious Answers

The plot thickens. In this chapter we discover (1) that only a transcendent source of human rights could logically establish a satisfactory justification for human dignity, but (2) that several major religious alternatives do not succeed in providing such a transcendental foundation, and (3) that ecumenical religiosity and religious natural rights theories are no more successful. We are left at best with inalienable rights lacking in specificity, and a broken order of nature crying out for redemptive solution.

''Midway in this our mortal life'' Dante took stock of himself, or so the opening lines of the *Divine Comedy* suggest. Midway in the present investigation let us see to what point we have arrived.

Sobering Recapitulation

A survey of existing human rights protections, international and domestic, governmental and nongovernmental, left us with a plethora of rights-claims, but with no underlying justification of the purported entitlements other than their embodiment, to varying degree, in conventions, constitutions, and other instruments of positive law. Our examination of the meaning of the concept of "right" yielded an understanding of human rights as entitlements to human dignity, but it did not reveal whence such entitlements properly arise. And a survey of the most challenging philosophies of human rights has left us with no adequate foundation for human dignity.

Shall We Jettison Rights-Analysis?

In the face of such conceptual and philosophical discouragement, some thinkers are prepared to jettison any link between morals and rights. R. G. Frey provides a homely illustration.

> Consider an example: Cathy loves fried eggs for breakfast, and her husband, Heathcliff, knows this; but though Heathcliff makes scrambled eggs, poached eggs, boiled eggs, and omelettes, he never makes fried eggs for breakfast. Heathcliff and Cathy are married, there are duties on both sides, and marriage is, we say, a matter of mutual accommodation; yet, though he knows Cathy's desires and preferences perfectly, Heathcliff never makes fried eggs for breakfast.
>
> Now I can imagine a third party saying that it is wrong of Heathcliff not to make fried eggs occasionally or that he ought to or even that, given that he is married, knows Cathy's desires, and finds making fried eggs no more trouble than making any other sort of eggs, he has a duty to make fried eggs occasionally; but does anyone really think we can move from saying these things to the view that Cathy has a moral right to fried eggs for breakfast? And if you think we *can* make this move, then how are you going to prevent the complete trivialization of the notion of a moral right, since there appears no end to the possible development of similar examples?[176]

It will be observed that neither Cathy's status as an individual human person nor her contextual, institutional relations with others (here, her marriage to Heathcliff) can adequately establish the alleged moral right in question.

For Frey, this problem is to be resolved by short-circuiting rights analysis totally.

> What is wrong with torturing and killing someone is not the violation of some right of his, but the sheer agony and suffering he undergoes, the snuffing out of his hopes, desires, and wishes, and so on. What is wrong with depriving someone of a decent wage is not that it infringes some alleged right of his to this or that income but that it ruins his life and the lives of those who depend upon him. What is wrong with depriving someone of his liberty is that it thwarts his hopes and plans, circumscribes his future and what he can make of it, and so impoverishes his life. In short, there is no need to postulate moral rights as intermediaries between pain and agony, or thwarted hopes, desires, and plans, or ruined lives and the wrongness of what was done.[177]

Yet surely this is a colossal begging-of-the-question, for one is immediately faced with the same issue in another guise: how do we justify the wrongness of killing, torturing, paying inadequate wages, depriving people of their liberty, or, in general, impoverishing their lives? The wrongfulness of such conduct requires demonstration, not mere assertion.

"Prima Facie" Rights Won't Do

It will be remembered that, at Nuremberg, Robert Jackson described our recent history thus: "No half-century ever witnessed slaughter on such a scale, such cruelties and inhumanities, such wholesale deportations of peoples into slavery, such annihilations of minorities."[178] These "overshadowing historical facts" have made contemporary thinkers less and less happy with an intuitive ethic (who's intuition? Eichmann's?) or with a relativistic, contextual approach to human rights. Thus, critics have pointed out that the "prima facie" rights theory of my former philosophy professor at Cornell University, Gregory Vlastos,[179] reduces to the notion that rights "should be exercised under the condition that better reasons cannot be cited for not exercising them."[180] Surely this is not enough: we need *inalienable* rights.[181] Even Marxist thinkers (who by definition make human rights a function of shifting economic and social conditions and the variable will of the Party) are now trying to employ "inalienable rights" terminology meaningfully.[182]

Inalienable Rights Require Transcendence

But how could "inalienable rights" be established, even in principle? And why have the ofttimes brilliant philosophical attempts to do so (such as those discussed in the last chapter) always failed? The answer, quite simply, is that

Wittgenstein

given aphoristically by Ludwig Wittgenstein in his *Tractatus Logico-Philosophicus:* "The sense of the world must lie outside the world. . . . Ethics is transcendental."[183]

Water does not rise above its own level. Human efforts at formulating, promoting, and protecting human rights suffer from the limitations and prejudices of those engaged in these activities. This should not appear the least strange, since all systems of human law display exactly the same failings. Prior to the U.S. Civil War, the common law of chattels was extended in a sophisticated manner to cover the ownership (and even the hypothecating—the mortgaging) of slaves. National Socialist law did not recognize the humanity of the Jew. The Union of South Africa today gives jurisprudential sanction to apartheid.

A Cannibalistic Illustration

One can well imagine a society of anthropophagi who formulate third-generation environmental rights standards in some such terms as the following: "We hold as self-evident the right to a clean environment, and therefore categorically forbid the leaving of femurs or other human bones in public places after picnicking." This fine statement of human rights could be incorporated into a ratified international convention between two or more anthropophagous states.

Kurt Baier, the analytical ethicist, has concluded that from within the human situation ethical values can never logically rise above the societal level; indeed, "outside society, the very distinction between right and wrong vanishes."[184] This is Wittgenstein's point: one's ethic always reflects one's stance in society; and an absolute ethical stance (inalienable human rights) would require an absolute vantage point, which is precisely what fallible and limited human beings lack. An absolute ethic—if there were one—would have to be *transcendental.*

Archimedes

The physical principle involved is classically set forth by Archimedes (figure 4). His pioneer work in mechanics was summed up by the line attributed to him: *δός μοι ποῦ στῶ καὶ κινῶ τὴν γῆν* ("Give me a place to stand and I will move the earth").[185]

Expressed otherwise, the necessary condition for moving even the most gigantically heavy object is a fulcrum outside the object itself. Pulling oneself up by one's own bootstraps is always hard on the derrière—and does not succeed in any case.

Rousseau

Rousseau—remarkably—saw the application of this principle to jurisprudence and political science when he wrote in the *Contrat Social* :

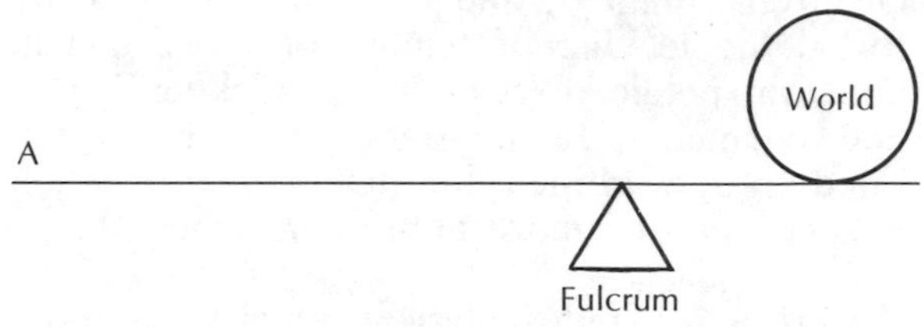

Figure 4
Archimedes' Lever

> In order to discover the rules of society best suited to nations, a superior intelligence beholding all the passions of men without experiencing any of them would be needed. This intelligence would have to be wholly unrelated to our nature, while knowing it through and through; its happiness would have to be independent of us, and yet ready to occupy itself with ours; and lastly, it would have, in the march of time, to look forward to a distant glory, and, working in one century, to be able to enjoy in the next. It would take gods to give men laws.[186]

Francis Schaeffer observed in much the same vein:

> Even Will and Ariel Durant, who were avowed humanists, and who received the humanist pioneer award in 1976, said in *The Story of Civilization:* "Moreover, we shall find it no easy task to mold a natural ethic strong enough to maintain moral restraint and social order without the support of supernatural consolations, hopes and fears." History, experience, and logic prove that is [*sic*] is not only difficult, as the Durants suggest, but *impossible*.[187]

In a word, to find an absolute foundation for human rights, one is obliged to move beyond the relative human situation to divine absolutes.

Flew's Roadblock Removed

But would not such a derivation of human rights be vacuous? Antony Flew argues—supporting his position by Plato's *Euthyphro*—that to establish human rights as creatures of the divine will is to "disclaim all possibility of praising that will as itself good" and that the rights conferred under God's prescriptive law would be "only the most empty and formal of custom-built necessary truths."[188] Aside from noting Flew's misattribution of this view to Hugo Grotius (a common mistake, easily correctable if one recalls that Grotius was one of the pioneers of Protestant Christian apologetics),[189] I reply that the derivation of human rights from God's will might well be a "formal, necessary truth" (in the sense that there would be no independent means of proving that God knew what He was doing in setting forth these rights!), but the rights set forth need hardly be "empty": their content could presumably be as full revelationally as God desired to make it. I am also at a loss to determine—in light of Wittgensteinian analysis—how an atheist such as Flew could even in principle establish the necessary absolute standard of goodness by which to "praise" (or blame) the prescriptive laws of God or man. From flux, nothing but flux, as Heraclitus well observed.

Rosenbaum is quite correct that "very few recent philosophers are inclined to found or even discuss human rights at the cosmic or spiritual levels. Most of them prefer to analyze the concept of human rights only within the moral dimension in terms of the status of personhood in the 'good society.' "[190] But this restriction of philosophical analysis to purely societal, immanent, nonreligious considerations is now seen to be the very reason why such analyses could not succeed even in principle. We must therefore turn our attention to religio-transcendental claims to justify human rights.

Religions of the Far East

Let us begin with the Far East. In his important article, "A Metaphysical Approach to Human Rights from a Chinese Point of View," Professor Peter Woo has argued that the Chinese world-view was shaped by "the Taoistic ideal of natural harmony, the ideal of the compassionate man of Confucianism, and the universal benevolence of Buddhism"; as a result, the Chinese "were, for a long time, . . . strangers to the concepts of human rights."[191] Specifically, "in view of the acceptance of universal unity and harmony, the issue of individual rights among men did not take the shape of a problem"; as for Confucianism, it "was to inculcate the acceptance of fate or of any living conditions, since all forms of revolt were ruled out."[192] Professor Elaine Pagels, discussing the same theme, writes:

> A similar pattern has prevailed for centuries in Hindu societies of India, Cambodia, Nepal, and in Pakistan: the social and political order reflect the divine order which the ruler embodies. The caste system, endorsed as the reflection of that order, fixed the ranks of society into the three upper classes, defined by their privileges, the fourth class, consisting of people who maintained minimal rights, and, below these, the "untouchables," who remained outside of society, and outside any system of rights. Buddhist society, which for centuries prevailed in China, Japan, Korea, Mongolia, Burma and Ceylon, similarly, revered the ruler as the embodiment of divine order. The laws of Buddhist society, which in its Indian form included the caste system, were religious laws which allowed no recourse for what we call "the individual."[193]

After a decade-long frustration with Marxism, Arthur Koestler drank deeply at the founts of

Eastern wisdom; his rejection of the Buddhist path was due principally to its lack of any clear moral direction, as exemplified by Zen monks who had no difficulty in becoming kamikaze pilots.[194] Francis Schaeffer writes:

> One of the distinctions of the Judeo-Christian God is that not all things are the same to Him. That at first may sound rather trivial, but in reality it is one of the most profound things one can say about the Judeo-Christian God. He exists; He has a character; and not all things are the same to Him. Some things conform to His character, and some are opposed to His character. This is in clear distinction, for example, from the Hindu or the Buddhist concept of God. To these gods, everything is the same, so that there is no distinction between good and evil, cruelty and non-cruelty, between tyranny and non-tyranny. In such a setting, speaking of inalienable rights or human rights would be meaningless, because to the Hindu or Buddhist the final reality—their concept of God as the all, the everything—would give no voice, no word, as to why anything is bad; why anything is humanness or anything is lack of humanness. In such a setting, human rights are meaningless. The proof of this is very easy to ascertain. All one has to do is to look at the Hindu situation in India itself with its caste systems. There are no intrinsic human rights. I would say in passing one only has to walk the streets of Bombay to feel the implications of this in practice.[195]

Though not a Christian, Gandhi acknowledged that it was the Christian missionaries and not his co-religionists who awakened in him a revulsion for the caste system and for the maltreatment of outcastes. And it is also worth pointing out that the Tantristic sacralizing of animal life has been one of the roots of the denigration of human values in the contemporary animal rights movement.[196]

Buddhist Enlightenment

Professor Chamarik endeavors to touch up this somber picture by stressing the Buddhist ideal of "internal self-control": "instead of relying on the external control on behaviour which is currently characteristic of both libertarian and egalitarian lines of approach . . . Buddhism goes further and deeper into the inner world of man himself; that is, the problem of deliverance from the transient self to the true self."[197] We have already noted—and the last chapter of this book will particularly stress—the overarching need for a change in man's inner perspective in order for true respect for human dignity to come about. Chamarik's recognition of this need is most commendable. The question remains, however, as to whether Buddhism can demonstrably fulfill that need. As Koestler observed, the nonpropositional, noncognitive nature of Buddhist ethics has left it with no absolute principles, and the enlightened sages of Buddhism did nothing to remove the appalling evil of the caste system. We are told that "Buddhism perseveringly takes to an optimistic view of man for his aptitude for goodness," that "the deliverance from the self to the true self can be accomplished and achieved solely through the individual's own endeavour," and that "man's altruistic outlook and attitude . . . is the result of his own deliverance through knowledge."[198] Sadly, human experience belies such optimism: the Germany of Hitler had a university tradition of cultural enlightenment second to none. Man is evidently incapable of attaining his "true self" through his own unaided efforts. To establish human rights, he requires absolute principles and transformation from outside himself, neither of which Buddhism offers or appears capable of supplying.

The Near East

Moving now from the Far East to the Near East, we come into contact with religious traditions which, in contrast with those just discussed, do indeed set forth explicit codes of rights and duties for man, with the claim that these codes are the product of divine revelation. Let us first consider human rights in the Islamic tradition, and then say a few words about Judaism and human rights.

Islam, a Religion of Law

Considerable scholarship in recent years has been devoted to the implications of Islamic religion for human rights. Such interest is understandable in light of the facts that the Koran is in itself a law code, that Islam ideally makes no distinction between divine law and human law, and that the Islamic way of salvation is strictly legalistic (on the Day of Judgment, one's good and bad deeds—as defined by the Koran—are meticulously weighed to determine whether one will go to Paradise or to Hell).[199]

The Positive Side of the Ledger

Islamic human rights principles include the right to life (Koran 5:35); the right to education without sex- or class-distinction—in light of the Prophet's insistence that all knowledge comes from God (Koran 96:1–5; 39:12; 35:20); the right to work (Koran 94:7–8; 53:40) and to form trade unions; and the right to possess property—in the capacity of a steward or life tenant, not as an absolute owner, since only Allah holds property in fee simple absolute (Koran 3:186; 2:27).[200] Such principles as these have been presented as illustrations of "the sublime morality and legal precepts of the Quran"[201] by Muslim scholars in a number of international colloquia, such as the Kuwait seminar on human rights in Islam, held in December 1980 under the co-sponsorship of the International Commission of Jurists, the University of Kuwait, and the Union of Arab Lawyers; and the earlier 1972–74 colloquia on Muslim dogma and human rights in Islam, held in Riyad, Paris, the Vatican, Geneva, and Strasbourg, sponsored by the government of Saudi Arabia.[202]

M'Bow Again

On 19 September 1981, at UNESCO headquarters in Paris, the European Islamic Council proclaimed their "Islamic Universal Declaration of Human Rights" in the setting of an international conference on human rights in Islam.[203] UNESCO director-general Amadou Mahtar M'Bow, himself a Muslim (we have met him earlier as the administrator most responsible for U.S. withdrawal from UNESCO),[204] waxed oratorical on Islamic human rights ideals. In the course of his address, he offered two illustrative anecdotes: during a famine in Medina, the future caliph Othman would not allow merchants to raise prices on necessaries, but insisted on giving away free the contents of his caravan shipment (showing Islam's concern with social and economic rights); and Muhammad's admission, on being asked whether his plan for the battle of Al Khandag was divinely inspired or his own idea, that the battleplan was only the result of his own thinking, and therefore his willingness to change the plan on the advice of others (showing Islam's respect for such civil and political liberties as individual freedom of expression and nondiscrimination).[205]

Islamic Doctrine and Human Rights

However, after all that can be said is said along the above lines, it will come as no surprise to the reader that Islam has some very serious human rights defects. We refer here not to inconsistencies between Islamic doctrine and practice (every system of thought has its unworthy disciples and fellow-travelers) but to unfortunate teachings built into the very fabric of Islamic jurisprudence through the Koran.

Thus, Sir Norman Anderson, formerly director of the Institute of Advanced Legal Studies of the University of London and probably the foremost present-day scholar of Muslim law outside of the Muslim world, notes the following doctrinal deficiencies of Islam vis-à-vis human rights: (1) The "cast-iron view of Predestination," supported by the Koran, leading to a "fatalism [which] plays a large part in the daily lives of millions of Muslims. To this the lethargy and lack of progress which, until recently at least, has for centuries characterized Muslim countries can be partially attributed." (2) "Islam sanctions slavery and the slave-trade, and the unlimited right of concubinage which a Muslim enjoys with his female slaves. . . . This extends even to married women captured in war, and opened the door to terrible abuse during the early wars of expansion, when almost any woman in a conquered land could be considered a slave by capture. . . . The would-be reformer of the position of women finds that polygamy, slave-concubinage, unilateral divorce and the beating of refractory wives is permitted by divine authority." (3) "The last section of the Shari'a deals with 'Punishments' or criminal sanctions. These provide, *inter alia,* for the murderer to be executed by the family of his victim; for one who causes physical injury to another to be submitted to the like; for the thief to have his right hand cut off; and for the adulterer to be stoned and the fornicator beaten." (4) Though the UN Universal Declaration of Human Rights has been "approved by all Muslim states, except Sa'udi Arabia and the Yemen, which are members of the United Nations Organization, yet the clause which affirms a man's right to change his religion if he so wishes runs directly counter both to the Islamic law of apostasy and to the practice of most of the Muslim states concerned."[206]

From Doctrine to Practice

These criticisms are by no means cavalier or able to be dispensed with on the ground that in enlightened Muslim countries modern civil and criminal codes have rendered Shari'a principles obsolete. President Sadat was assassinated by Muslim fanatics primarily because of his refusal to make Egypt a fundamentalist Islamic state;[207] the human rights violations of Khomeini's Iran have been documented *ad nauseam;*[208] and a recent London *Times* report from Khartum informs us that

> One year after he imposed a stern Islamic Code on punishments on this 70 per cent Muslim nation, President Gaafar Nimeiry of Sudan says he remains convinced that surgically amputating hands and feet of habitual thieves is a good thing.
>
> "Cutting off hands and feet is justifiable, because it has been prescribed by God in the Koran," said Mr Fuad El-Amin, the Cornell University-trained chief judge of Khartum Emergency Court Two.[209]

Why Accept the Koran?

But far more devastating for Islamic human rights theory than these specific deviations from accepted standards of human dignity is the epistemological problem of establishing that the Koran indeed constitutes divine revelation. We have no difficulty with the fact (to return to M'Bow's illustration) that Muhammad declared his military strategy to be mere human opinion; our problem is to find an adequate ground for accepting his assertions that in writing the Koran he was the unique Prophet of God, conveying infallible judgments. To *claim* divine inspiration is surely not the equivalent of *proving* it. (Consider also Father Divine and Jim Jones—examples suggesting that a false religious claim may be more dangerous than even an inadequate secular ethic, for the former not infrequently trades on its pseudo-absolutism to ruin lives and trod on human rights with olympian impunity.) Elsewhere I have analyzed in depth the paucity of supporting evidence for Islamic revelational claims, particularly in comparison with Christian claims.[210] It should be of more than passing interest that Sir Norman Anderson (whom I quoted at length above), while one of the foremost living specialists on Islamic law, is a Christian and author of a treatise titled, *The*

Evidence for the Resurrection.[211] No such attesting evidence for Muslim revelational claims can be marshalled, for it simply does not exist.

Judaism

Islam accepts Old Testament religion as one of its legitimate forerunners. What can be said of Judaism and human rights? We shall not go into detail here, for the general biblical approach to human dignity will occupy our attention in later chapters. But we do need to examine the claim of Judaism per se to supply the transcendental-revelational answer to the dilemma of human rights.

Professor Abraham Kaplan, chairman of the University of Haifa's Department of Philosophy, handsomely summarizes the Jewish approach to human rights:

> In short, the basis of human rights and their content rest, for Judaism, on the divine order of things. Because man, like the rest of nature, has also been created by God, this order has its counterpart in man's makeup, in his conscience and reason. Laws governing relations between man and man, if they accord with the divine law, stand to reason and satisfy our native sense of justice. "Reason," says Saadya Gaon, "prescribes that human beings should be forbidden to trespass upon one another's rights by any sort of aggression"—any sort, even that which claims to be justified by its noble goals. Commentators have explained that the Law proclaims "Justice, justice shall you follow!" (Deut. 16:20), repeating the word "justice" to convey that we must pursue justice in the means we employ as well as in the ends to which we aspire.
>
> God is the Author of human rights, and of man's capacity to discern and defend them. In this discernment, we come to know the divine. We know God by exercising justice and righteousness, says the Mishnah (Avot 1), echoing such prophets as Jeremiah (22:16). When this knowledge is the guide to action, we are in the service of the divine.

The sage joins the prophet in insisting that to do justice is more acceptable to God than to perform the sacrifices (Prov. 21:3). Above all, economic needs must be acknowledged and fulfilled. When a poor man stands at the door, says the Talmud, God stands at his right hand. If the poor are invited to share our own food, the dining table takes the place of the altar (Berachot 55a).

Human rights, like other moral ideals, make apparent the emptiness and even hypocrisy of what is often only a lip service. Action has a fundamental role in Jewish doctrine, to the point, indeed, that Judaism must be defined by characteristic actions rather than by a set of beliefs. It is a faith, not a creed, a faith which can find expression only in commitment to appropriate action. "Both the palm tree and the cedar stand tall," said the Baal Shem Tov, "but only the palm bears fruit—be like the palm!" Theories and symbols also have their contribution to make. "Between the mind and the heart," said another Hassidic master, Simchah Bunam, "the distance is as great as that between heaven and earth." Then he added, "Yet the earth is nourished by rain from heaven."[212]

Actions, Not Simply Beliefs

Unfortunately, however, this is only part of the story. On the doctrinal side, it is true, the Old Testament is free of the debilitating principles of social and familial intercourse that we have found to be integral to the Koran.[213] But Professor Kaplan insists that "Judaism must be defined by characteristic actions rather than by a set of beliefs." Viewed from the standpoint of "characteristic actions," Judaism does not have an enviable human rights record. During most of her history, the Jewish people have manifested an extreme racial exclusivism; rabbinic Judaism has displayed a fascination with legalistic minutiae unparalleled elsewhere—a legalism that has often crushed the human person under the weight of rule and alleged spiritual authority; the State of Israel today has a sorry history of documented human rights violations vis-à-vis her neighbors (Left-Bank Palestinians, Lebanese civilians, etc.) and her own people (e.g., the anti-proselytizing law which in principle chills Christian missionary efforts and religious freedom in the country).[214]

Even if such conduct can somehow be explained away, the same epistemological watershed exists for Judaism as for Islam: How do you know that your purported revelation is indeed from God? Suppose that the human rights contributions of Eastern religions, or of Islam, or of Judaism were unqualifiedly positive (which, as we have seen, is hardly the case)—would even such a record establish the divine authority of the faith in question? One of the most distinguished living analytical philosophers, Willard Van Orman Quine, puts it devastatingly:

Social Benefits ≠ Truth

> Social benefits, unlike mere wishful thinking, are a sound reason for propounding religious doctrine. Whether they are a sufficient reason, I hesitate to say; *but they afford no evidence of truth*.[215]

Wanted: An Epistemological Messiah

One can indeed show, in the case of the Old Testament (unlike the Koran or even later rabbinic tradition) that its teachings are unique, standing—in the words of Harvard Old Testament scholar G. Ernest Wright—"against their environment."[216] But uniqueness is not the equivalent of divine origin. Without a provably divine Messiah to stamp biblical revelation with His approval and to distinguish true law from merely legalistic accretions, how could Judaism even in principle meet the need for a transcendental standard of human dignity? In human rights, as in *Heilsgeschichte* (salvation-history), Judaism offers a beguiling but unfinished canvas: a picture lacking only a Messiah for ethical and epistemological completeness.

Ecumenicity as a Basis for Human Rights?

If the individual religious claims we have discussed do not succeed in providing a demonstrably transcendent foundation for human rights, could we not achieve that goal by showing the "natural agreement" of these—and, indeed, all great religious traditions—on the core values of human dignity? Just such evidence of common human values was collected by Jeanne Hersch in the UNESCO volume, *Birthright of Man*[217]; and distinguished Christian writer C. S. Lewis, in an appendix to his *Abolition of Man,* provides a catena of citations from the world's religious literature illustrating what he terms the "Tao," or basic ethical values.[218]

Three Anti-Ecumenical Salvoes

Sad to say, this ecumenical endeavor is doomed to failure, and for at least three reasons. (1) As Hersch herself perceived by quoting Mariano Moreno's classic line, "Any tyrant can compel his slaves to sing hymns in praise of liberty," even if one cites common human rights principles from diverse religious traditions, this is no guarantee that people do or will follow them; i.e., the key problem of transforming man's motivations still remains unsolved.

(2) Professor Werblosky is doubtless correct in his rather uncharitable comment about anthologies of religious "golden sayings" concerning human rights: "The trouble with this noble and well-intentioned parlour-game is that it is so utterly and depressingly childish."[219] The naïveté of the anthologies comes from at least two sources. First, the anthologist is generally unaware of the principle of selection which he employs in culling one aphorism rather than another from the vast literature of the world's religions: C. S. Lewis' anthology sounds wonderfully Christian because it is! (Lewis, as a Christian, had already derived his ethics from Christian revelation before he proceeded to

anthologize the religious traditions.) Secondly, the world's religions do not in fact agree in their core teachings about human value, the meaning of human dignity, or man's capacity to put human rights into practice. To be specific, they differ radically in their understanding of the nature of man and how he can be "saved."[220] René Cassin is simply incorrect when he declares, "It is plain to see that for the Christian, as for the Muslim and the Buddhist, doing one's duty constitutes the very essence of virtue for the believer who is desirous of aspiring to eternal rewards."[221] In reality, the Buddhist and Muslim views of man and ways of salvation (as we have seen) are by no means identical even as between themselves, and the Christian faith is 180 degrees removed from both of them on these cardinal points. Christianity asserts that man, being radically self-centered, can only be saved and transformed so as to treat his neighbor with proper dignity when he admits that he *cannot* "do his duty" or save himself—and relies entirely on God in Christ for salvation.[222]

(3) Finally, even if all the great religions of the world agreed on fundamental human rights principles (we here ignore the thorny problem of identifying which religions are truly "great"—Toynbee thought Islam was great but not Judaism!), their agreement would not *justify* those rights, since the revelatory character of no one of those religions has been established. Their common tenets could well represent no more than common human opinion—with no binding force for anyone who disagreed with them. D. L. Perrott of the University of Exeter makes the point strongly when he writes:

> Even if research revealed the existence of such rules, their ubiquitousness would not by itself justify calling them Natural Law. They might, although wide-spread, be very bad rules. Surveys carried out at various points before the eighteenth century might well have revealed, for example, that

slavery, or an inferior legal status for women, were well-nigh universal institutions. Alternatively the widespread rule might be a very trivial or arbitrary one; conceivably one day all the world may have to drive on the right of the road, or obtain two witnesses for a valid will, but we would probably not call such rules Natural Law.[223]

Natural Rights in the Spirit of the Declaration of Independence

But doesn't the extent of natural agreement on human rights in the various religious traditions say *anything* to help us in our quest? Perrott's references to "natural law" remind us of the classical natural rights position, dominant in Western jurisprudence before the rise of legal positivism, by which fundamental rights were defended. In the previous chapter, we briefly discussed John Finnis' attempt to rehabilitate natural law thinking on a purely philosophical basis, and we saw that modern neo-Kantian rights theorists (Rawls, Gewirth) and even the Marxists have a natural law flavor to their thinking.[224] Might not the search for an adequate justification of human rights be found in the stirring natural rights philosophy of the American Declaration of Independence: "We hold these truths to be self-evident, that all men are created equal; that they are endowed by their Creator with certain unalienable rights; that among these are life, liberty, and the pursuit of happiness"?[225]

Expressions of This Viewpoint in the Ancient World

What we term the classical—or religious—natural rights tradition can be traced back to Greco-Roman antiquity. Prior to the Christian era and the medieval scholastic labors of Thomas Aquinas, it was expressed most attractively by the Stoics and by their greatest jurisprudential representative, Cicero. That noble Roman lawyer declared:

> I find that it has been the opinion of the wisest men that Law is not a product of human thought, nor is

> it any enactment of peoples, but something eternal which rules the whole universe by its wisdom in command and prohibition. Thus they have been accustomed to say that Law is the primal and ultimate mind of God.[226]

The Justinian Code, which summed up Roman law in a Christian spirit, set forth the most quoted description of the natural law in the tripartite phrase, *Honeste vivere, neminem laedere, suum cuique tribuere* ("Live honestly, harm no one, give to each his own).[227]

Roman Catholic Affirmations of Natural Rights

Thomas Aquinas, in his *Summa Theologica,* declared the natural law to be rooted in the cosmic order and in the God-given nature of each human being,[228] and modern Thomists such as Jacques Maritain have argued for the validity and universality of human rights on this same ground:

> The true philosophy of the rights of the human person is . . . based upon the idea of natural law. The same natural law which lays down our most fundamental duties, and by virtue of which every law is binding, is the very law which assigns to us our fundamental rights. It is because we are enmeshed in the universal order, in the laws and regulations of the cosmos and of the immense family of created natures (and finally in the order of creative wisdom), and it is because we have at the same time the privilege of sharing in spiritual nature, that we possess rights vis-à-vis other men and all the assemblage of creatures.[229]

Appeals to natural rights have not been limited to the Thomist frame of reference in contemporary Catholicism. "The unbreakable link that is said to exist between human rights and human nature has been poignantly expressed by Gabriel Marcel, the late religious existentialist, as a human right written, as it were, into the very structure of a slave's own nature, for example, the slave can never entirely rid himself of the feeling that his body is his own."[230]

Conflict on Natural Rights Among the Protestants

In Protestantism, with its formal principle of *Sola Scriptura,* the key question as to natural rights has always been whether the Bible allows for such a teaching. Principally on the basis of Romans 1 and 2 (in particular, 1:20 and 2:14–15), the Reformers maintained that even after man's Fall into sin, a limited general knowledge of the universal principles of morality remained, indelibly inscribed on man's heart. This was Luther's position, and Calvin's also.[231] In the twentieth century, following the collapse of the old modernism, or religious liberalism, which in effect jettisoned biblical revelation in favor of a saving view of general revelation, a powerful reaction set in. Karl Barth in particular cried *Nein* to Emil Brunner's relatively mild endeavor to maintain natural revelation (as in the case of the Reformers, not as a means of salvation, but only as a partial and imperfect knowledge of divine standards for human life and thus an objective judgment on man's sinful conduct toward his fellows).[232] Brunner's position was in fact little more than a restatement of the classic Reformation doctrine of the *Schöpfungsordnungen* (Orders of Creation), declaring on the basis of Scripture that even after the Fall, God in his grace structured human life through government, the family, education, etc., to prevent sinful man from destroying himself through unrestrained selfishness.[233] The weight of Evangelical scholarship has concluded that Barth's total rejection of natural theology—and, with it, natural rights theory—is scripturally unwarranted.[234]

But even if such a natural law theory is accepted, does it provide the necessary grounding for human rights? Norwegian theologian Einar Molland contends that

> It is enough to believe in the value of man and in a written law which is valid for all mankind at all times, that is, in the law which ancient thinkers

called the natural law. This is not what the natural sciences understand by natural law, since the law they refer to raises us above nature. The law in question here is concerned with man and corresponds to man's nature. For human co-existence, it is enough to believe that such a natural law exists and that we can all more or less clearly discern it.[235]

Natural Rights: The Predicament of Justifying Their Content

I doubt very much that this is "enough for human co-existence." The problem is not that formal natural rights structures or orders are absent from human society. The trouble is that, though ubiquitously present, they *are* "formal": what universal substantive content they possess in line with Romans 1–2 seems incapable of independent epistemological justification. Perrott's theory of fundamental rights highlights the root difficulty, when he concludes that "there are what may be called Natural Areas of Legal Concern rather than Natural Law principles with a specific content," and that "the precise content of the rules, within limits, does not matter very much; what does matter is that legal discriminations should be drawn, and then generally adhered to. We *do* need to decide which side of the road to drive on; the choice of sides is, within limits, arbitrary."[236]

And Content Is All-Important

With respect, this is simply inadequate. In a footnote to the quoted passage, Perrott states that "of course, it [the choice of substantive legal content] matters enormously from an evaluative or emotional point of view." Does it only matter emotionally? Is it just an arbitrary question of which side of the road one drives on? A little earlier in his essay, Perrott declares that "a number of different definitions of murder may be equally acceptable"! In point of fact, the substantive definition of particular human rights is all-important, and it is these clear definitions that natural law fails to provide or to justify epistemologically. Carl J. Friedrich noted that the formula of the Justinian Code is so "imprecise" that it does little more than to underscore the need for "some kind of equity."[237] I observed at the Buchenwald death camp in East Germany that the *Digest's* vague expression, "Give to each his own," was inscribed in German translation (*Jedem das seine*) on the metal doors leading into that place of horror.

Natural Rights Are Real, but They Cry Out for Definition

This is not in any sense to deny the reality of natural rights: it is only to say that their content is left epistemologically ill-defined by natural law thinking, and it is precisely their content that is essential to solve the human rights dilemma. C. S. Lewis is correct that all human societies operate—and must operate—with ethical values;[238] but in order effectively to oppose the myriad variations of man's inhumanity to man, we must be able to determine *which* ethical values are good, bad, and indifferent. (Is torture wrong? What about cannibal environmentalists cleaning their plates?) The Orders of Creation are a reality; but it is not enough to know that the family has been instituted by God—one must be able to determine whether polygamy and polyandry are assets or liabilities to human dignity. The Declaration of Independence properly asserts that human beings are endowed by their Creator with the inalienable rights to life, liberty, and the pursuit of happiness; but, without more, what does this guarantee? "Life" remains undefined (does it include the fetus?), likewise "liberty," and—vaguest of all—"happiness." Even if John Locke's original trilogy of "life, liberty, and property" had been retained by the Founding Fathers, "property" would no less have required substantive definition.

Natural Rights Theories Are Like John the Baptist

The best that can be said of religious natural rights theories is that, like John the Baptist, they point beyond themselves. The same is true of the secular moral philosophies, such as Rawls' theory of justice and Gewirth's conscious endeavor to rehabilitate the Golden Rule, that draw indirectly upon the natural law tradition.[239] They remind us of ethical patterns without which we would cease to be human, but they do not flesh out these patterns so that we can confidently identify genuine human rights and with equal confidence stigmatize violations of human dignity.

A Corrupt Natural Order Requires Redemptive Human Rights

Moreover, as Daniel Vidal well observes, the natural order cannot simply be equated with the original order of creation. Because of the brokenness of the human situation, one will forever be frustrated in "a search for the basis of human rights in the natural order."

> Historically, the natural order is always, or almost always, self-justifying, basing itself on situations of inequality, and therefore of injustice. It is not difficult to discern at the very foundation of naturalism a pattern of rich-poor, powerful-weak, even indeed, oppressor-oppressed. But the existence of this pattern serves precisely to prove that what is "natural" for the one who is rich and powerful is not at all natural for the one who is poor and weak, although the latter does not and cannot act except in the hope of reversing the situation—the hope of an opposite inequality.[240]

Vidal's conclusion: "Human rights can only build on the proper foundation, the order of redemption." The final chapters of this book are devoted to that very programmatic.

chapter six

A Revelational Solution

Whatever their positive features, the philosophical and religious approaches to human rights we have discussed so far offer no demonstrable proof of transcendence. The Christian claim, however, is in an entirely different category epistemologically. In this chapter we test its revelatory assertions by accepted canons of legal evidence: we examine the documentary reliability and testimonial soundness of its central declarations that God has spoken in Jesus Christ and that the Bible provides a transcendental foundation for human dignity.

The Potential Value of Revealed Human Rights

Man's inhumanity to man cries out for the kind of unqualified condemnation that only a philosophy of inalienable rights can provide. Inalienable rights, however, cannot be built on the shifting sands of human opinion or social values. Religious natural law theory reflects the common conviction of men of good will that absolute standards of ethical conduct exist, but the content of these standards remains elusive. Perrott sharpens the issue considerably when he writes:

> Traditionally, two kinds of answers have been given to the question of how to identify the source and content of Natural Law rules. (Sometimes, as in Aquinas, both kinds of answer have been combined in a unified theory). We are said to be able to discover what are the principles of Natural Law, because either they are statements of what God requires of us, of which He has adequately informed us, or alternatively, they are those principles which our ordinary human reason, given the chance, forces us to realise to be necessary.
>
> Of these two, the first kind of answer strikes the writer as *logically* more satisfactory. Of course, it will be factually unacceptable to the non-religiously inclined, and downright unintelligible to some atheists. But, if it were granted, for the sake of argument, that the proposition "God exists" is meaningful, that God does in fact exist, and that He has informed us of His wishes for us, there would be no particular logical difficulty about conceiving His instructions to be highly specific, at least in some areas.[241]

In much the same vein, Shestack declares:

> Once the leap to belief has been made, religion may be the most attractive of the theoretical approaches. When human beings are not visualized in God's image then their basic rights may well lose their metaphysical raison d'être. The concept of human beings created in the image of God certainly endows men and women with a worth and dignity from which there can logically flow the components of a comprehensive human rights system.[242]

Both Perrott and Shestack are legal scholars, not theologians, and they do not pursue these tantalizing insights further. Opines Perrott: "The objections to this approach . . . turn on questions of theology and religious philosophy, not of legal philosophy or general logic, and no more will be said here on this point."

The Leap of Faith Can Be a Fall Into the Void

We readily admit that existential, blind "leaps to belief" can be and often are suicide jumps, with no criteria of truth available, by definition, before the leap is made. But suppose the truth of a revelational claim did not depend upon an unverifiable, subjectivistic leap of faith? What if a revelational truth-claim did not "turn on questions of theology and religious philosophy"—on any kind of esoteric, fideistic method available only to those who are already "true believers"—but on the very reasoning employed in the law to determine questions of fact?

Christianity Takes a Different Route

The historic Christian claim differs qualitatively from the claims of all other religions at the epistemological point: on the issue of testability. Eastern faiths and Islam, to take examples with which we are already familiar from the previous chapter, ask the uncommitted seeker to discover their truth experientially: the faith-experience will be self-validating. Unhappily, as analytical philosopher Kai Nielsen and others have rigorously shown, a subjective faith-experience is logically incapable of "validating God-talk"—including the alleged absolute ethical values and human rights principles about which the God in question does the talking.[243] Christianity, on the other hand, declares that the truth of its absolute claims rests squarely on certain historical facts, open to ordinary investigation. These facts relate essentially to the man Jesus, His presentation of Himself as God in human flesh, and His resurrection from the dead as proof of His deity.

Paul on the Areopagus

Thus, the rabbinic lawyer, Christian convert, and apostle—Paul of Tarsus—offered his gospel to Stoic philosophers at Athens as the historically verifiable fulfillment of natural religion and of the natural law tradition, with their vague and insufficiently defined content.

> Certain Epicurean and Stoic philosophers encountered [Paul at Athens]. And some said, What will this babbler say? Others said, He seems to be setting forth strange gods—for he had been preaching Jesus and the resurrection to them. And they took him to the Areopagus, saying, May we know what this new doctrine is of which you are speaking? . . .
>
> Then Paul stood at the center of the Areopagus and said, You men of Athens, I note that in all things you are too superstitious. For as I passed by and beheld your devotions, I found an altar with this inscription: TO THE UNKNOWN GOD. Whom therefore you ignorantly worship I declare to you. . . . The times of this ignorance God winked at, but now commands all men everywhere to repent, for he has appointed a day when he will judge the world in righteousness by the Man whom he has ordained, and he has given assurance of it to all in that he has raised him from the dead.[244]

At one point in his speech, Paul asserted that human life is the product of divine creation, "as certain also of your own [Stoic] poets have said," thereby making clear that classical natural law thinking was correct as far as it went, though it did not by any means go far enough.[245] Its completion could be found in Jesus, the Man whom God ordained, and His divine character was verifiable through His resurrection from the dead.

Why Legal Reasoning?

Elsewhere I have argued this case by using standard, accepted techniques of historical analysis.[246] Here, consistent with the juridical character of the international and comparative law of human rights, we shall use legal reasoning and the law of evidence. The advantage of a jurisprudential approach lies in the difficulty of jettisoning it: legal standards of evidence develop as essential means of resolving the most intractable disputes in society (dispute settlement by self-help—the only alternative to adjudication—will tear any society apart). Thus one cannot very well throw out legal reasoning merely because its application to Christianity results in a verdict for the Christian faith and its approach to human rights![247]

Testimonials to the Value of Legal Evidence in Arbitrating Ultimate Claims

Significantly, both in philosophy and in theology, there are moves to introduce juridical styles of reasoning. Stephen Toulmin, professor of philosophy at Leeds and one of the foremost analytical philosophers of our time, presents a veritable call to arms:

> To break the power of old models and analogies, we can provide ourselves with a new one. Logic is concerned with the soundness of the claims we make—with the solidity of the grounds we produce to support them, the firmness of the backing we provide for them—or, to change the metaphor, with the sort of *case* we present in defence of our claims. The legal analogy implied in this last way of putting the point can for once be a real help. So let us forget about psychology, sociology, technology and mathematics, ignore the echoes of structural engineering and *collage* in the words "grounds" and "backing", and take as our model the discipline of jurisprudence. Logic (we may say) is generalised jurisprudence. Arguments can be compared with law-suits, and the claims we make and argue for in extra-legal contexts with claims made in the courts, while the cases we present in making good each kind of claim can be compared with each other.[248]

Mortimer Adler, at the end of his careful discussion of the question of God's existence, employs, not the traditional philosophical ideal of Cartesian absolute certainty, but the legal standards of proof by preponderance of evidence and proof beyond reasonable doubt:

> If I am able to say no more than that a preponderance of reasons favor believing that God exists, I can still say I have advanced reasonable grounds for that belief. . . .

> I am persuaded that God exists, either beyond a reasonable doubt or by a preponderance of reasons in favor of that conclusion over reasons against it. I am, therefore, willing to terminate this inquiry with the statement that I have reasonable grounds for affirming God's existence.[249]

And from the jurisprudential side, Jerome Hall recognizes the potential for arbitrating central issues of religion and ethics by the sophisticated instrument of legal reasoning.

> Legal rules of evidence are reflections of "natural reason," and they could enter into dialogues in several ways, for example, to test the validity of theological arguments for the existence of God and to distinguish secular beliefs, even those held without any reasonable doubt, from faith that is so firm (Job's) that it excludes the slightest shadow of doubt and persists even in the face of evidence that on rational grounds is plainly contradictory. In these and other ways the rationality of the law of evidence in the trial of an issue of fact joins philosophical rationalism in raising pertinent questions about faith.[250]

The Four Key Questions

In terms of our discussion, what are the "pertinent questions about faith"? Four overarching questions need to be answered: (1) Are the historical records of Jesus solid enough to rely upon? (2) Is the testimony in these records concerning His life and ministry sufficiently reliable to know what He claimed about Himself? (3) Do the accounts of His resurrection from the dead, offered as proof of His divine claims, in fact establish those claims? (4) If Jesus' deity is established in the foregoing manner, does He place a divine stamp of approval on the Bible so as to render its pronouncements covering human dignity apodictically certain? Let us see how legal reasoning helps to answer each of these key questions.

(1) The Documentary Question

Basic to any determination of the soundness of Christian claims is the question of the reliability of the pertinent historical documents. The documents at issue are not (*pace* the man on the Clapham omnibus) Josephus, Tacitus, Pliny the Younger, or other pagan references to Jesus, though these do of course exist. Such references are secondary at best, since none of these writers had firsthand contact with Jesus or with His disciples. The documents on which the case for Christianity depends are the New Testament writings, for they claim to have been written by eyewitnesses or by close associates of eyewitnesses (indeed, their origin in apostolic circles was the essential criterion for including them in the New Testament).

NT Documents as Competent Evidence

How good are these New Testament records? They handsomely fulfill the historian's requirements of *transmissional reliability* (their texts have been transmitted accurately from the time of writing to our own day), *internal reliability* (they claim to be primary-source documents and ring true as such), and *external reliability* (their authorships and dates are backed up by such solid extrinsic testimony as that of the early second-century writer Papias, a student of John the Evangelist, who was told by him that the first three Gospels were indeed written by their traditional authors).[251] Harvard's Simon Greenleaf, the greatest nineteenth-century authority on the law of evidence in the common-law world, applied to these records the "ancient documents" rule: ancient documents will be received as competent evidence if they are "fair on their face" (i.e., offer no internal evidence of tampering) and have been maintained in "reasonable custody" (i.e., their preservation has been consistent with their content). He concluded that the competence of the New Testament documents would be established in any court of law.[252]

Fakes Can't Stand the Test of Time

The speculation that the Gospel records were "faked" some three hundred years after the events described in them (a viewpoint gratuitously proffered by Professor Trevor-Roper) is dismissed by Lord Chancellor Hailsham, England's highest-ranking legal luminary, with an apt lawyer's illustration.

> [What] renders the argument invalid is a fact about fakes of all kinds which I learned myself in the course of a case I did in which there was in question the authenticity of a painting purporting to be by, and to be signed by, Modigliani. This painting, as the result of my Advice on Evidence, was shown to be a fake by X-ray evidence. But in the course of my researches I was supplied by my instructing solicitor with a considerable bibliography concerning the nature of fakes of all kinds and how to detect them. There was one point made by the author of one of these books which is of direct relevance to the point I am discussing. Although fakes can often be made which confuse or actually deceive contemporaries of the faker, the experts, or even the not so expert, of a later age can invariably detect them, whether fraudulent or not, because the faker cannot fail to include stylistic or other material not obvious to contemporaries because they are contemporaries, but which stand out a mile to later observers because they reflect the standards, or the materials, or the styles of a succeeding age to that of the author whose work is being faked.[253]

To Throw Jesus Out, You Must First Discard Tiberius Caesar

As for the skepticism of the so-called "higher critics" (or redaction critics) in the liberal theological tradition, it stems from an outmoded methodology (almost universally discarded today by classical and literary scholars and by specialists in comparative Near Eastern studies), and from unjustified philosophical presuppositions (such as antisupernaturalistic bias and bias in favor of religious evolution).[254] A. N. Sherwin-White, a specialist in Roman law, countered such critics in his 1960–61 Sarum Lectures at the University of London.

It is astonishing that while Graeco-Roman historians have been growing in confidence, the twentieth-century study of the Gospel narratives, starting from no less promising material, has taken so gloomy a turn in the development of form-criticism that the more advanced exponents of it apparently maintain—so far as an amateur can understand the matter—that the historical Christ is unknowable and the history of his mission cannot be written. This seems very curious when one compares the case for the best-known contemporary of Christ, who like Christ is a well-documented figure—Tiberius Caesar. The story of his reign is known from four sources, the *Annals* of Tacitus and the biography of Suetonius, written some eighty or ninety years later, the brief contemporary record of Velletus Paterculus, and the third century history of Cassius Dio. These disagree amongst themselves in the wildest possible fashion, both in major matters of political action or motive and in specific details of minor events. Everyone would admit that Tacitus is the best of all the sources, and yet no serious modern historian would accept at face value the majority of the statements of Tacitus about the motives of Tiberius. But this does not prevent the belief that the material of Tacitus can be used to write a history of Tiberius.[255]

Autobiographical Excursus

The conclusion is inescapable: if one compares the New Testament documents with universally accepted secular writings of antiquity, the New Testament is more than vindicated. Some years ago, when I debated philosophy professor Avrum Stroll of the University of British Columbia on this point,[256] he responded: "All right. I'll throw out my knowledge of the classical world." At which the chairman of the classics department cried: "Good Lord, Avrum, not *that*!"

(2) The Testimonial Question

If, as we have seen, the New Testament records are sound historical documents, how good is their testimony to Jesus? This is a question of great importance, since the accounts tell us plainly that Jesus claimed to be nothing less than God-in-the-flesh, come to the earth to reveal God's will for man and to save humankind from their sins. Moreover, the same testimony meticulously records Jesus' post-resurrection appearances, so a decision as to its reliability will also bear directly on our third major question, the historicity of Jesus' resurrection.

In a court of law, admissible testimony is considered truthful unless impeached or otherwise rendered doubtful. This is in accord with ordinary life, where only the paranoiac goes about with the bias that everyone is lying. (Think of Cousin Elmo, convinced that he is followed by Albanians.) The burden, then, is on those who would show that the New Testament testimony to Jesus is not worthy of belief. Let us place the Gospel testimony to Jesus under the legal microscope to see if its reliability can be impeached.

Here we employ a construct for attacking perjury that has been labeled "the finest work on that subject."[257] McCloskey and Schoenberg offer a fourfold test for exposing perjury, involving a determination of *internal* and *external* defects in the *witness himself* on the one hand and in the *testimony itself* on the other.[258] We can translate their schema into diagrammatic form (see figure 5).

Internal Defects in the Witnesses?

(a) Internal defects in the witness himself refer to any personal characteristics or past history tending to show that the "witness is inherently untrustworthy, unreliable or undependable." Were the apostolic witnesses to Jesus persons who may be disbelieved because they were "not the type of person who can be trusted"? Did they have criminal records or is there reason to think that they were pathological liars? If anything, their simple literalness and directness is almost painful. They seem singularly poor candidates for a James Bond thriller or for being cast in the role of "Spy and Counterspy." But perhaps they were mythomanes—people incapable of distinguishing fact from fantasy? They themselves declare precisely the contrary: "We have not followed cunningly devised fables [Gk. *mythoi,* 'myths']," they write, "when we made known to you the power and coming of our Lord Jesus Christ, but were eyewitnesses of his majesty."[259]

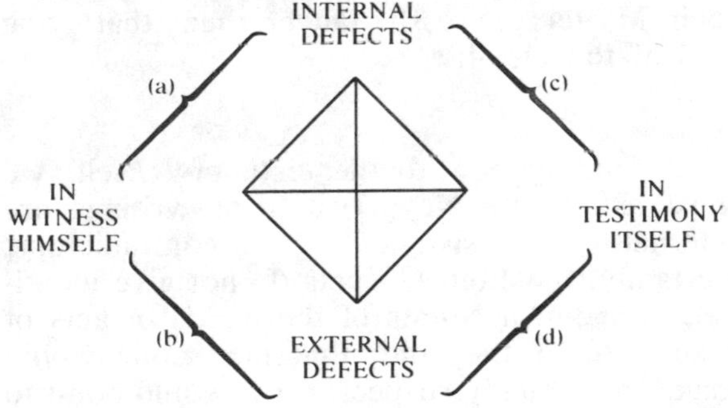

Figure 5
A Construct for Exposing Perjury

External Motives to Falsify?

(b) But did the apostolic witnesses perhaps suffer from external defects, that is, "motives to falsify"?

Not all perjurers have committed prior immoral acts or prior crimes. Frequently, law abiding citizens whose pasts are without blemish will commit perjury, not because they are inherently unworthy, but because some specific present reason compels

> them to do so in the case at bar. Motive, then, becomes the common denominator. There is a motive for every act of perjury. The second major way in which the cross-examiner can seek to expose perjury, therefore, is to isolate the specific motive which causes the witness to commit perjury.[260]

Surely no sensible person would argue that the apostolic witnesses would have lied about Jesus for monetary gain or as a result of societal pressure. To the contrary: they lost the possibility both of worldly wealth and of social acceptability among their Jewish peers because of their commitment to Jesus.[261] Might that very affection for and attachment to Jesus serve as a motive to falsify? Not when we remember that their Master expressly taught them that lying was of the Devil.[262]

Internal Defects in the Testimony?

(c) Turning now to the testimony itself, we must ask if the New Testament writings are internally inconsistent or self-contradictory. Certainly, the Four Gospels do not give identical, verbatim accounts of the words or acts of Jesus. But if they did, that fact alone would make them highly suspect, for it would point to collusion.[263] The Gospel records view the life and ministry of Jesus from four different perspectives—just as veridical witnesses to the same accident will present different, but complementary accounts of the event. If the objection is raised that the same occurrence or pericope is sometimes found at different times or places in Jesus' ministry, depending on which Gospel one consults, the simple answer is that no one Gospel contains or was ever intended to contain the complete account of Jesus' three-year ministry,[264] and Jesus (like any preacher) certainly spoke the same message to different groups at different times. And suppose He did throw the moneychangers out of the temple twice: is it not strange, in light of their activity and His principles, that He *only* threw them out twice? (We would have expected it every Saturday—Sabbath—night.) Observe also how honestly and in what an unflattering manner the apostolic company picture themselves in these records. Mark, Peter's companion, describes him as having a consistent case of foot-in-the-mouth disease; and the apostles in general are presented (in Jesus' own words) as "slow of heart to believe all that the prophets have spoken."[265] To use New Testament translator J. B. Phillips' expression, the internal content of the New Testament records has "the ring of truth."[266]

External Defects in the Testimony?

(d) Finally, what about external defects in the testimony itself, i.e., inconsistencies between the New Testament accounts and what we know to be the case from archaeology or extrabiblical historical records? Far from avoiding contact with secular history, the New Testament is replete with explicit references to secular personages, places, and events. Unlike typical sacred literature, myth, and fairytale ("once upon a time . . ."), the gospel story begins when "there went out a decree from Caesar Augustus that all the world should be taxed."[267] Typical of the New Testament accounts are passages such as the following:

> Now in the fifteenth year of the reign of Tiberius Caesar, Pontius Pilate being governor of Judaea, and Herod being tetrarch of Galilee, and his brother Philip tetrarch of Ituraea and of the region of Trachonitis, and Lysanias the tetrarch of Abilene, Annas and Caiaphas being the high priests, the word of God came unto John the son of Zacharias in the wilderness. And he came into all the country about Jordan, preaching the baptism of repentance for the remission of sins.[268]

Modern archaeological research has confirmed again and again the reliability of New

Testament geography, chronology, and general history.[269] To take but a single, striking example: after the rise of liberal biblical criticism, doubt was expressed as to the historicity of Pontius Pilate, since he is mentioned even by pagan historians only in connection with Jesus' death. Then in 1961 came the discovery at Caesarea of the now famous "Pilate inscription," definitively showing that, as usual, the New Testament writers were engaged in accurate historiography.

Thus, on no one of the four elements of the McCloskey-Schoenberg construct for attacking perjury can the New Testament witnesses to Jesus be impugned.

The Complexities of Deception

Furthermore, one should realize (and nonlawyers seldom do realize) how difficult it is to succeed in effective lying or misrepresentation when a cross-examiner is at work. Richard Givens, in his standard work, *Advocacy,* in the McGraw-Hill Trial Practice Series, diagrams ordinary truthful communication and then contrasts it with the tremendous complexities of deceitful communication (figures 6a and 6b).[270]

Successful Lying Requires Tremendous Skill and Energy

Observe that the witness engaged in deception must, as it were, juggle at least three balls simultaneously, while continually estimating his chances of discovery: he must be sure he doesn't say anything that contradicts what his examiner knows (or what he thinks his examiner knows); he must tell a consistent lie ("liars must have good memories"); and he must take care that nothing he says can be checked against contradictory external data. Givens' point is that successful deception is terribly difficult, for the psychological strain and energy expended in attempting it makes the deceiver exceedingly vulnerable.

> The wider the angles of divergence between these various images, the more confusing the problem, and the more "higher mathematics" must be done in order to attempt to avoid direct conflicts between these elements. The greater the angle of deception employed, the greater the complexity and the lower the effectiveness of these internal mental operations. If this is conscious, we attribute this to lying. If it is unconscious we lay it to the "bias" of the witness.
>
> If one is lying or strongly biased, it is not enough to simply dredge up whatever mental trace there may be of the event and attempt to articulate it in answer to a question. Instead, all of the various elements mentioned must be weighed, a decision made as to the best approach, a reply contrived that is expected to be most convincing, and then an effort made to launch this communication into the minds of the audience.
>
> The person with a wide angle of divergence between what is recalled and the impression sought to be given is thus at an almost helpless disadvantage, especially if confronting a cross-examiner who understands the predicament.
>
> If the audience includes both a cross-examiner and a tribunal, the number of elements to be considered becomes even greater. The mental gymnastics required rise in geometric proportion to the number of elements involved.[271]

Why the Apostolic Company Could Not Have Put Over the "Big Lie"

Now, wholly apart from the question as to whether the New Testament witnesses to Jesus were the kind of people to engage in such deception (and we have already seen, in examining them for possible internal and external defects, that they were not): *had* they attempted such a massive deception, *could they have gotten away with it*? Admittedly, they were never put on a literal witness stand, but they concentrated their preaching on synagogue audiences, thus putting their testimony at the mercy of the hostile Jewish religious leadership who had had intimate contact with Jesus' ministry and had been chiefly instrumental in ending it.

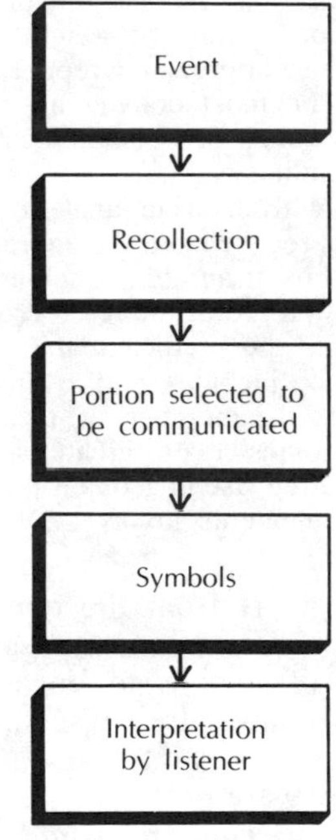

Figure 6A
The Mental Process in "Simple"—i.e., Truthful—Communication

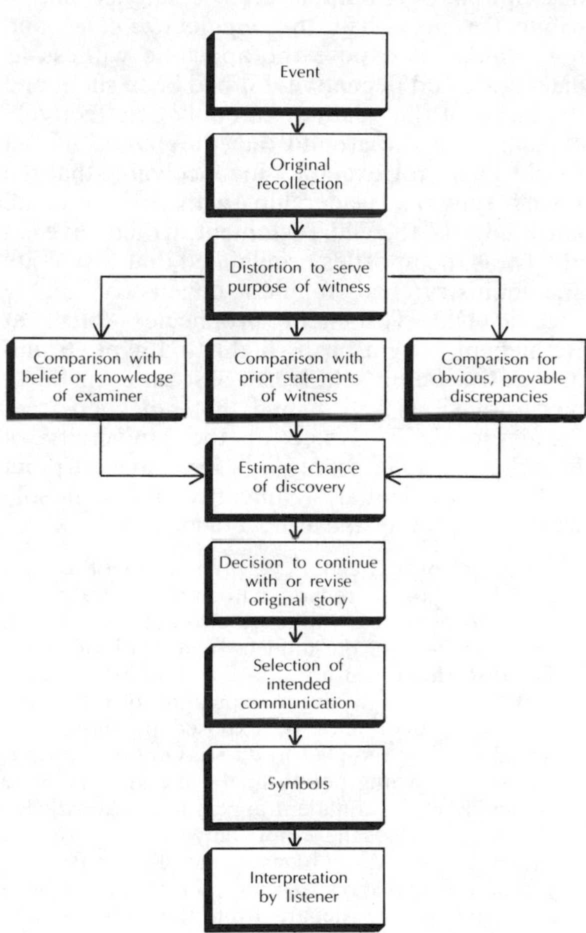

Figure 6B
The Lying Witness

Hostile Witnesses as *De Facto* Cross-Examiners

Such an audience eminently satisfies Givens' description of "both a cross-examiner and a tribunal": they had the *means, motive,* and *opportunity* to expose the apostolic witness as inaccurate and deceptive if it had been such, and the fact that they did not can only be effectively explained on the ground that they *could not*. It would seem, for example, inconceivable that the Jewish religious leadership, with their intimate knowledge of the Old Testament, would have sat idly by as the apostles proclaimed that Jesus' life and ministry had fulfilled dozens of highly specific Old Testament prophecies (birth at Bethlehem, virgin birth, flight to Egypt, triumphal entry, being sold by an associate for thirty pieces of silver, etc.), had that not been true. Professor F. F. Bruce of the University of Manchester underscores this fundamental point as to the evidential significance of the hostile witnesses in the apostolic era:

> It was not only friendly eyewitnesses that the early preachers had to reckon with; there were others less well disposed who were also conversant with the main facts of the ministry and death of Jesus. The disciples could not afford to risk inaccuracies (not to speak of willful manipulation of the facts), which would at once be exposed by those who would be only too glad to do so. On the contrary, one of the strong points in the original apostolic preaching is the confident appeal to the knowledge of the hearers; they not only said, "We are witnesses of these things," but also, "As you yourselves also know" (Acts 2:22). Had there been any tendency to depart from the facts in any material respect, the possible presence of hostile witnesses in the audience would have served as a further corrective.[272]

Insanity, Anyone?

We do not waste time on the possibility that the disciples suffered from insane delusions. First, because the law presumes a man sane, and the accounts have no hint the disciples were otherwise. Second, because the point Professor

Bruce has stressed concerning the hostile witnesses applies with equal force to the insanity suggestion: had *anything*, even a deluded state of mind, caused the disciples to distort Jesus' biography, the hostile witnesses would surely have used this against them.

The Hearsay Issue

The functional equivalence of hostile witnesses with formal cross-examination goes far to answer the occasionally voiced objection that the apostolic testimony to Jesus would be rejected by a modern court as "hearsay," i.e., out-of-court statements tendered to prove the truth of their contents. Let us note at the outset the most severe problem with hearsay testimony: the originator of it is not in court and so cannot be subjected to searching cross-examination. Thus, even when New Testament testimony to Jesus would technically fall under the ax of the hearsay rule, the hostile witnesses as functional cross-examiners reduce the problem to the vanishing point.

In the second place, the hearsay rule exists in Anglo-American common law (no such rule is a part of the Continental civil law tradition) especially as a technical device to protect juries from secondhand evidence. Following the virtual abolition of the civil jury in England, the Civil Evidence Act of 1968 in effect eliminated the hearsay rule by statute from civil trials—on the ground that judges can presumably sift even secondhand testimony for its truth value.[273] In the United States, and in English criminal trials, the exceptions to the hearsay rule have almost swallowed up the rule, and one of these exceptions is the "ancient documents" rule (to which I referred earlier), by which the New Testament documents would indeed be received as competent evidence.

To be sure, the underlying principle of the hearsay rule remains vital: that a witness ought to testify "of his own knowledge or observation," not on the basis of what has come to him indirectly from others. And the New Testament writers continually tell us that they are setting forth that "which we have heard, which we have seen with our eyes, which we have looked upon, and our hands have handled, . . . the Word of life" (1 John 1:1).

A Challenge to the Reader

Simon Greenleaf's summation of the testimonial case for Jesus' life, ministry, and claims about himself offers a perennial challenge to the earnest seeker for truth.

> All that Christianity asks of men on this subject, is, that they would be consistent with themselves; that they would treat its evidences as they treat the evidence of other things; and that they would try and judge its actors and witnesses, as they deal with their fellow men, when testifying to human affairs and actions, in human tribunals. Let the witnesses be compared with themselves, with each other, and with surrounding facts and circumstances; and let their testimony be sifted, as it were given in a court of justice, on the side of the adverse party, the witness being subjected to a rigorous cross-examination. The result, it is confidently believed, will be an undoubting conviction of their integrity, ability, and truth. In the course of such an examination, the undesigned coincidences will multiply upon us at every step in our progress; the probability of the veracity of the witnesses and of the reality of the occurrences which they relate will increase, until it acquires, for all practical purposes, the value and force of demonstration.[274]

(3) The Question of the Resurrection

At the heart of the apostolic testimony and proclamation is the alleged resurrection of Jesus Christ from the dead. During His ministry, Jesus offered His forthcoming resurrection as the decisive proof of His claim to deity.[275] Did the Resurrection in fact occur?[276]

Testimonial Evidence, Not Metaphysics, the Key

The first point to consider is that the accounts of the Resurrection and of detailed post-Resurrection appearances over a forty-day period[277] are all contained in the very New Testament documents whose historical reliability we have confirmed, and they are testified to by the same apostolic witnesses whose veracity we have just established. To do an abrupt *volte-face* and now declare those documents and witnesses to be untrustworthy because they assert that Jesus rose from the dead would be to substitute a dubious metaphysic ("resurrections from the dead are cosmically impossible"—and how does one establish *that* in a relativistic, Einsteinian universe?) for careful historical investigation. We must not make the mistake of eighteenth-century philosopher David Hume, who thought he could avoid evidential drudgery by deductively reasoning from the gratuitous premise that "a firm and unalterable experience has established the laws of nature" to the (entirely circular) conclusions: "There must be a uniform experience against every miraculous event" and "That a dead man should come to life has never been observed in any age or country."[278]

The Missing Body

Secondly, we should reflect upon the force of the "missing body" argument of Frank Morison,[279] who was converted to Christianity through his investigation of the evidence for Jesus' resurrection. Morison argues that if Jesus didn't rise, someone must have stolen the body; the only people involved were the Roman authorities, the Jewish religious leaders, and Jesus' disciples; the Romans and Jewish religious leaders would certainly not have taken the body, since to do so would have been against their own interests (for the Romans, to keep Palestine quiet; for the Jews, to preserve their religious influence),[280] and the disciples would hardly have stolen the body and then died for what they knew to be untrue. *Ergo*—by process of elimination—Jesus rose from the dead just as the firsthand accounts declare.

We Have No Bias in Favor of Biological Miracles

I have shown elsewhere that Antony Flew's attempt to avoid the impact of this argument is unsuccessful.[281] When Flew says that Christians simply prefer a biological miracle (the Resurrection) to a psychological miracle (the disciples dying for what they knew to be false), he completely misses the point. The issue is not metaphysical preference; it is testimonial evidence. No such evidence exists to support a picture of psychologically aberrant disciples, while tremendously powerful testimonial evidence exists to the effect that Jesus physically rose from the dead.

But We Aren't Crazy About Wild Speculations

During the last few years, more inventive attempts to explain away the Resurrection have appeared. Schonfield's *Passover Plot* argues that Jesus induced His own crucifixion, drugging Himself so as to survive just long enough in the tomb to convince the fuddled disciples that He had risen.[282] (*Quaere:* How does this square with Jesus' own moral teachings? And does it not leave us with precisely the same problem as to what finally happened to the body?) Von Daniken—who turned to pseudo-scientific writing while serving a prison sentence in Switzerland for embezzlement, fraud, and forgery[283]—"explains" the Resurrection by suggesting that it was the product of a close encounter of the third kind: Jesus was a kind of Martian cleverly dressed in a Jesus suit who knew a few tricks such as how to appear to rise from the dead.

Legal Reasoning Is Probabilistic

Aren't such hypotheses *possible*? Doubtless, in our contingent universe, anything is possible (as one philosopher said) except squeezing toothpaste back into the tube. But legal reasoning operates on *probabilities,* not possibilities: preponderance of evidence in most civil actions; evidence beyond reasonable (not beyond *all*) doubt in criminal matters.[284] The *Federal Rules of Evidence* define relevant evidence as "evidence having any tendency to make the existence of any fact that is of consequence to the determination of the action more probable or less probable than it would be without the evidence."[285] Suppose a jury brought in a verdict of "innocent" because it is always *possible* that invisible Martians, not the accused, were responsible for the crime! Judges in the United States carefully instruct juries to pay attention *only* to the evidence in the case, and to render verdicts in accord with it. A guilty verdict in a criminal matter should be rendered only if the jury cannot find any reasonable explanation of the crime (i.e., any explanation *in accord with the evidence*) other than that the accused did it. The tone and value of discussions about Jesus' resurrection would be considerably elevated if equally rigorous thinking were applied thereto.

Probability Is the Only Justifiable Basis for Factual Decision-Making, Even as to Life and Death

Can we base ultimates (Jesus' deity, our commitment to Him for time and eternity) on mere probabilities? The analytical philosophers have shown that we have no other choice: only formal ("analytic") truths (e.g., the propositions of deductive logic and of pure mathematics) can be demonstrated absolutely—and the absoluteness here is due to the definitional nature of their axiomatic foundations, as with Euclid's geometry. All matters of fact ("synthetic" assertions) are limited to probabilistic confirmation, but this does not immobilize us in daily life. We still put our very lives in jeopardy every day on the basis of probability judgments (crossing the street, consuming packaged foods and drugs, flying in airplanes, etc.). And the law in every land redistributes property and takes away liberty (if not life) by verdicts and judgments rooted in the examination of evidence and probabilistic standards of proof.

What Weight of Evidence Would Substantiate a Resurrection?

But the issue here is a *miracle:* a resurrection. How much evidence should a reasonable human being require in order to establish such a fact? Could evidence ever justify accepting it? Thomas Sherlock, master of the Temple Church (owned by two of the four guilds of English barristers, the Honourable Societies of the Inner and Middle Temple) and bishop of London, well answered these questions in the eighteenth century:

> Suppose you saw a Man publickly executed, his Body afterwards wounded by the Executioner, and carry'd and laid in the Grave; that after this you shou'd be told, that the Man was come to Life again: What wou'd you suspect in this Case? Not that the Man had never been dead; for that you saw your self: But you wou'd suspect whether he was now alive. But wou'd you say, this Case excluded all human Testimony; and that Men could not possibly discern, whether one with whom they convers'd familiarly, was alive or no? Upon what Ground cou'd you say this? A Man rising from the Grave is an Object of Sense, and can give the same Evidence of his being alive, as any other Man in the World can give. So that a Resurrection consider'd only as a Fact to be proved by Evidence, is a plain Case; it requires no greater Ability in the Witnesses, than that they be able to distinguish between a Man dead, and a Man alive: A Point, in which I believe every Man living thinks himself a Judge.[286]

Needed: Enough Evidence to Show (A) Death and (B) Life

Bishop Sherlock is certainly correct that a resurrection does not in principle create any insuperable evidential difficulty. Phenomenally (and this is all we need worry about for evidential purposes) a resurrection can be regarded as *death followed by life,*

D, then L.

Normally, the sequence is reversed, thus:

L, then D.

We are well-acquainted with the phenomenal meaning of the constituent factors (though we do not understand the "secret" of life or why death must occur), and we have no difficulty in establishing evidential criteria to place a person in one category rather than in the other. Thus the eating of fish[287] is sufficient to classify the eater among the living, and a crucifixion is enough to place the crucified among the dead. In Jesus' case, the sequential order is reversed, but that has no epistemological bearing on the weight of evidence required to establish death or life. And if Jesus was dead at point A, and alive again at point B, then resurrection has occurred: *res ipsa loquitur*.[288]

But How Reliable Are Eyewitness Identifications?

However, does not the unreliability of eyewitness testimony cast doubt on an event as extraordinary as the Resurrection? Psychologists such as Loftus have pointed up genuine dangers in eyewitness testimony.[289] Nonetheless, as we have already seen, it remains the cornerstone of legal evidence. As for the reliability of identifying acquaintances (the precise issue in the disciples' post-resurrection identifications of Jesus), specialists on the subject agree that "the better acquainted a witness is with a subject, the more likely it is that the witness' identification will be accurate" and that "in an eyewitness context, the greatest challenge to the advocate's power of persuasion is presented by the attempt to argue, without support from expert testimony, the unreliability of an unimpeached eyewitness' identification of a prior acquaintance."[290] And this is precisely what we have in the instant case: disciples like Thomas provide "unimpeached eyewitness identification'' of the resurrected Jesus with whom they had had the most intimate acquaintance for the immediately preceding three-year period.[291] No advocate's ''power of persuasion'' is going to make a difference to that kind of identification evidence.

Henry, Nash, Gerstner, Sproul, Geisler, and Rat on Facts and Interpretations

Finally, the objection may be offered: even granting Jesus' resurrection, is that fact alone enough to establish His deity and the truth of His claims? Theological presuppositionalists Carl F. H. Henry and Ronald H. Nash tell us that there are no self-interpreting facts,[292] and Calvinists John Gerstner and R. C. Sproul, as well as Evangelical neo-Thomist Norman L. Geisler, insist that an independent theistic structure must be established to make any theological sense out of Jesus' resurrection.[293] I profoundly disagree. Even Rat—famous for his leading role in Kenneth Grahame's *The Wind in the Willows,* but hardly an accomplished epistemologist—becomes exasperated with his companion for not recognizing that facts can be self-interpreting:

> ''Do-you-mean-to-say,'' cried the excited Rat, ''that this doormat doesn't *tell* you anything?''
>
> ''Really, Rat,'' said the Mole quite pettishly, ''I think we've had enough of this folly. Who ever heard of a doormat *telling* anyone anything? They simply don't do it. They are not that sort at all. Doormats know their place.''
>
> ''Now look here, you—you thick-headed beast,'' replied the Rat, really angry, ''this must stop. Not another word, but scrape—scrape and scratch and dig and hunt round, especially on the sides of the hummocks, if you want to sleep dry and warm tonight, for it's our last chance!''

Historical Facts Can Be Self-Interpreting

Elsewhere I have argued in detail that facts—historical and otherwise—''in themselves provide adequate criteria for choosing among variant interpretations of them.''[294] Philosopher

Paul Feinberg has defended that case with inexorable logic:

> Let us consider an example from recent history. It can be substantiated that some 6 million Jews died under German rule in the second World War. Let me suggest two mutually exclusive interpretations. First, these events may be interpreted as the actions of a mad man who was insanely anti-Semitic. The deaths were murders, atrocities. Second, it might be asserted that Hitler really loved the Jews. He had a deep and abiding belief in heaven and life after death. After reviewing Jewish history, Hitler decided that the Jews had been persecuted enough, and because of his love for them he was seeking to help them enter eternal blessedness. If no necessity exists between events and interpretation, then there is no way of determining which meaning is correct. We would never be justified in claiming that one holding the latter view is wrong. This is both repugnant and absurd. There must be an empirical necessity that unites an event or fact with its correct interpretation.[295]

Likewise Legal Facts

Beyond this, I merely remind the reader that the very nature of legal argument (judgments rendered on the basis of factual verdicts) rests on the ability of facts to speak for themselves. As a single illustration, take the leading U.S. Supreme Court case of *Williams v. North Carolina* (the "second Williams case"), which stands for the proposition that a divorce on substituted or constructive service in one state need only be given full faith and credit by another state when the parties have acquired a bona fide domicile in the divorcing state. In the course of its opinion, the Court declared:

> Petitioners, long time residents of North Carolina, came to Nevada, where they stayed in an auto-court for transients, filed suits for divorce as soon as the Nevada law permitted, married one another as soon as the divorces were obtained, and promptly returned to North Carolina to live. *It cannot reasonably be claimed that one set of*

inferences rather than another regarding the acquisition by petitioners of new domicils [sic] in Nevada could be drawn from the circumstances attending their Nevada divorces.[296]

Two Reasons to Accept the Deity of the Resurrected Jesus

Geisler misrepresents me when he says that I hold that "the resurrection is so bizarre, so odd, that only a supernatural explanation will adequately account for it."[297] In my view there are two compelling reasons to accept Jesus' resurrection as implicating His deity, neither of which is its "oddness" per se. First, "this miracle deals effectively with the most fundamental area of man's universal need, the conquest of death"[298]—a truth recognized in law by the "dying declaration" exception to the hearsay rule (even the declaration of the homicide victim without religious faith is admissible in evidence, on the ground that one is particularly likely to tell the truth when conscious of the immanence of that most terrible of existential events).[299] If death is indeed that significant, then "not to worship One who gives you the gift of eternal life is hopelessly to misread what the gift tells you about the Giver."[300]

In the second place, there are logically only two possible kinds of explanation or interpretation of the fact of the Resurrection: that given by the person raised and that given by someone else. Surely, if only Jesus has been raised, He is in a far better position (indeed, in the *only* position!) to interpret or explain it. Until Von Daniken, for example, rises from the dead, I will prefer Jesus' account of what happened. And Jesus said His miraculous ministry is explicable because He was God in human form: "I and my Father are one"; "he who has seen me has seen the Father."[301] Theism, then, becomes the proper inference from Jesus' resurrection as He Himself explained it—not a prior metaphysical hurdle to jump in order to arrive at a proper historical and evidential interpretation of that event.

(4) Jesus Places His Divine Stamp of Approval on the Bible

Jesus' deity in itself gives us a foundation for human dignity, in the fact that the God of the universe chose to clothe Himself in human garb. And Jesus' teachings per se, being God's teachings, represent an infallible guide to human rights and duties. But Jesus does more even than this. By His direct statements concerning the Old Testament as divine revelation[302] and by His consistent quoting of it as trustworthy and divinely authoritative in all respects,[303] Jesus put upon it His (i.e., God's) *imprimatur*. By giving His apostles a special gift of the Holy Spirit to recall infallibly what He had taught them,[304] and, by implication, to recognize apostolicity in others, He proleptically stamped with approval as divine revelation the future writings of apostles (the original twelve, minus Judas Iscariot, plus Paul—grafted in as Apostle to the Gentiles)[305] and writings by their associates (Mark, Luke, etc.) whose accuracy the apostles were in a position to verify. As a result, the entire Bible—Old Testament and New—becomes an unerring source of absolute principles, from which a revelational philosophy of human rights can be derived.[306]

Two Objections to Deriving Biblical Authority From a Divine Jesus

Two objections may be raised to the argument just presented: Why should the mere fact that God says something guarantee its truth? and What if the incarnate Christ was so limited to the human ideas of His time that His stamp of approval on the Bible represents no guarantee of its absolute accuracy?

The Nonsensicality of a Lying God

The first of these arguments is reflected in Descartes's discussion of God as a possible "Evil Genius"—a cosmic liar. But if He were,

He would be a divine and, therefore, consummate liar, so you would be incapable of catching Him at it. In short, He would be a better liar than you are a detective. So the very idea of God-as-liar is meaningless—an analytically unverifiable notion in principle. Once you have met God incarnate, you have no choice but to trust Him: as to the way of salvation, as to the reliability of the entire Bible, and as to human rights.

The Absurdity of a Kenotic Christ

The suggestion that Jesus was limited to human and fallible ideas (the so-called Kenotic theory[307] of liberal theology) also collapses under its own weight. On Kenotic reasoning, either Jesus chose to conform His statements to the fallible ideas of His time (in which case He was an opportunist who, in the spirit of Lenin, committed one of the most basic of all moral errors, that of allowing the end to justify the means);[308] or He couldn't avoid self-limitation in the very process of incarnation (in which case incarnation is of little or no value to us, since there is then no guarantee that it reveals anything conclusive). And note that if such a dubious incarnation mixed absolute wheat with culturally relative chaff, we would have no sufficient criterion for separating them anyway, so the "absolute" portion would do us no good! To meet people's desperate need for apodictic principles of human dignity, an incarnate God must not speak with a forked tongue. In light of man's inhumanity to man, the last thing we need is additional fallible opinion, even if it is disguised in divine dress.

Now to Biblical Human Rights

With solid epistemological ground beneath our feet, and an incarnate God who does not stutter, let us now see what biblical revelation can tell us about human rights.

chapter seven

The Revelational Content of Human Rights

Now that the case for the Bible's transcendent, revelational character has been developed evidentially, we need to know what difference biblical revelation will make in solving the theoretical and practical problems of human rights. First, we examine threshold objections to the clarity and applicability of scriptural teaching, and set forth some hermeneutic ground rules for construing its meaning. Then we offer a schematic overview of the revelational foundations for specific human rights of all three generations. Particular attention is devoted to the biblical perspective on religious freedom, on the distinction between derogable and nonderogable rights and the unsoundness of ethical hierarchicalism, and on the legislation of morals in general and of human dignity in particular. The chapter concludes with a look at the advantages of biblical revelation over philosophical theory in furthering human rights and fundamental freedoms.

A Transcendent Explosion

In his posthumously published "Lecture on Ethics," Ludwig Wittgenstein employed a metaphor to describe the qualitative distinction that would exist between a transcendent value system and the relativistic value systems that are the products of fallible humanity: "If a man could write a book on Ethics which really was a book on Ethics, this book would, with an explosion, destroy all the other books in the world."[309] We have seen that such a book does indeed exist: the Bible, attested as revelatory by God himself, who in Jesus Christ "showed himself alive after his passion by many infallible proofs."[310] What kind of explosion does biblical revelation create in the sphere of human rights?

The Bible Is Not a Wax Nose

A mere fizzle, some would say, on the ground that "you can get anything out of the Bible." You can—but only if you are allowed to bring anything you want to the Bible.[311] Diverse interpretations of the Bible result from bringing alien ideas to the Bible and forcing it to say what one wants it to say. Luther referred to this as turning the Scriptures into a "wax nose" which could be twisted in any direction. In criticizing Erasmus, he wrote:

> The notion that in Scripture some things are recondite and all is not plain was spread by the godless Sophists (whom now you echo, Erasmus)—who have never yet cited a single item to prove their crazy view; nor can they. And Satan has used these unsubstantial spectres to scare men off reading the sacred text, and to destroy all sense of its value, so as to ensure that his own brand of poisonous philosophy reigns supreme in the church. I certainly grant that many passages in the Scriptures are obscure and hard to elucidate, but that is due, not to the exalted nature of their subject, but to our own linguistic and grammatical ignorance. . . . Who will maintain that the town fountain does not stand in the light because the people down some alley cannot see it, while everyone in the square can see it?[312]

The issue of scriptural perspicuity or clarity is not hard to test. Take a passage such as "there went out a decree from Caesar Augustus, that all the world should be taxed" (Luke 2:1); could it legitimately be construed as referring to the banana crop in Tanganyika? English actor Alec McCowen, whose solo recitations of St. Mark's Gospel have electrified audiences on both sides of the Atlantic, maintains that the ordinary meaning of that book would be plain to us even if the book were unearthed for the first time yesterday.[313] McCowen's view is powerfully reinforced by the fact that, whatever their differences, all branches of Christendom—Orthodox Eastern, Roman Catholic, and Protestant—find the very same central teachings in the Bible, for they all accept the same ecumenical creeds: the Apostles' Creed, the Nicene Creed, and the Athanasian Creed. The Apostles' Creed, for example, sums up the major themes of scriptural teaching as expressly set out in passages like 1 Corinthians 15:1–3:

> I believe in God, the Father Almighty, Maker of heaven and earth;
> And in Jesus Christ, his only Son, our Lord,
> Who was conceived by the Holy Spirit,
> Born of the Virgin Mary, suffered under Pontius Pilate, was crucified, dead, and buried:
> He descended into Hell, the third day he rose again from the dead,
> He ascended into heaven, and sitteth on the right hand of God, the Father Almighty:
> From thence he shall come to judge the quick and the dead.
> I believe in the Holy Ghost; the holy catholic (i.e., Christian, universal) Church, the Communion of Saints; the forgiveness of sins;
> The Resurrection of the body, and the life everlasting. Amen.

One should not therefore be surprised to find that the Bible contains a consistent and comprehensible body of teaching on human dignity.

Scriptural Applicability: From One Extreme to the Other

Though the meaning of biblical commands and principles is remarkably unambiguous ("Thou shalt not steal"; "Love thy neighbor as thyself"), there are admittedly differences of theological opinion as to their *applicability*. At one extreme stand some hyper-Calvinist "reconstructionists," who view virtually all of Old Testament legislation as properly applicable to life today. R. J. Rushdoony, for example, even goes so far as to assert that, with regard to adultery, "a godly law-order will restore the death penalty, but the church must live realistically with its absence and protect itself."[314] At the other end of the spectrum are those "dispensationalists" who divide the Bible into a series of more or less airtight historical compartments (the number varies, *The Scofield Reference Bible* using the perfect number seven), claiming that only the laws relating to the current dispensation are now applicable.

Some extreme dispensationalists too easily miss the unity of Scripture: that only one way of salvation has ever existed, that Abraham no less than Paul was saved by grace through faith.[315] The only unarguable division into "dispensations" is the separation between the Old Testament and the New Testament, and, as we have just seen, a single way of salvation bridges even that gap.

Reconstructionists, in line with their Calvinistic roots, tend to swallow up the New Testament in the Old, viewing the Old Testament as the foundation of the New rather than as its preparation.[316] In theological parlance, they "confuse law and gospel" by overextending the applicability of Old Testament legislation and by transforming the New Testament gospel into a higher law.[317]

Is the Inerrant Old Testament Ever Inapplicable?

Dispensationalists and reconstructionists account for a very small proportion of the Christian community, whether viewed historically or in present-day terms. Classical theological thought has taken a middle path, based upon the following principles: (1) Though both Old and New Testaments are equally revelatory, the New fulfills the Old and therefore finally determines its true meaning and applicability. This approach, not so incidentally, is in full conformity with general juridical principle.

> "The latest pronouncement of the law-maker is the law." According to this axiom where two laws have been made by the same authority, or by different authorities of the same dignity, the one last made will prevail over the earlier one in so far as the two conflict. Applying this principle to Biblical law, when a rule of the Old Testament disagrees with one of the New, the older rule must be considered as "abrogated" or "repealed" and the newer rule as being the effective and existing law. So even if a commandment of Jesus were regarded as of the same authority as one given by Moses, the new commandment nevertheless is of greater force and supersedes the old by virtue of its being the latest expression of the law-maker.[318]

(2) Because of the unique nature of Israel as the vehicle for the coming of the Messiah, her purely *national* and *ceremonial* legislation is not mandatory for other peoples or for the church of the New Testament. Such national and ceremonial legislation may not be made obligatory, and (3) must in fact be rejected when (a) the New Testament expressly abolishes it (as in the case of strict sabbatarianism—Col. 2:16–17),[319] or (b) the New Testament abolishes it by clear implication (as in the case of the stoning of prostitutes—John 8:1–11),[320] or (c) such practices militate against the effective preaching of the gospel of the free grace of God in Jesus Christ (as in the case of circumcising Gentiles—Acts 15; Gal. 2, 5, and 6). Moreover, (4) even when general principles of Old Testament legis-

lation remain in force because of their absolute moral content (appellate justice, equitable restitution, etc.), their adjectival law aspects (such as a particular appellate court organization) or detailed remedies (e.g., restitution plus one-fifth in specified circumstances) may be so limited to Hebrew national life as not to be binding on the future.[321]

OT Moral Law Is Forever Applicable

The *moral* law of the Old Testament does not come under these strictures; it remains permanently in force. Liberal Old Testament scholar Walter Harrelson tells us that in relating the Ten Commandments to present-day human rights concerns, "we are not likely to find it necessary to depart greatly from the contents of our present Decalogue," but that, for example, where it is a question of the Seventh Commandment ("Thou shalt not commit adultery"), "it cannot be claimed that this commandment should become an absolutistic and unbreakable norm, issuing in a commitment never to have sexual relations with anyone other than the marriage partner."[322] Such a treatment of the permanent moral law of the Old Testament has more affinity with Mel Brooks' *History of the World, Part One* than with Jesus' respect for the Ten Commandments, and it places the Christian human rights advocate in the awkward position of cutting off the limb on which he is sitting.

The Law Interiorized

Jesus accepts the Decalogue unqualifiedly—and then goes beyond it. "Think not that I am come to destroy the law, or the prophets," He declared in the Sermon on the Mount: "I am not come to destroy, but to fulfil" (Matt. 5:17). He illustrates the fulfillment with some examples:

> Ye have heard that it was said by them of old time, Thou shalt not kill; and whosoever shall kill shall be in danger of the judgment: But I say unto you, That

> whosoever is angry with his brother without a cause shall be in danger of the judgment. . . .
>
> Ye have heard that it was said by them of old time, Thou shalt not commit adultery: But I say unto you that whosoever looketh on a woman to lust after her hath committed adultery with her already in his heart.[323]

Jesus here and elsewhere *interiorizes* the Old Testament law. He insists not only on outward obedience but also and principally on the internal condition of the heart. He is concerned with *motivation,* not just with external conformity to absolute standards. This interiorizing of the law places every man under judgment and in equal need of salvation from self-centeredness. As we shall see in the final chapter, the problem of motivation touches the nerve of man's inhumanity to man and starkly points up the need for personal and societal redemption to make human rights more than an unattainable ideal.

A Synoptic Overview of Human Dignity

Now that we have obtained a perspective on the clarity and applicability of biblical law in general, we are in a position to ask the specific question of concern to us in this book: What does transcendent scriptural revelation have to say about human rights? Perhaps the most helpful way of answering that question is to begin with a synoptic overview of major human rights principles together with their biblical justification. The following tabular summary employs categories and terminology that lean heavily on the European Convention, the most sophisticated of modern international human rights treaties, but its inclusions extend beyond the limits of that Convention.[324] No attempt has been made to give an exhaustive list of all human rights justifiable by biblical revelation: our modest purpose is to show the broad sweep and wide scope of the scriptural protections of human dignity (figure 7).

It will be seen at a glance that this chart of biblically supported human rights embraces all three generations of rights we discussed in chapter 2. Some matters relating to each of the generations as viewed from the Christian position warrant special attention at this point.

A. *Procedural Due Process (cf. European Convention, Articles 5, 6, 7)*[325]

—Impartiality of tribunal	Mal. 2:9; 1 Tim. 5:21
—Fair hearing	Exod. 22:9
—Speedy trial	Ezra 7:26
—Confrontation of witnesses	Isa. 43:9
—No double jeopardy	Nah. 1:9[326]

B. *Substantive Due Process: Nondiscrimination (cf. European Convention, Article 14)*

—Versus unjust discrimination in general	Acts 10:34; Deut. 16:19; Prov. 24:23
—The just and the unjust stand equally before the law	Matt. 5:45
—Likewise all races and both sexes; condition of servitude irrelevant (versus slavery)	Gal. 3:28; Amos 9:7; Exod. 21:2
—Likewise rich and poor	James 2:1–7; Amos 5:12; Isa. 1:16–17
—Likewise citizens and foreigners	Exod 12:49; Lev. 23:22; 24:22; Num. 9:14; 15:15–16
—Even the sovereign is under the law	2 Sam. 11–12

C. *Miscellaneous Basic First-, Second-, and Third-Generation Rights*

—Right to life (cf. American Convention)	Exod. 20:13; Ps. 51:5; Matt. 5:21–22; Luke 1:15, 41[327]
—Right to family life	1 Tim. 5:8
—Versus inhuman or degrading treatment/punishment and torture	Luke 6:45 (cf. Publications of Action des Chrétiens pour l'Abolition de la Torture, 252 rue St-Jacques, Paris)
—Freedom of thought, conscience, religion, expression, assembly, association, movement	John 7:17
—Social and economic rights in general	1 Cor. 6:19–20
—Right to universal education	Deut. 6:7; 11:19
—Right to work, to a fair remuneration, and to good working conditions (protection of labor)	Luke 10:7; 1 Tim. 5:18; Deut. 23:25–26; 24:6, 10, 12–13, 15.
—Right to protection of honor and personal reputation	Exod. 20:16

Biblical Influences on First-Generation Rights

First-generation human rights (civil and political liberties) have been widely acknowledged to stem from biblical influence. "Due process finds its roots at Runnymede"[329]—and the Magna Charta was a profoundly Christian document. John C. H. Wu, emeritus professor of law at Seton Hall and former chief justice of the Provisional Court of Shanghai, writes:

—Right to leisure time	Exod. 20:8–11
—Right to asylum	Exod. 21:13; Josh. 20; 1 Chron. 6:67; et al. (cities of refuge)
—Right to equitable distribution of land	Num. 33:54; Lev. 25:14–18, 25–34
—Environmental rights	"Scripture expresses horror over murder, for example, by personifying matrix earth being forced to drink the blood of her offspring. In the biblical imagery, crimes *pollute* the soil and the land will *vomit* its polluting population into exile. The modern concern with preventing the extinction of various species of animal life is in resonance with the biblical prescription not to collect the dam with her chicks but to release her to hatch another generation. Cruelty to animals is proscribed in such prescriptions as not to yoke animals of different strengths (ox and ass) to the plough or not to muzzle the ox which treads the grain. Ecological considerations are exemplified in the prohibition of sowing the vineyard's aisles with a second crop or the destruction of defenseless fruit trees while waging war in enemy territory. Such concerns must be perceived for what they are—a sensitivity to the human capacities for greed, rapaciousness, wanton cruelty, and ingratitude, capacities which cross over from the human realm into the non-human."[328]

Figure 7
Revelational Foundations for Specific Human Rights

Magna Charta

I cannot dismiss the Magna Carta without mention of Cardinal Stephen Langton, Archbishop of Canterbury, who was actually the soul of the whole movement. To me it is not without significance that the father of the Magna Carta was also the author of the magnificent hymn to the Holy Ghost, *Veni Sancte Spiritus*. The same Spirit that inspired that hymn motivated and energized, on a lower plane, the movement which was crowned by the Magna Carta; and I think that the same Spirit has enlivened the common law by breathing into it the liberalizing influence of natural justice and equity.[330]

John Locke

The dean of American constitutional historians, Edward S. Corwin, in a classic monograph, argued the case for *The "Higher Law" Background of American Constitutional Law,* and other equally celebrated historians of political theory have come to the same conclusion.[331] John Locke's contract theory, philosophy of limited government, and affirmation of inalienable rights were the most immediate ideological influences on the founding documents of American constitutionalism—and Locke, author of the apologetic treatise, *The Reasonableness of Christianity,* was simply putting his faith into practice.[332]

Checks and Balances

In particular, the consistent theme of checks-and-balances in the U.S. Constitution harks back to the biblical word that "in a multitude of counselors there is much wisdom" (Prov. 11:14; 15:22; 24:6), and this principle in turn is grounded in the scriptural view of man as a fallen, sinful, self-centered creature whose independent judgment is not to be trusted. A healthy biblical fear of the autocratic domination of one man by another led directly to the restraints on arbitrary power which make our Federal Constitution the great political instrument it is.[333]

The Reformers

The German jurist Georg Jellinek, followed by the great historian of ideas Ernst Troeltsch,[334] argued that American constitutionalism has been far more important than the secularistic French Revolution for the growth of true freedom in the modern world, and that the American colonists drew their inspiration from the Protestant Reformers' battle for liberty of faith and conscience in the sixteenth century and the struggles of Puritans, Dissenters, and Congregationalists a century later. Indeed, these same strivings for religious liberty created the ideological backdrop from the 1789 Declaration of the Rights of Man. Jellinek's thesis has been challenged, and doubtless it goes too far, but it points up the central importance of religious freedom to first-generation human rights in general.

Is the Biblical Gospel Compatible With Religious Freedom?

A common misconception, especially on the part of modern secularists, is that Christianity is at root opposed to religious liberty—that it only favors liberty for its own belief-system. Here confusion reigns between Christianity's assertion that it is indeed the truth (John 14:6; Acts 4:12), and the illogical inference that, therefore, all views contradicting the Christian gospel should be repressed or at least discouraged. The true biblical view is 180 degrees removed from that expressed by Rabbi Meir Kahane, leading reactionary rightest in the Israeli Knesset: "Judaism is truth. People cannot have the right to choose falsehood."[335] The scriptural gospel cannot be forced on anyone: if it is not freely accepted, it is not accepted at all. The risen Christ declares: "Behold, I stand at the door, and knock: if any man hear my voice, and open the door, I will come in to him, and will sup with him, and he with me" (Rev. 3:20). Jesus never forces Himself on man, and the true Christian believer can hardly justify doing what his Master will not do. Thus, even viewed from the standpoint of the absolute truth of the gospel, repressing non-Christian beliefs is indefensible: in removing freedom of religious choice, one removes in principle the opportunity genuinely to choose Christ himself.

Christianity Insists on Maximum Freedom of Religious Practice

Marxist Constitutions typically protect the right "to conduct religious worship or atheistic propaganda" and separate "the school from the church."[336] This is a transparent attempt to eliminate evangelism and religious influence in education. The biblical viewpoint insists on freedom to proselytize and to educate religiously (Matt. 28:18–20—the "Great Commission"). Thus, the U.S. Supreme Court's rationale in the nineteenth-century Mormon polygamy cases[337] can hardly be satisfactory (even if we agree with the result): that the Constitution protects only freedom of religious *belief,* not freedom to *practice* one's belief! The biblical approach is surely not to restrict religious conduct unless there is a compelling state interest—and the only properly compelling interest is to oppose practices that in themselves violate the common law of crimes (at the *malum in se* level) or the civil law applicable to all citizens (human sacrifice; torts against the person or property; fraud and undue influence, including tax fraud; ritual use of illegal drugs; etc.—and doubtless also violation of laws for the protection of the family). The establishment of a state religion—as in the case of the Anglican church—is not per se wrong, as long as its privileges do not otherwise restrict the religious activities and free choice of nonadherents.[338] To prohibit religious practices on the ground of "compelling state interest" is always dangerous, and the phrase must not be given a scope permitting governments to repress religion in the interests of political ideology or established belief systems. Though the World Council of Churches is not famous for the depth of its scriptural exegesis, its 1948 Amsterdam Assembly certainly expressed the biblical approach to religious liberty in the four fundamental principles it set forth:

(1) Every man has the right himself to choose his faith and creed. (2) Every man has the right to express his religious convictions in worship, in instruction and in practice, and to give public expression to the conclusions he draws from them regarding social and political relations. (3) Every man has the right to assemble with others and to form with them a common organization for religious purposes. (4) Every religious organization formed or maintained in accordance with the rights of the individual is entitled itself to determine fundamental rules and practice in order to serve the aims it has itself chosen.[339]

The Bible and Second- and Third-Generation Rights

Our tabular summary of the Revelational Foundations for Specific Human Rights should leave no doubt that the Bible, though appealed to again and again as the source and justification of first-generation rights, by no means limits itself to the category of civil and political liberties. What today are termed economic, social, educational, and solidarity rights are likewise woven into the very fabric of biblical revelation.

Revelational Concern for the Needy

The enormous significance of a transcendent, revelational grounding for second- and third-generation rights should not escape our attention. We have already noted the less defined, more fluid character of these rights in international law, and the degree to which they are often regarded as little more than expressions of goals for attainment someday. Moreover, what Freeman has termed "manifesto" rights (adequate housing, nutrition, medical care, a clean environment, etc.) do not impose duties upon anyone in particular to provide the needed services.[340] But if God Almighty declares—as He has done in the Scriptures—that widows, orphans, the disenfranchised, and the downtrodden are to be taken care of by the more fortunate—then the rights involved are made highly specific and the corresponding duties fall on every person in a position to help.

Versus Unbiblical Libertarianism

What of the oft-expressed libertarian argument (reiterated, sadly, by some churchmen to the right of Genghis Khan politically) that second- and third-generation rights do not accord with "the biblical work-ethic": "This we commanded you, that if any would not work, neither should he eat" (2 Thess. 3:10). The answer is, of course, that this sound principle deals with malingerers; it hardly justifies an attitude of social indifference toward the genuinely needy. And the viewpoint that governments ought not to enter a realm appropriate to private charity (since this will presumably deaden the charitable instinct) suffers from a lamentable absence of focus on the one in need, who should not be left in want because of philosophical disputes between government and private charity as to their respective spheres of activity.

Scripture regards with scorn the hypocrisy of saying "be warmed and filled" (by someone else) instead of doing something personally to bring it about (James 2:15–16)—and this applies as much to corporate entities as to individuals. Even if one takes a minimalistic view of government (first-generation rights do indeed encourage such a view), the moment one agrees to the legitimacy of taxation—as Jesus did (Matt. 22:17–22)—one admits in principle the positive duty of government to use its income for the best interests of its people. These interests, on scriptural grounds, surely include the social and economic rights, as well as the major solidarity rights, of the second and third generation.[341]

On the Frontiers of Human Rights

There is no reason for Christians to feel uncomfortable about even the most innovative of third-generation rights. Granted, these can be misused for political ends, but ever since Cain, fallen human beings have been employing neutral objects for bad ends. What Christian could scripturally question the right to peace[342]—as long as peace is not a cloak for preserving an even greater evil than war, such as an inhuman, totalitarian regime like the Third Reich? As for the so-called New International Economic Order, the biblical perspective I have been describing would favor *conditional* redistribution of wealth—the conditions, laid down by developed donor states, being that the donees institute and observe civil and political liberties and use the donated resources to increasc distributive justice and aid the poor in their territories.[343] It should not be necessary to add that from the biblical (as contrasted with a revolutionary) standpoint, any redistributions of wealth must be *voluntary:* "Thou shalt not steal."

In Biblical Perspective, All Three Generations of Rights Are Equal

In discussing the several qenerations of human rights in chapter 2, we noted the ideological pitched battle between those arguing for the superiority of one generation of human rights over another (in general, Westerners claiming the primacy of civil and political liberties, Socialists of the Eastern bloc maintaining the supremacy of social and economic rights, and Third World peoples elevating solidarity rights to chief position). A revelational philosophy of human rights will have none of this: it regards the entire controversy as misconceived. Man in the Bible is a psychosomatic unity, and to put one generation of rights over another is to split that unity. Declared Jesus, in summing up the whole law: "Thou shalt love the Lord thy God with all thy heart, and with all thy soul, and with all thy mind, and with all thy strength: this is the first commandment. And the second is like, namely this, Thou shalt love thy neighbour as thyself" (Mark 12:30–31). Neighbor-love is grounded in the love of God, and all proper love involves the whole person: physical, mental, spiritual, environmental.

Some frequently cited biblical passages seem on the surface to contradict this psychosomatic holism but do not in fact do so. The verse "Man shall not live by bread alone, but by every word that proceeds out of the mouth of God" (Matt. 4:4, quoting Deut. 8:3) does not denigrate physical needs in favor of spiritual needs. Observe that it makes bread a necessary (though not a sufficient) condition of human life: "Man *shall* live by bread, but not by bread *alone*." Likewise passages contrasting the "spirit" with the "flesh": these scriptural terms do not refer to more or less valuable, separable parts of man, in the sense of a faculty psychology, but to the whole man viewed in or out of relation to God (in the language of the Reformers, *Totus homo est caro, totus homo est spiritus*).

Beams, Motes, and Radical Selfishness

Biblical anthropology offers profound insight into the true reasons for pitting one generation of rights against another. Scripture delineates in bold strokes the universality of sin and selfishness: "All have sinned and fallen short of the glory of God" (Rom. 3:23). A corollary of original sin is the universal human tendency to see faults in others rather than in ourselves. So the West has no difficulty in condemning the Socialist world for its cavalier attitude to civil and political liberties—the West taking for granted that its own strengths correspond to the highest values for humanity. The Socialists and the Third World perform the identical operation in terms of their own strengths and interests, and express equal but opposite outrage at the West's denigration of second- and third-generation rights. To all three ideological camps, our Lord thunders: "Why beholdest thou the mote that is in thy brother's eye, but perceivest not the beam that is in thine own eye? . . . Thou hypocrite, cast out first the beam out of thine own eye, and then shalt thou see clearly to pull out the mote that is in thy brother's eye" (Luke 6:41–42).

Concretely, for Westerners—and especially, perhaps, for Americans addicted to rugged individualism—this means facing our own insensitivity to social, economic, and solidarity rights. Louis Henkin does not exaggerate: "Planning is still uncongenial and Americans are reluctant to sacrifice—or even act with restraint—now for future generations."[344] And if we would defend ourselves by citing our enviable record of constitutional liberty, Jesus would surely reply: "These [things] ought ye to have done, and not to leave the other undone" (Luke 11:42).

Derogable and Nonderogable Rights

If the biblical approach to human rights rejects a hierarchicalism among the three generations of rights, what would it say to the distinction in many international human rights instruments between derogable and nonderogable rights? The category of nonderogable rights generally includes freedom from unlawful or arbitrary deprivation of life, from torture and inhuman punishment, and from slavery—and states bound by covenants so designating them may not derogate from these rights under any circumstances. Does this distinction not constitute a hierarchy of rights, making some rights more fundamental than others? What is the revelational viewpoint in the matter?

There is a sense in which, to paraphrase George Orwell's *Animal Farm,* all human rights are equal but some are more equal than others. Stephen P. Marks rightly speaks of an "indestructible core" of human dignity: "prohibition of torture, slavery, degrading or humiliating treatment or punishment, the arbitrary deprivation of life, adverse discrimination and judicial guarantees recognized as indispensable."[345] The right to life logically precedes other rights, since once the victim is deprived of this right, all others become moot. The Bible recognizes this. For example, Jesus said, "For what is a man profited, if he shall gain the whole world, and lose his own soul [Gk., *psyche*: "personhood"]?

Or what shall a man give in exchange for his soul?'' (Matt. 16:26). Elsewhere, Jesus speaks of ''the weightier matters of the law'' (Matt. 23:23), implying that some are weightier than others.

Versus Ethical Hierarchicalism

But we cannot emphasize too strongly that these passages do not commit the Scriptures or Christian faith to a neo-Thomist ethic of ''hierarchicalism,'' in which ''not all absolutes are absolutely absolute,'' ''some are only relatively absolute,'' and it can be affirmed that ''when one obeys a higher norm in favor of a lower and opposing one, he is not really breaking the lower one but transcending it.''[346] Revelational absolutes *are* absolutely absolute and will brook no relativizing. When, as a result of the conditions of a fallen world, they come into conflict, this is not due to any fault in God's law but to the mess human beings have made of God's creation. In these situations, one must choose the lesser of evils—and go to the Cross for forgiveness for one's participation in and contribution to the fallen world. Evangelicals, like medieval Catholics, have felt very uncomfortable with this thoroughly Reformation viewpoint, doubtless because, like their monastic predecessors and following John Wesley's preoccupation with ''Christian perfection,'' they must justify their every action in the quest for empirical sanctification and a life entirely pleasing to God. Sad to say, such a goal is chimerical in this life (1 John 1:8–10) and diverts attention from the biblical truth that true holiness is to be found only as we return daily to the Cross for forgiveness. As Kierkegaard well put it, ''No Christian is more than one day old.''[347]

Guard Against Relativizations of Human Dignity

Applied to the issue of derogable versus nonderogable rights, a nonderogable human right will be seen biblically as a right whose violation presumably would *never* constitute a lesser of evils. Choosing to violate it would therefore never be a legitimate course of action juridically. But we must not forget that from the scriptural standpoint, the violation of *any* genuine human rights—including the derogable ones—is always an evil. "A lesser evil does not turn out to be a good by the fact that it's less evil than something else."[348] Because of the ease with which derogations by states-parties to international human rights conventions become means of avoiding their spirit and intendment, they should certainly be discouraged as much as possible, in the interests of opposing all relativizations of human dignity.

Do Biblical *Ideals* = *Rights?*

Suppose one were to argue, after examining the biblical passages cited in our schematic presentation of Revelational Foundations for Specific Human Rights and the discussion leading from it to this point, that, in reality, the Bible at best sets forth *moral ideals* for human life, and ideals fall far short of *rights*. In what sense (if any) can the ethical ideals in Holy Scripture be regarded as *entitlements*?[349] Once one sees that the Bible presents the "ideals" in question, not as abstract Platonic ideas but as divine commands or orders, the problem essentially vanishes. Shestack, though not writing from a Christian perspective, sees the point clearly:

> There is a positivist aspect to divine orders since obedience derives from one's duty to God, not from one's inherent nature. Still, the fact remains that once the duties are ordered by God, those duties accrue to the individual's benefit and may be inviolate from denigration by the state, which is an important objective of any human rights system.[350]

Entitlement comes about by divine fiat. (This, of course, does not preclude—and in fact suggests—that the rights established would conjoin precisely with man's true nature and needs.) Granted, in the terms of Albert Ellis' rational-emotive therapy,[351] human beings will fall into irrational anger or depression if they think that there is some way, in a fallen world, to force others always to treat them as they ought. Nonetheless, God's judgment—immanent, transcendent, and final—stands over human conduct, and man's inalienable rights are not one whit diminished by the foolish disregard or violation of them.

The Legislation of Human Dignity

But how far should we go, in domestic or international law, to legislate the human rights to which Scripture entitles us? We need to face this important variant on the general question, how far should we legislate morality? Our specific question is: To what extent ought one to try to legislate human dignity?

Some General Principles

In my book *The Shaping of America,* I deal with the wider, "Moral Majority" issue of legislating morals. On the one hand, there is certainly no biblical justification for the quietistic view of some separationist Christians that morality ought not to be legislated at all. The Old Testament prophets insist that God's ethical standards be incorporated into the very fabric of government, and since all law necessarily reflects a moral value system of some kind, there is every reason to have it reflect the proper (absolute, revelational) value system.

On the other hand, "It is no solution to legislate . . . even genuinely scriptural moral teachings when they do not have direct and demonstrable social necessity."[352] To legislate biblical truth whose social necessity cannot be demonstrated to unbelievers (even when we can get away with it by mobilizing a "Christian majority") is to win a Pyrrhic victory: what we gain in higher moral standards will surely be lost in our alienation of the unbeliever. The non-

Christian will hardly respond to our offer of the free grace of God in Jesus Christ after he has been forced against his will to conform to the ethical standards of a religion he has not accepted. (The Moral Majority's obtuseness to this practical truth not only testifies to the movement's insensitivity in regard to what constitutes effective evangelism in a pluralistic society but also illustrates its continual confusion of law and gospel.)[353] To follow a genuinely biblical approach, then, "we should actively strive to legislate all revelational standards whose societal importance can be demonstrated to our fellow citizens, and where we are unsuccessful in legislating them we should do all in our power to create a climate of opinion in which they will eventually become acceptable."[354]

Human Rights in Particular

The issue of legislating morality becomes considerably less agonizing when one turns to the specific area of human rights and fundamental freedoms. Here there is much more agreement (at least on paper) among believers and unbelievers, and among those in opposing ideological camps, as to the legitimacy of the rights involved. Thus, when Christians spearhead human rights legislation in international and domestic law, they create no significant barriers to evangelism. Moreover, as one moves up the scale of rights to those universally regarded as nonderogable—what Marks termed the "indestructible core" of human dignity—the concern not to imperil evangelism by legislating what non-Christians will not agree to diminishes to the vanishing point. Unbelievers who seriously oppose the right to life or advocate slavery, torture, and inhuman treatment are doubtless (in human terms) too far gone to respond to evangelistic appeals, even though we may refuse to offend them on these issues.

Core Rights Versus Evangelism

In any case, it would be monstrous to use the victims of such human rights violations as hostages to this kind of evangelism. No human beings should have their lives arbitrarily snuffed out or be enslaved or tortured for the sake of the possible future conversion of their executioner, slaver, or torturer, when Christians could reduce the extent of the practice or perhaps even legislate it out of existence. A concrete example: The arbitrary destruction of fetal life should be outlawed, even if to do so deeply offends abortionists and reduces the chances of their conversion. The life of the unborn child must not be sacrificed to the possible conversion of those who violate indestructible core values of human dignity. There is, after all, a Last Judgment to consider. Roland de Pury has put it this way:

An Eschatological Reminder

> We can only welcome the Kingdom in engaging body and soul in the struggle for human rights. Otherwise, how could we be among those to whom the Shepherd, Judge, and Lamb will say on the Last Day, "Come my sheep, for I was hungry, I was cold, I was a prisoner, and you did something about it—you respected my right to be fed, clothed, healed, liberated, treated with dignity." The Shepherd doesn't here condemn just those who starve, exile, imprison, and torture others—all the horrible monsters of history and their police who create misery for the peoples of this world—but also everyone who lets it happen by his indifference, who does not intervene in favor of the oppressed and the stricken, whether at our door or across the globe.[355]

The Christian Philosophical Corrective

Now that we have obtained an overview of the revelational philosophy of human rights, it might be helpful to see at a glance the tremendous advantages this approach has over previously discussed secular philosophical attempts to justify human dignity. The following tabulation (figure 8) includes those secular philosophies of human rights treated at length in chapter 4.

PHILOSOPHICAL POSITION	FAILING	CHRISTIAN CORRECTIVE
1. Utilitarianism (Bentham)	Utility undefined	Utility defined revelationally
2. Legal Positivism/Realism (Hart, Kelsen, Dworkin)	Human rights restricted to existing legal order or societal values (e.g., equal concern and respect)	Transcendent standard of human dignity established
3. Natural Law (Finnis)	Human nature and the content of natural law undefined	Human nature and natural law defined revelationally
4. Sociological Jurisprudence (Pound, Stone)	Naturalistic fallacy and quasi-absolutes	The "ought" and genuine absolutes established revelationally
5. Neo-Kantian Moral Philosophy (Rawls, Gewirth)	Gratuitous apriorism	Universals justified by evidentially verifiable divine revelation and sanctioned by Last Judgment
6. Marxism	Concentration on altering a person's external environment without any means of changing the inner motivations	Personal redemption available to alter human motivations and thus the external environment and human rights conditions
7. Policy-orientation	Policies lacking justification except sociologically; the human heart left unchanged	Sound policies established revelationally and a new heart available redemptively

Figure 8
Secular Philosophies of Human Rights Critiqued

Not Loss but Gain

Perhaps the most important lesson to be learned from this tabulation is that in the philosophical realm—as in the realm of non-Christian religions, for that matter—a biblical approach does not so much destroy as fulfill: it provides an ultimate grounding for the human values sought in vain by men of good will everywhere. Acceptance of the Christian answer to human rights therefore results not in loss but gain, both in terms of the quest for the true nature of human dignity and in the epistemological effort to justify it.

Not a Magic Wand

I do not claim that a revelational philosophy of human rights offers instant answers to every conceivable practical problem in this exceedingly complex area. In a sinful and fallen world, there are no simplistic solutions to such human rights dilemmas as that posed by Professor (and Watergate Special Prosecutor) Archibald Cox:

> Suppose that a vacancy occurs in a racially mixed, public housing project. Ten families apply, one white and nine black. There should be equality of opportunity without regard to race, you will say; selection should be according to need, or priority of application, or some other racially neutral principle. Suppose further that experience shows that if the percentage of black families in a public housing project exceeds an established figure, the white families will leave the project, ending the racial integration. Racially integrated housing is widely believed to be a desirable measure, perhaps one of the best ways to overcome prejudice and resulting discrimination against minorities. Suppose that our hypothetical housing project is just at the tipping-point. Must the State award the vacancy to the black family entitled by colour-blind rule or may it discriminate against that particular family because it is black and prefer the white family because it is white, in order to benefit the black minority generally by residential integration? When we speak of "equality of opportunity" whose, and what, opportunity are we to focus upon? The particular black

> family's opportunity to get this housing? The opportunity to live in a racially mixed community? The opportunities of black people generally to overcome the obstacles resulting from slavery and segregation?[356]

What Christianity offers is not a pat formula to apply to every such human rights enigma, but an underlying justification of the absolute values (here: racial equality, equality of treatment and opportunity) that must never be compromised or relativized politically if these problems are to be dealt with even tolerably well in a broken world.

What About Human Rights Violations by Christians?

But are not violations of human rights also chargeable to Christians? What is to be said of the persecutions of Jews in the Middle Ages, the atrocities committed during the Spanish Inquisition, the intolerance of the Puritans, the rule of apartheid in South Africa, etc.? Without in any way whitewashing such tragic events, two points need to be made. First: though human rights violations have certainly been committed "in the name of Christ," it is hardly fair to attribute to the Christian religion acts or opinions that in fact are in direct opposition to Christ's own teachings. Unlike the human rights violations in certain other religious traditions (e.g., discrimination against women and cruel and unusual punishments in Islam), "Christian" violations of human dignity occur *in spite of,* not because of, Jesus' teaching. One should judge a belief-system by the acts of its consistent disciples, not those of its inconsistent fellow-travelers.

In the second place, Christian belief does not guarantee moral perfection in this world. True Christians are by definition born again, but they do not reach complete ethical maturity in this life. Christians suffer from environmental and historical blindspots too. The failures of Christians must not be laid at Christ's door, for He has allowed mankind (including believers) to make free moral decisions and to take the consequences of them. As the Reformers so trenchantly put it, Christians are *simul justi et peccatores:* sinners and justified at the same time. Their sin is their own, and ought not be attributed to the One who saves them by His acts of grace and love. The gospel and the Scriptures remain the answer to man's ultimate human rights dilemmas, whether or not the human race—or the church itself—follows the revelation given to it.

Biblical Superiority in Human Rights

Even if Christianity is incapable of bringing in a human rights millennium (according to the Bible, only Christ himself at his return is able to do that!), it can go considerably further than its secular rivals in advancing human rights doctrine. Four brief examples will illustrate this.

My Brother's Keeper

(1) A revelational philosophy of human rights will be capable of seeing further into the requirements of human dignity than even the best and longest established systems of domestic jurisprudence. The Anglo-American common law, which Professor Wu goes so far as to refer to as a "cradle Christian,"[357] nonetheless (in contrast to the Continental civil law tradition) enshrines the "Bad Samaritan" principle: defendant who, being under no special duty to plaintiff, refuses to help him when in need, is not legally liable to him in tort or criminally. (Example: ignoring the cries of a drowning child.) The biblical position that each person is his brother's keeper (Gen. 4:9–10) and that one's neighbor is simply any person in need (Luke 10:25–37) flatly contradicts the common law doctrine that nonfeasance in situations of human need leaves one without culpability. There *is* a human right to be helped, and this right should surely be given legal sanction. The adherent to a Christian philosophy

of human rights would therefore go even beyond D'Amato, who proposes criminal but not civil liability for the Bad Samaritan:[358] the latter should suffer all the weight the legal system can put upon him (civil penalties often being the most effective deterrents).

Protecting the Right to Life All the Way

(2) The right to life is the most basic of all human rights—surely the very center of the "indestructible core of human dignity." But when does human life begin? Without an answer to that fundamental question, we are incapable of protecting life as we ought. Revelationally, human life is seen to begin at conception (Ps. 51:5; Luke 1:15, 41). So Christians will strive—well beyond others—to support and extend those (rare) international instruments such as the American Convention on Human Rights which recognize that beginning point.[359]

Human Rights Without Partiality

(3) At the heart of the frustration many feel toward the human rights movement is the endemic redefinition of rights in terms of one's own interest group. The violators to be condemned always seem to be one's political or ideological opponents, never one's friends. To the Eastern bloc, the Vietnam War and the invasion of Grenada are clearly imperialistic; but not the Russian presence in Afghanistan! To Western nations, the Gulags are a monstrosity, but not the torture and disappearance of untold numbers of people in Central and South American rightist dictatorships. Claude Lelouch's 1980–81 film, *Les Uns et les Autres,* makes the point nicely in its title, taken from George Orwell's *Animal Farm:* "All the animals were equal, but some were more equal than others." The Christian can have no illusions in the matter: all human beings have equal rights—their human rights entitlements are identical (Gal. 3:28). The Christian will, therefore, con-

demn without partiality violations of human rights whenever they occur and without regard to the politics of the violators; and he will strive to promote and protect the dignity of every man, without fear or favor.

The Best of All Worlds

(4) The Christian's revelational perspective not only keeps him from unjustified favoritism in human rights practice; it likewise protects him from myopia in his human rights theories. He is not forced, like the doctrinaire secularist, to cram all human rights thinking into the procrustean bed of a single ideology or methodology (a particularly sad example being the Marxist dogma that all human rights problems are explainable by inequities in the ownership of the means of production in society). The Christian can "hang loose": his anchor is in eternity, not in human ideology. He will, thus, eclectically gather the best from the several schools of human rights theory and practice and try to apply their several insights as the needs of the human situation best dictate. Most importantly, he will have *an absolute, revelational criterion* for distinguishing the good from the bad in these diverse positions, so the results will not consist of the blind leading the blind. Hugo Grotius, the acknowledged "father of international law" and the first modern Protestant apologist for the historic truth of Christianity, made the point elegantly:

A Seventeenth-Century Word from Hugo Grotius in Conclusion

> For my part, both here and elsewhere I avail myself of the liberty of the early Christians, who had sworn allegiance to the sect of no one of the philosophers, not because they were in agreement with those who said that nothing can be known—than which nothing is more foolish—but because they thought that there was no philosophic sect whose vision had compassed all truth, and none which had not perceived some aspect of truth.[360]

chapter eight

Human Dignity and the Human Heart

The path we have traveled in search of human dignity began in the realm of jurisprudence; it ends in theology. We have weighed secular philosophies of human rights and other religious options in the balance and found them wanting, and we have provided a solid evidential foundation for the biblical value system. Now, in conclusion, we examine liberal and classical theological approaches, and arrive at the preeminent Christian doctrines of creation *and* redemption *as the keys to human dignity.*

The Forest, Not Just the Trees

To appreciate fully the significance of the biblical approach to human dignity, one must not just consider isolated scriptural texts bearing on particular human rights issues. The forest has to be seen as well as the trees (and not only when dealing with third-generation environmental rights!). Our final chapter therefore concentrates on the general theological themes most pertinent to human dignity. Treatment of these themes will put in bold relief the unique value of the Christian message in solving the most intractable difficulties of human rights theory and practice.

Theological styles may be roughly divided into two camps: liberal and classical. This distinction, between those who regard themselves as capable of constructing theology *de novo* and those who maintain commitment to existing biblical and confessional formulations, is today far more significant—even sociologically—than the differences between, say, Roman Catholics and Protestants.[361] Let us begin with a word about liberal theologies and human rights.

Theological Liberalism: Emasculating Revealed Truth

In our previous encounter (this term is *de rigueur* in any liberal theological dialogue) with Professor Walter Harrelson on the Ten Commandments,[362] we observed that liberalism's critical attitude toward the Bible (1) was inconsistent with Jesus' attitude toward it, and (2) undercut the liberal's own laudatory effort to find a solid basis for ethics and human rights. Once the liberal theologian has unnecessarily and unjustifiably reduced biblical content to mere human opinion, he has so emasculated it that it offers no advantages over secular philosophies of human rights. The pabulum-like results can be seen, for example, in an issue of the World Council of Churches' *Ecumenical Review* devoted to human rights.[363]

A glance at three influential liberal theologies (process theology, existentialism, situationism) will reinforce this point and make us even more appreciative of the need for a reliable biblical revelation to establish inalienable rights.

Process Theology

Process theology, represented especially by John B. Cobb, Jr., Norman Pittenger, and

Schubert Ogden, derives from the philosophical thought of Alfred North Whitehead and Charles Hartshorne. It reverses the ontological position of the Greek philosophy of the Golden Age that Being precedes Becoming, and maintains that change ("process") is the ultimate category of understanding. God himself is interlocked with the world in a panentheistic fashion (though God is not merely to be identified with the world, as in pantheism, the world exists in God and therefore he changes as it changes).[364] In Roman Catholic circles, Teilhard de Chardin's evolutionary theology—the world growing into a divine, cosmic "Omega Point"—has affinities with the process orientation, as does the liberal Reformed theologian Jürgen Moltmann's eschatological "theology of hope."[365]

Its Epistemological and Doctrinal Miseries

Process theology has a number of crippling deficiencies. Harry K. Wells, endeavoring to shore up Whitehead's view, argued that if process is all, one cannot any longer use traditional, formal logic (based on the static law of noncontradiction): one should shift to Hegel's dialectic logic![366] But Bertrand Russell, in his devastating critique of Hegel, demonstrated that Hegelian "logic" presupposes traditional logic anyway—as does all meaningful thinking.[367] In logic as in life, one cannot start from flux. Moreover, theologically, process thought pays no serious attention to the biblical doctrine of sin (God presumably sins as the world sins—or *neither* sins), and it has no room for a meaningful Incarnation (the world is already in God: why should God bother with a distinctive entry into human history?).

Its Debility for Human Rights

As for human rights, process theology is a total washout. By definition, it cannot offer inalienable rights—or inalienable *anything*. Its approach at root denies the "static" category of absoluteness. Rights, therefore, become part of the continually changing process—much as in Marxism, where they are forever conditioned by changing modes of production. But the problem cuts even deeper: man *himself* cannot be regarded as a constant entity. "In the most concrete terms, according to Hartshorne, there is no permanently or continuously enduring human ego or soul or self."[368] Human rights thus lack all permanence, not only because rights are impermanent but more especially because the very notion of humanity is thoroughly processive. Yet the Bible says Jesus Christ, the Second Adam, is "the same yesterday, and today, and for ever" (Heb. 13:8).

Existential Theology

Existential theology has very different roots from process theology: its modern progenitor, Søren Kierkegaard, arrived at it in full reaction against the dominant philosophical ideology of his time (nineteenth-century Hegelianism). But in common with process theology, existential theology opposes the static. As process thought rejects Being as a fundamental category, so existentialism rejects Essence. *Existence* is substituted for Essence (thus the name, "existentialism"). By Existence is meant, not change or any similar abstraction, but personal reality—the subjective perception and creation of meaning in one's innermost self. Theological existentialism is impatient with all formal, abstract, propositional statements of doctrine or ethics, believing, in Kierkegaard's phrase, that "truth is subjectivity" and that one must discover it in the particulars of experience, not in any alleged universal, timeless generalities.

Bishop Pike's Existential Ethic

A good example of the ramifications of this approach in legal ethics is provided by the late Resigned Episcopal Bishop James A. Pike (a lawyer before he was ordained).[369] In his 1962

Rosenthal Lectures at Northwestern University Law School, published under the significant title, *Beyond the Law,* Pike declares expressly that he is an existentialist.[370] He goes on to apply that perspective to the Ten Commandments and biblical precepts in general. He admits that "they give us a very good rule of thumb as to standard situations, thus saving us from the necessity of going through a great moral struggle of repeated contextual patterns." But they are at root conventional, like traffic lights. "One could perhaps make a better case for green being the proper color for stop and red the proper color for go, but it is better for all-round reliability simply to follow the mores and stop on red and go on green. . . . But such rules, whether they be traffic regulations or commandments from Mount Sinai, do not exhaust the full moral dimension of things."[371]

A Mess of Subjective Pottage

I am not prepared to argue the metes and bounds of "the full moral dimension of things," but I suggest that such an approach leaves one in a moral quagmire. If biblical morality is only conventional, what criteria are to be used to determine when it is applicable, and, if it isn't, what is to be substituted? The existential feelings of the individual as he encounters each new ethical or human rights dilemma? Jesus certainly did not take this view of biblical commandments; for Him, "Till heaven and earth pass, one jot or one tittle shall in no wise pass from the law, till all be fulfilled" (Matt. 5:18). It should go without saying that in today's life-or-death struggle for inalienable human rights, an existential theological ethic sells its biblical birthright for a mess of subjectivistic pottage.

Fletcher's Situation Ethics

Closely related to the existential theological ethic is Joseph Fletcher's situationism. Its core propositions are: "Only one thing is intrinsically good, namely, love"; "only the end justifies the means"; and "decisions ought to be made situationally, not prescriptively."[372] As in existential theology, there is powerful resistance to the binding, absolute force of scriptural principle. Ethical decisions are to be made, not on the basis of God's prescriptive commands, but out of "love"—and the achievement of a loving end justifies any means to bring it about.[373]

Love: Undefined and Dangerous

In my public debate with Professor Fletcher at San Diego State College in 1971,[374] I stressed the hopeless inadequacy of such an ethic for dealing with practical moral problems. Because love remains undefined in Fletcher's (essentially utilitarian) philosophy, *any* ethical results can flow from its operation. It should not take George Orwell's *1984* to remind us that human rights violators have always twisted vocabulary propagandistically, so that slavery becomes freedom—and hate becomes love. Essential to an adequate philosophy of human dignity are consistent, binding norms, and an absolute, nonsituational justification of proper ethical standards.

Consequences for Medical Ethics

The incredible dangers for human rights that flow from situationism are particularly evident when one examines Fletcher's views in the areas of abortion, treatment of the handicapped, and genetic engineering. In his capacity as professor of medical ethics, he has taken positions reflecting a denial of the human personhood of the fetus; he favors unrestrained termination of lives that are allegedly lacking in sufficient "quality of life"; and he has no ethical objections to virtually unlimited experimentation with human genetic-chromosomal material.[375] Without the Bible's unqualified respect for the human person, such aberrations are almost inevitable in a situational context.[376]

The Common Thread: Relativism

What all three of the liberal theologies we have just discussed have in common is endemic *relativism*. And relativism is the last thing needed for human rights. Inalienable rights require a constant (nonprocess) human nature, and norms of human dignity that do not alter with every change of existential perception or contextual situation. Jacques Maritain might as well have been speaking of the consequences of liberal theology as of secularism when he declared that since the eighteenth-century Enlightenment man has asserted

> the absolute independence of the human subject and a so-called absolute right—which supposedly pertains to everything in the human subject by the mere fact that it is in him—to unfold one's cherished possibilities at the expense of all other beings. When men thus instructed clashed on all sides with the impossible, they came to believe in the bankruptcy of the rights of the human person. Some have turned against these rights with an enslaver's fury; some have continued to invoke them, while in their inmost conscience they are weighed down by a temptation to scepticism which is one of the most alarming symptoms of the present crisis. A kind of intellectual and moral revolution is required of us, in order to re-establish on the basis of a true philosophy our faith in the dignity of man and in his rights, and in order to rediscover the authentic sources of this faith.
>
> The consciousness of the dignity of the person and of the rights of the person remained implicit in pagan antiquity, over which the law of slavery cast its shadow. It was the message of the Gospel which suddenly awakened this consciousness, in a divine and transcendent form, revealing to men that they are called upon to be the sons and heirs of God in the Kingdom of God.[377]

Theological Liberalism at a Dead End

The theologian should be doing his utmost to preserve and extend that message of the gospel rather than (as in theological liberalism) diluting it. Where dilution occurs, the result is an inability on the theologian's part to say anything significant about human rights. Characteristically, of the five contemporary theological models of human rights identified by Huber and Tödt,[378] no less than two (including Tödt's) come to the conclusion that "we must give up trying to justify or legitimize human rights on theological grounds" and that "there is no question of seeking a theological foundation for human rights."[379]

Classical Theology in Three Varieties

What of the classical theologies of Christendom, which (unlike theological liberalism) have on the whole sought to remain within scriptural and confessional boundaries? Let us try to discover the particular motifs of three such theologies of human rights, those of Roman Catholicism, Lutheranism, and Calvinism.[380] We shall endeavor to set forth their distinctives vis-à-vis human rights, as they themselves emphasize them.

(1) Roman Catholicism: Nature and Grace

In classical Roman Catholicism, the key human rights motif is the dichotomy between nature and grace.[381] This scholastic distinction is still maintained,

> even though in recent decades a more biblically-oriented approach has emerged, bringing with it a more holist outlook, which sometimes shows signs of slipping over into a monist theology. In the traditional Roman Catholic view, however, which is still dominant in its confessional utterances, the realm of grace stands over and beyond the realm of nature. Nature is viewed as relatively immune to the affects of sin. Grace, however, is lost by man's fall into sin, to be restored by the grace of the sacraments. Grace, therefore, does not renew and redeem nature, but complements and elevates it. The realm of nature, the public sector of life, accordingly, is good, but the state of grace is better.

Each realm has its own peculiar God-given standards of conduct. In the higher realm of church life the controlling norm is faith. The lower realm of societal life stands under the rule of reason.

On this Roman Catholic view, human rights issues belong to the lower order of reality. Its problems are, therefore, essentially reduced to the level of natural human concerns. They fall basically within the mandate of natural theology. Yet, since the realm of natural things is subservient to the realm
of grace, the world's agenda, including human rights issues, also falls properly under the tutelage of the church. For the church, as the locus of authority for the kingdom of God on earth, is the divinely appointed custodian of all truth. Accordingly, it is called to serve as the conscience of society. Therein lies its authority to speak out on human rights issues, especially when states and other societal institutions either tolerate or are themselves instruments of their violation and abuse.[382]

The Weaknesses of This Motif

There are at least two grave dangers in a theology of human rights that is built on the nature-grace dichotomy. First, because the effects of the Fall are not seen to permeate nature thoroughly (contrast Rom. 8:22), there is a strong tendency to overvalue natural theology and natural law teaching.[383] The result is reliance on immanent, moralistic remedies to human rights problems instead of stressing the need for transcendent, revelational solutions. Secondly, the nature-grace dichotomy tends to encourage withdrawal from the secular realm of human rights to a spiritual, ecclesiastical realm of grace—the monastic failing, where separation from the world and concentration on liturgical holiness and official pronouncements offer a retreat (in both senses of the term) from the agonies of man's inhumanity to man. The ease with which not a few Roman Catholic theologians in recent years have embraced Liberation theology (with its double dose of weaknesses: those of process theology and of Marxism) can in part be explained as a reaction against the inability of traditional, scholastic Catholic theology to cope with the dilemmas of the contemporary human rights scene.[384]

(2) Lutheranism: Law and Gospel and Two Kingdoms

Lutherans have been in the forefront of the modern human rights movement. Pastor O. Frederick Nolde, to take but one example, is singled out by René Cassin for his "zealous support of the Universal Declaration of Human Rights."[385] Such zeal has clear precedent in the Reformer's own career. Within six years of the posting of the Ninety-Five Theses, Luther

> was faced with the issue of human rights in a very concrete fashion. Duke Georg of Saxony wanted to ban from circulation the New Testament translated by Luther and stem the progress of the evangelical movement across his land. This gave Luther an opportunity to express in writing his views on secular authority and the limits of the obedience due to it (1523), stressing those limits in vigorous terms: «the soul eludes any form of human ascendancy and pertains to the power of God alone, . . . faith is a divine work which issues forth from the Spirit and consequently shall not be imposed or created by any external power». (Weimar Edition, vol. 11, p. 263, 14). . . .
>
> The attitude reflected in these writings is, in embryo, one mindful of the fundamental liberty to which man is entitled as a creature of a God who calls for freedom of faith in a world otherwise governed by duress. The theme of justification by faith, that is to say of immediate and direct relations between God and man, in a sense gives weight to the idea of man as an individual.[386]

What has been termed without exaggeration Luther's "Copernican revolution in theology" centered on the formal and material principles of all truly biblical religion: Scripture alone (as the only final revelational authority) and salvation by grace through faith alone (as the only way human beings, dead in trespasses and sins, could be restored to fellowship with a holy and loving God). From this new appreciation of Bible and gospel came Luther's realization that law (what people ought to do) can never be gospel, i.e., can never save people individually or societally but, at best, will show how far short we fall of God's demands and serve as a "schoolmaster to bring us unto Christ" (Gal. 3:24).[387] Scrupulous care not to confuse law and gospel gave rise to the correlative doctrine of the "two kingdoms,"[388] dramatically expressed in Luther's image of the two hands of God.

> Luther spoke of "the two hands of God." The "left hand of God" is a formula meaning that God is universally at work in human life, through structures and principles commonly operative in political, economic, and cultural institutions that affect the life of all. The struggle for human rights occurs within this realm of divine activity. However, no matter how much peace and justice and liberty are experienced in these common structures of life, they do not mediate "the one thing needful." This is the function of the gospel of God in Jesus Christ, the work of the "right hand of God." The scandal of the gospel is that salvation is a sheer gift of grace, given freely by God for Christ's sake, and received through faith alone. It is meritorious for a society to grant and guarantee to all its citizens the basic human rights, but high marks in this area do not translate into the righteousness that counts before God in the absolute dimension.[389]

The Two Kingdoms Doctrine Unjustly Criticized

The Lutheran doctrine of the two kingdoms and its underlying law-gospel distinction have been severely criticized as *quietistic*—productive of inaction in the face of social injustice (Troeltsch)—and *dualistic*—limiting Christ's lordship to personal salvation rather than recognizing his sovereignty over all areas of life and of the world (Calvinist critics).[390] These criticisms misunderstand the Lutheran view, which does not at all deny God's action in the secular realm.

Though the secular world is the kingdom of the left hand, the hand involved is, after all, *God's* hand! Professor Althaus provides helpful clarification when he emphasizes that Luther

> intends to view secular life, insofar as Christians participate in it, as being under the lordship of Christ. In fact he does not claim that Christ is lord within the *orders* as such but only in the *men* who act within these orders. Thus the secular kingdom does not stand under the lordship of Christ in the same way that the kingdom of Christ or Christendom does. On this, Jesus and the New Testament agree with Luther. The New Testament itself speaks of the lordship of Christ only as his lordship in persons, that is, in their faith. Such Christians will, in fact, work in the world so that the orders and relationships which God has established to serve human life may be reestablished and set free from misuse and distortions. Even though this is true, however, this goal cannot be defined in terms of "Christ's lordship in the orders"—as though there were a Christocracy.[391]

The key to Luther's understanding of social ethics is that the individual Christian serves as the point of contact—the connecting link—between the two kingdoms and has the responsibility (and privilege) of remedying social injustice by becoming a "little Christ" to his neighbors. This is anything but quietism; it is faith active in love, based upon a "theology of the Cross."[392] What Lutherans will not tolerate is a "theology of glory"—a utopian, millennial triumphalism in which God's participation in secular life offers believers the possibility of creating a perfect society. A sinless society must wait for Christ's personal return, when "the kingdoms of this world will become the kingdoms of our Lord and of his Christ" (Rev. 11:15).[393]

Revolution Always an Evil

Two related emphases in the Lutheran human rights ethic deserve mention. First, in line with the two-kingdoms doctrine and based squarely on apostolic teaching in Romans 13, Lutheran theology has viewed political revolution as always an evil. Cases such as the generals' plot against Hitler illustrate that usurpation of power may be a *lesser* of evils; but, being a genuine evil, even such an act will necessarily drive the believer back to the Cross for forgiveness. The Bible regards governmental authority as "ordained of God" for our ultimate benefit, and bad government as preferable to no government at all. Revolution, in other words, can easily produce the worst of all conditions for man as a political animal: total anarchy. Lutherans are therefore especially sensitive to the ethical ambiguity in any struggle against constituted authority and insist that the advocate of revolution discharge a heavy burden of proof.[394]

My Neighbor's Rights, Not My Own

Second, Lutheran theology makes an important distinction between one's own rights and the rights of others. In his treatise *On Temporal Authority,* Luther wrote:

> A Christian should be so disposed that he will suffer every evil and injustice without avenging himself; neither will he seek legal redress in the courts but have utterly no need of temporal authority and law for his own sake. On behalf of others, however, he may and should seek retribution, justice, protection, and help, and do as much as he can to achieve it.[395]

From such passages Lienhard concludes: "Luther's ideas are determined by one decisive principle. According to him, a Christian accepts his own rights being endangered, but watches zealously over the preservation of his neighbour's rights."[396] Such an approach is very characteristic of Luther: since the believer has received everything from Christ by grace, his life is to be expended not for himself but in behalf of his neighbor (1 John 4:19–21).[397] The great value of this theme for a theology of human rights is that it serves as a counterweight to the egotistic special pleading so common in the human rights movement. The activist obnoxiously pushing for the furtherance of his own rights and interests is replaced by the Christian employing his full energies to defend the rights of others.

(3) Calvinism: the Covenant of Liberation

Classical Calvinism begins and ends its theologizing with the sovereignty of God, who by his eternal decrees established a covenantal relationship with human beings and makes them office-holders in His creation.

> In the beginning [God] covenanted the world into existence, and covenantally defined man's place and task in it. All creation stands in covenant relationship to the Creator, either in a covenant-keeping or a covenant-breaking way. Man as imager of God lives always at the intersection-point of three fundamental relationships: he is servant of God, steward and caretaker of creation, and his brother's keeper (Genesis 4:9), guardian of the human rights of his fellowmen. In the covenant embedded in creation, God holds sovereign rights, charter rights, divine rights. Man holds creational rights, human rights. On the ground of the covenant, we have rights (amazing thought!) with respect to God, and God maintains his rights toward us. We also have rights in relation to others, and others may lay their rightful claim upon us.
>
> The Calvinist tradition at its best has understood human rights as related to *office*. Man is placed in office. By virtue of creation he holds office. Being man means being an officer. Involved in this office is a basic threefold relationship: Man is servant to God, guardian of his fellowmen, and steward of creation. All human life has a built-in deeply religious *unity* to it (which individualism violates). Life is fundamentally of one piece. We can therefore speak in the singular of man's central, integrally unified *office*. But we can also speak of the *multi-dimensional* character of life. Man's single office manifests itself concretely in a rich diversity of *offices* (which collectivism violates). As a single

ray of light passing through a prism gets refracted into a multi-faceted rainbow of colors, so man's single office opens up into a richly variegated spectrum of offices. Our offices are as many as our tasks, such as being marriage partners, parents, children, students, teachers, ministers, laborers, artists, scientists, journalists, and all the rest. Each of these offices is lodged in one or another societal institution, such as home, school, church, industry, studio, laboratory, news media, and so forth. Such a social order, formed in obedient response to the creation order, is the normed context for fulfilling our callings in life. Guaranteeing human rights therefore means safeguarding the elbowroom and freedoms which men need in order to exercise their offices in a responsible way.[398]

Barth

Calvinist emphasis on God's covenant with man as the source of human rights has easily led to a focus on related themes, particularly among neo-orthodox and progressive theologians of Calvinist persuasion. Karl Barth has argued, for example, that "true Church law is exemplary law," i.e., that the Christian community ought to be a model for society at large. Ideally, God's divinely decreed church order should be exemplary for the juridical ordering of the secular state. In this sense, the church is in a position to offer a human rights paradigm for the world.[399]

Moltmann

The most prominent contemporary spokesman for a Reformed theology of human rights is Professor Jürgen Moltmann of Tübingen. In his "original" and "definitive" study papers for the World Alliance of Reformed Churches, he utilized the theme of liberation as the key to a theology of human dignity, associating it with the traditional Calvinist motif of the covenant.

> By reflecting the liberation, the covenant, and the claim of God according to biblical witnesses, Christian theology also discovers the freedom, the covenant, and the rights of human beings today,

> and therefore brings out the pain caused by their present inward and outward enslavements, as well as the struggle for their liberation from these enslavements, towards a life of dignity, rights, and duties in fellowship with God. In a world which is not yet the kingdom of God, Christians cannot leave any area of life without witness to the divine liberation, the covenant of God, and the dignity of human beings. The biblical witness to liberation, covenant, and God's claim leads to a corresponding Christian practice and theology.[400]

By 1980, Moltmann's liberation focus had undergone a subtle but significant shift. Now the "biblical witnesses" to liberation and covenant are of less immediate importance than the "praxis of liberation" in "one's own life experience." Indeed, for Moltmann, covenantal liberation moves into the orbit of Liberation theology: "Experience in the praxis of liberation from inhumanity is for Christians and churches the concrete starting point for the commitment to human rights."[401]

Liberation = Confusion

Dr. Richard Mouw calls Moltmann's liberation starting-point for a theology of human rights "rather murky."[402] U. Scheuner is even less charitable: "One cannot find the theological justification of human rights in Christian liberty without perverting the very idea. True Christian freedom is liberation from the weight of sin and it occurs through an act of divine reconciliation. . . . No one has the right to receive God's grace."[403] Scheuner's judgment could equally be brought to bear on the Puritan and contemporary supporters of the Calvinist revolutionary tradition (Samuel Rutherford, John W. Whitehead, et al.), who have moved unjustifiably from the liberation passages of the Old Testament (Exod. 3:7–8; 20:2; et al.) to the belief that opposition to constituted authority can be not merely a lesser of evils but actually a positive good. And as for "liberation experience," neither it nor any other existential experience is capable of validating God-talk, theological truth, or absolute values.[404]

Societal Pluralism

The most ambitious ecclesiastical attempt to date by traditional Calvinists to formulate a theology of human rights introduces the concept of "societal pluralism."

> It is a central thesis of this report that a biblically-illumined and biblically-directed view of societal pluralism most faithfully reflects the genius of the Judeo-Christian tradition. It embraces a view of our life together in God's world, of human relationships, and within that context of human rights which captures most clearly and fully the rich insights and wide perspectives of the Reformed world-view. This pluralist view of society has built into it two basic dimensions. First is that aspect called *structural pluralism*—the idea that by virtue of the creation order we discover the true meaning of our lives within the structured framework of various spheres of activity, each with its own divinely ordained identity and integrity (such as marriage, family, work, worship, play, governance, art, science, journalism, etc.). Second is that aspect known as *confessional pluralism*—the recognition that as a result of our fall into sin and as a fruit of redemption we now lived [*sic*] in a religiously divided world with various faith communities (Protestant, Catholic, Jewish, Islamic, Humanist, Buddhist, etc.), and that the human rights, the religious liberties, and the freedom of all these groups to express their deepest convictions openly must be assured in an equitable way.[405]

Onward to Creation and Redemption

The careful reader of this somewhat dense passage will observe that the components of societal pluralism—"structural pluralism" and "confessional pluralism"—relate directly to the classic theological *loci* of *creation* and *redemption*. Indeed, it can be argued (and I shall argue) that these two fundamental Christian doctrines provide the common denominators for all the sound human rights teaching which we have met in the classical theologies of Christendom. Let us, therefore, examine in turn the human rights implications of each of these two great core doctrines of biblical revelation.

Creation Is the Origin of Human Rights

The significance of the biblical doctrine of creation for human rights cannot be exaggerated. Elaine Pagels, professor of history and religion at Barnard College of Columbia University, locates the very origins of modern human rights theory in the Book of Genesis.

> Where, then, do we get the idea on which contemporary human rights theory rests: that ultimate value resides in the individual, independent from and even prior to participation in any social or political collective? The earliest suggestion of this idea occurs in the Hebrew account which describes Adam, whose name means "humanity," as being created in the "image of God." . . . This account implies the essential equality of all human beings, and supports the idea of rights that all enjoy by virtue of their common humanity.[406]

In the New Testament, God becomes man in Jesus Christ, hallowing the human condition anew.

> *Man has supreme value*. This is the first and most important truth that can be deduced from Christ's statements about and treatment of man. Each and every man is, *coram deo,* a creature of infinite worth. Jesus saw beyond the externals of life, the distinctions of class, the disparities of conditions and the shame of corruption, to the priceless value of human life itself. It was through Jesus Christ that this estimate of man first found revolutionising expression in human history. Herein indeed lies one of the most distinctive contributions of Christianity to civilisation. . . . The canker at the heart of paganism was the absence of certainty that life had any final meaning or permanent value. For Jesus, man was not a creature of passing time, a bearer of

borrowed values, a worthless thing whose failures bring no reason for shame or destruction and no occasion for regret.[407]

Physicist Donald MacKay of the University of Keele, a specialist on the communication mechanisms of the brain, finds in the Old and New Testament witness the key to human dignity:

> What then is so special about man? What is so special about John Smith, about you or me? The biblical answer is that what makes us special, is the amazing fact that our Creator was prepared to do for us all that Christ did and suffered in his incarnation, crucifixion and resurrection. Our dignity has nothing to do with our occupying a geographical hub of the universe, or being the product of a special process, or being constructed of special materials, or being inexplicable at one or another scientific level. We matter simply because he, our Creator, has conceived us in his own image so that he can address us, plead with us, rescue us, and forgive us.[408]

Man's status as creature of God has definite human rights consequences. The general principle has been well articulated by Professor Lienhard:

> What the Creator thus grants to created man, no man can refuse him or withdraw from him. His aim should rather be to act in accordance with the will of God and, as Luther put it, to help him preserve his assets and improve his means of subsistence. What therefore is freely accorded by God becomes, between men, a right which must be recognized and respected.[409]

More specifically, in terms of the issues with which we have dealt in this book, man's creaturehood solves (1) the problem of the entitlement nature of human rights, (2) the issue of equality and the perennial conflict between individual versus collective rights, and (3) the relationship between human rights, the environment, and the future.

Creation Is the Source of Human Beings' Entitlement to Dignity

It will be recalled that our study of the complexities involved in defining human rights (chapter 3) led us to the conclusion that rights are entitlements, and that entitlements, being relational, necessarily look beyond themselves to a source of title. Only a transcendent Creator can supply the needed title for inalienable rights. R. C. Sproul, after linking the biblical understanding of man's dignity to the Hebrew word "glory," with its root meaning of "heaviness" (as in Ps. 8:4–8), writes:

> It is because God has assigned worth to man and woman that human dignity is established. Man's glory is derived, dependent upon God's glory for his own. It is because mankind bears the image of God that he enjoys such an exalted rank in the nature of things. From his creation to his redemption, man's dignity is preserved. He is created by One who is eternal and is made for a redemption which stretches into eternity. His origin is significant—his destiny is significant—he is significant.[410]

Our discussion of the will theory of rights (Hart) versus the interest theory (MacCormick) took us in the same general direction. Interest theory is preferable to will theory, if only to preserve the rights of children and others incapable of appreciating or defending their own rights; but how can one justify the required interests without opening the floodgates to indiscriminate rights for fauna, flora, and even inanimate objects?[411] The scriptural doctrine of creation resolves this otherwise insoluble dilemma by declaring man and man alone to have received the *imago Dei* (Gen. 1:26–27; 2:7; 5:1–2). The Bible also asserts that man is genuinely human from the moment of conception (Ps. 51:5; Luke 1:15, 41).[412] Thus, we must reject all functionalist definitions of human personhood and the philosophy of Professor Tooley, who argues for the moral legitimacy of abortion and even early infanticide on the ground that an entity is not genuinely a human person "unless it possesses, or has previously possessed, the capacity for thought."[413]

Creation Is the Source of Human Equality and Community

The great Eastern church father St. Basil declared, on the basis of clear scriptural teaching: "By nature every human being has equality according to nature."[414] The creation account establishes male-female interdependence and the interrelatedness of all people as their brothers' keepers (Gen. 2:20–24; 4:9–14). "The Bible starts with a solidarity of the race in Adam. And from the beginning the awareness of the larger unity was strong, based on the belief of God's creation of humanity in the first man."[415] Christ's role as Second Adam in the New Testament powerfully reinforces and extends this teaching: all believers, with their diverse gifts, are equally members of the Body of Christ (1 Cor. 12:26; 14:12); their oneness in Christ transcends racial, national, social, and sex differences (Gal. 3:28); indeed, they form, with each other and with Christ Himself, a single edifice, the church (1 Peter 2:5).

It follows that the biblical approach to human dignity cannot be identified with the barren extremes either of eighteenth-century Western liberal individualism and Nozick's contemporary libertarian philosophy or of Marxist-Socialist collectivisms. Opposed as it is to what the United Nations system of human rights protection terms "consistent patterns of gross and massive violations,"[416] Scripture has no less concern with the fall of a sparrow (Matt. 10:29–31): even a single human life is of infinite value in the eyes of its Creator, and thus it deserves every protection. Moreover, rights and duties are necessarily interlocked, for mankind is united in a universal brotherhood (cf. the preamble to the American Declaration of the Rights and Duties of Man).[417] Christopher

Wright draws out the implications of this biblical stance with great precision:

> Now, to what extent we can disclaim guilt for the plight of others—particularly in the realm of international relationships, the world order of which we are inevitably part, which operates unjustly to our benefit and the deprivation of others—is a matter of complex moral debate. There are questions of direct and indirect guilt, of corporate and individual guilt, of inherited guilt, and guilt by association, and of "moral distance." But my point is this: even if we could disclaim all guilt and genuinely say of a given situation "I am not responsible for *it* [the situation]," that in no way absolves us from our responsibility to *God* for the *persons* involved in the situation. Such responsibility, though not implying guilt, nevertheless entails obligations on our part and rights under God attaching to the persons concerned.[418]

Creation Is the Source of Solidarity With the Environment and With the Future

Though creation establishes man's uniqueness and the rights peculiar to him by virtue of the *imago Dei,* it also links him to nature and the environment. "The image of God means man conformed to God," and "man must be conformed to God in his relationship to the non-human creation. Man is called to subdue the earth and to live in communion with it, and by virtue of this he has essential economic rights and essential ecological duties."[419] Furthermore, the creation extends not only horizontally in terms of geography but also vertically in history. Therefore, "man must be conformed to God in the succession of generations. He is in this respect a historical being who has temporal rights and duties in the succession of generations."[420] In sum, the scriptural philosophy of human rights, by its doctrine of creation, not only offers an absolute foundation for "third-generation" solidarity rights (a category left awkwardly up in the air in most secular thinking on the subject) but is able to raise such concerns to an eschatological level of significance. For the rights of future generations extend to the very last moment of history, when Christ shall return and we shall all have to account to him for our stewardship of his creation.

A Secular Objection: Aren't Creation Rights Static?

We conclude our discussion of the doctrine of creation with two objections, one secular, the other theological. Non-Christians—particularly Marxists—sometimes suggest that to establish human rights on a revelational foundation is to arrive at a static view of rights, a view lacking the flexibility needed to meet the changing conditions of modern life.[421] If all basic human rights stem from creaturehood, is this the result? Answer: It *need* not be, and it *should* not be. True, Christians can become self-satisfied with their biblical knowledge and with long-recognized rights the Bible plainly sets forth—to the neglect of new problems and new discoveries in the Word. But the consistent believer will have such genuine concern for his neighbor's needs that he will be sensitive to new areas in which man's dignity is ignored, and these areas will drive him back to the inexhaustible treasure of Scripture for fresh perspectives.

The Secularist Is the One in Trouble

Our question to the secular critic should be more troubling than his question to us: Without any absolute standard of human rights, how can *you* justify as rights the entitlements you now claim—to say nothing of identifying authentic new rights were they to come along? Flux still breeds flux. This is truly the time to recall the insights we gained in our survey of existing human rights protections (chap. 2): a nation's deepest convictions as to human worth are far more important than its particular constitutional mechanisms (compare the United Kingdom with the U.S.S.R.), and the greater the shared value system the more effective the human rights protection (contrast the European and American regional systems with Asia). Thus, a stable and solid concept of human dignity is the most important factor for success in human rights, and it would be hard to imagine anything more inalienable than God's creative workmanship as seen in His own Book.

A Theological Objection: Didn't Rights Collapse at the Fall?

A theological objection to the grounding of human rights in the doctrine of creation is that the original creation is now a fallen creation: does not the Fall destroy or vastly attenuate original rights? The answer, in a word, is No! In the first place, the Fall did not destroy the original creation. It reduced man to a condition of total depravity, thereby making it impossible for him to save himself, and man's self-centeredness threw, as it were, a monkey wrench into the machinery of the natural world. But the Fall did not obliterate the *imago Dei*, and the *imago* is the source of man's rights as creature. Second, as Wright well puts it: "The Fall did not destroy responsibility. It has not, therefore, nullified rights. . . . Far from obliterating human rights . . . the effect of the Fall has rather been to sharpen the issue and render the pursuit of rights all the more important."[422] This is because fallen man has become so dangerous to his fellows that the promotion and protection of human rights is now a life or death matter. Indeed, "the Fall has resulted in a situation in which God holds one man responsible to assist another, even at sacrificial cost to himself" (Lev. 25:25ff.).[423] Third, to the extent that the original creation suffered, to the same extent restoration in Christ is available personally and individually (2 Cor. 5:17). But the second and third reasons just given take us to the doctrine of redemption—the other pillar of biblical human rights teaching.

Au Contraire!

Redemption

What is the significance of the doctrine of redemption for human rights? The Bible leaves no doubt that the panoply of human rights derive from man's status as creature of God, made in His image. The sun shines and the rain falls on the just and the unjust (Matt. 5:45): believers have no more human rights over against unbelievers than the latter have over against them. In what sense, then, is Vidal correct in declaring that "human rights can only build on the proper foundation, the order of redemption"?[424] To be sure, believers, by virtue of their incorporation into the body of Christ, acquire additional rights vis-à-vis other believers—and even vis-à-vis God Himself (see, e.g., Gal. 6:10; Rom. 8:28). But these intrachurch rights neither add to nor detract from the biblical catalog of human rights per se. Philosopher Henri Bergson offers a tantalizing hint as to the connection between redemption and human rights when he speaks of the Evangelical motivation behind democracy.

> The republican motto ["liberty, equality, fraternity"] shows that the third term dispels the oft-noted contradiction between the two others, and that the essential thing is fraternity: a fact which would make it possible to say that democracy is evangelical in essence and that its motive power is love. . . . The American Declaration of Independence (1776), which served as a model for the Declaration of the Rights of Man in 1791, has indeed a Puritan ring: "We hold these truths to be self-evident . . . that all men are endowed by their Creator with certain unalienable rights, etc." . . . The formula of non-democratic society, wishing its motto to tally, word for word, with that of democracy, would be "authority, hierarchy, immobility."[425]

Human Rights Standards and Philosophies Leave Man's Motivations Untouched

Let us pursue Bergson's hint by looking behind the formal expressions of human rights in covenants and in ethical systems, and focus on the question of human motivation. Professor Bassiouni, it will be remembered, spoke of the effect of human rights activity in "thickening the veneer of civilization."[426] Now we must penetrate beneath that veneer. What do we find? That not a single major philosophy of human rights is able to supply the motivation needed to carry out even its own best ideals.[427] Utilitarianism, were it to identify and prove what is truly useful for human beings (which it does not), would still not be able to motivate them to choose the useful. Neo-Kantian rights theories tell us, *inter alia,* that we ought to act in accord with the generic rights of the recipient as well as of ourselves (Gewirth); but we are given no inner stimulus to ethical universalization. Policy orientation is incapable of motivating the individual or the society to carry out what it claims (and, incidentally, has not proven) to be desirable policies. Marxism is caught in the vicious conceptual circle of believing that external economic factors are the ultimate source of all violations of human dignity; its refusal to face the dark side of human nature leaves it powerless to find any means of changing human beings from within so that they will no longer exploit each other.

Needed: Good News for the Inner Man

We noted in passing that Buddhist human rights theorists realize man's lack of "internal self-control."[428] Jesus expresses this truth with maximum generality: "There is nothing from without a man, that entering into him can defile him: but the things which come out of him, those are they that defile the man" (Mark 7:15; cf. Matt. 15:16–20). McClosky and Brill's recent study of tolerance concludes that intolerance is natural—an innate characteristic[429]—reminding me of a young, highly cultured French medical specialist who told me that "Algerians are just like Blacks in your country: you can't educate them, and when they move in, the property values go down." Unitarians and religious liberals to the contrary,[430] even Jesus' high ethical teachings—even His human rights standards—

carry no built-in guarantees that people are going to be motivated to follow them. As someone has said, what the world needs is not more good advice but *good news*.

Incarnation as Motivation

And this is precisely the message of the Incarnation ("gospel" *means* "good news"). Karl Barth expressed it elliptically in his aphorism, "From the moment God himself became man, man is the measure of all things."[431] Roland de Pury is more explicit:

> In Jesus Christ divine and human rights are conjoined and become inseparable. To violate the rights of a creature of God in the name of divine right is thus to serve another god—to commit idolatry.[432]

Motivationally, as René Coste recognizes, this incarnational fact is of paramount importance: "The more one believes in the mystery of the Incarnation, the more one's commitment to human rights becomes a matter of motivational urgency."[433]

Justification by Faith and Human Rights

Jesus came to earth "to seek and to save that which was lost" and "to give his life a ransom for many" (Luke 19:10; Mark 10:45). The purpose of the Incarnation was to redeem fallen mankind. Jesus' sacrificial, atoning death provides redemption for all and is personally appropriated by faith in Him. Concretely, then,

> Let us further note, with Hüber and Tödt, how the theme of justification by faith provides a set of criteria determining the interrelations between the Christian faith and human rights:
>
> (a) If the humanity of man is not the outcome of his own endeavours, recognition of that humanity cannot be linked to his social success, to the living standard he has achieved or to his contribution to the quality of life. Effort and success do of course betoken the activity of a

person and are an expression of it; but they cannot be made the criterion for defining the person. A society is truly human only if it also recognizes the humanity of the person who has failed or is incapable. In this context, there is no correlation between rights and duties. Rights must also be accorded to the person who has failed in his duties. This applies, for instance, to the penitentiary system.

(b) The freedom of a number of individuals cannot be achieved at the expense of that of a number of others. Care must be taken to ensure that a «new economic order» does not imperil freedom.

(c) Faith liberates man from the constraint of desiring to fulfil himself on his own. This freedom, thus received, also makes man capable, through love of his neighbour and in order to promote his freedom, of renouncing his own demand for freedom and his own right.

(d) Liberated from himself, man becomes capable of communicating with other men and of transcending ethnic, national, social and cultural frontiers. That in itself is a manner of postulating the right to freedom of communication and access to information.[434]

Becoming a "Little Christ" to One's Neighbor

Point (c) is the operative consideration. Only when an individual has been liberated from self-centeredness is there freedom to serve the needs and protect the rights of others. "Jesus answered, Truly, truly, I say to you, Whoever commits sin is the slave to sin. . . . If the Son shall make you free, you shall be free indeed" (John 8:34, 36). God's grace in Christ touches the world at the point of the redeemed sinner, and spreads out from him to those whose God-given rights have been violated and whose wounds need to be bound up.

Again to use Luther's felicitous expression, the redeemed man becomes a "little Christ" to his neighbor. Thus is the problem of motivation solved: God Himself takes up residence within the believer's heart and supplies the motivation personally. Old things pass away; all things become new (2 Cor. 5:17).

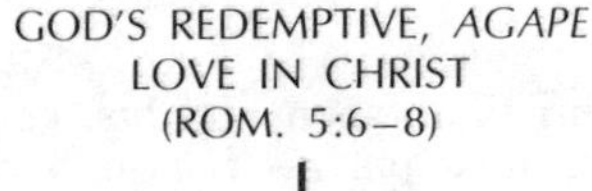

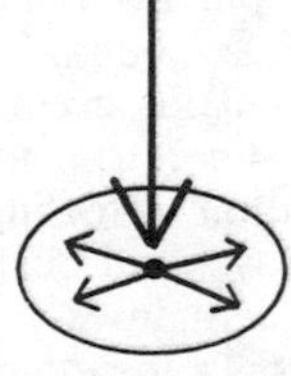

Figure 9
Redemptive Love

Other philosophies of human rights attempt to realize the goal of inalienable human dignity by climbing, as it were, from earth to heaven. Inalienable rights escape their grasp for the very same reason that the builders of the Tower of Babel failed to reach their goal. Transcendence, as Wittgenstein taught us, cannot be attained from below. "No man has ascended up to heaven," said Jesus, "but he who came down from heaven, even the Son of man" (John 3:13).

Human Rights by Grace Alone

Divine revelation informs us that human rights exist—paradoxically—by grace alone. "Man's dignity does not rest on itself but on the grace alone of the God of redemption. Man has no claim to it whatever; he receives pardon not by virtue of his merits but as the gracious gift of God."[435] Ultimately, it could be said that one has no "right" to human rights! But this realization is the *sine qua non* for a truly adequate philosophy of human dignity. If people's rights were of their own making, they could as easily unmake them. Since rights come as a divine gift from above, their inalienability is sure. "Every good gift and every perfect gift is from above, and cometh down from the Father of lights, with whom is no variableness, neither shadow of turning'' (James 1:17). And because our rights come as a gift and not by merit, the only hope lies in placing ourselves and our society in the hands of the Giver, to be changed into His likeness.

> The Christian, then, in his concern for the neighbour, must put his full support in the social and political realm behind the *Declaration on Human Rights;* but his greater concern will be to bring men and women to such an inner attitude of mind and orientation of feeling that their ideals can be embodied in laws and customs, translated from aspirations into actualities.
>
> This calls not only for education but for conversion—a radical change of heart until a man learns to forget himself in concentration upon the true well-being of the other.[436]

Secular Bankruptcy

Swiss jurist Dr. Peter Saladin sums up the dilemma and the challenge of human rights on the eve of century twenty-one.

> Last, but most important, it has to be realized that the philosophical bases traditionally underlying the idea of human rights—the philosophical systems of the Enlightenment, of liberalism, of utilitarianism—are now crumbling and no longer credible. After two world wars and numberless demonstrations of inhumanity we can no longer cling to the anthropological optimism on which those systems rest without sacrificing our intellectual and moral honesty. But the whole idea of human rights is then left in the air; and the flagrant lack of basis is bound to result in a loss of credibility if a new basis cannot be laid down. . . . So it is especially incumbent on Christians and the Christian churches to seek urgently for this new foundation.[437]

Only One Foundation for Human Dignity

The present study has been an effort to lay such a foundation. More accurately, I have tried to direct the reader to the already existing—and the only satisfactory—foundation for human dignity. ''No other foundation can a man lay than that which is laid, even Jesus Christ.''[438]

APPENDIX 1

Universal Declaration of Human Rights Approved by the General Assembly of the United Nations

Paris, 10 *December* 1948

PREAMBLE

WHEREAS recognition of the inherent dignity and of the equal and inalienable rights of all members of the human family is the foundation of freedom, justice and peace in the world,

WHEREAS disregard and contempt for human rights have resulted in barbarous acts which have outraged the conscience of mankind, and the advent of a world in which human beings shall enjoy freedom of speech and belief and freedom from fear and want has been proclaimed as the highest aspiration of the common people,

WHEREAS it is essential, if man is not to be compelled to have recourse, as a last resort, to rebellion against tyranny and oppression, that human rights should be protected by the rule of law,

WHEREAS it is essential to promote the development of friendly relations between nations,

WHEREAS, the peoples of the United Nations have in the Charter reaffirmed their faith in fundamental human rights, in the dignity and worth of the human person and in the equal rights of men and women and have determined to promote social progress and better standards of life in larger freedom,

WHEREAS Member States have pledged themselves to achieve, in co-operation with the United Nations, the promotion of universal respect for and observance of human rights and fundamental freedoms,

WHEREAS a common understanding of these rights and freedoms is of the greatest importance for the full realisation of this pledge,

NOW, THEREFORE,

THE GENERAL ASSEMBLY,

PROCLAIMS this Universal Declaration of Human Rights as a common standard of achievement for all peoples and all nations, to the end that every individual and every organ of society, keeping this Declaration constantly in mind, shall strive by teaching and education to promote respect for these rights and freedoms and by progressive measures, national and international, to secure their universal and effective recognition and observance, both among the peoples of Member States themselves and among the peoples of territories under their jurisdiction.

Article 1

All human beings are born free and equal in dignity and rights. They are endowed with reason and conscience and should act towards one another in a spirit of brotherhood.

Article 2

Everyone is entitled to all the rights and freedoms set forth in this Declaration, without distinction of any kind, such as race, colour, sex, language, religion, political or other opinion, national or social origin, property, birth or other status.

Furthermore, no distinction shall be made on the basis of the political, jurisdictional or international status of the country or territory to which a person belongs, whether it be independent, trust, non-self-governing or under any other limitation of sovereignty.

Article 3

Everyone has the right to life, liberty and the security of person.

Article 4

No one shall be held in slavery or servitude; slavery and the slave trade shall be prohibited in all their forms.

Article 5

No one shall be subjected to torture or to cruel, inhuman or degrading treatment or punishment.

Article 6

Everyone has the right to recognition everywhere as a person before the law.

Article 7

All are equal before the law and are entitled without any discrimination to equal protection of the law. All are entitled to equal protection against any discrimination in violation of this Declaration and against any incitement to such discrimination.

Article 8

Everyone has the right to an effective remedy by the competent national tribunals for acts violating the fundamental rights granted him by the constitution or by law.

Article 9

No one shall be subjected to arbitrary arrest, detention or exile.

Article 10

Everyone is entitled in full equality to a fair and public hearing by an independent and impartial tribunal, in the determination of his rights and obligations and of any criminal charge against him.

Article 11

1. Everyone charged with a penal offence has the right to be presumed innocent until proved guilty according to law in a public trial at which he has had all the guarantees necessary for his defence.
2. No one shall be held guilty of any penal offence on account of any act or omission which did not constitute a penal offence, under national or international law, at the time when it was committed. Nor shall a heavier penalty be imposed than the one that was applicable at the time the penal offence was committed.

Article 12

No one shall be subjected to arbitrary interference with his privacy, family, home or correspondence, nor to attacks upon his honour and reputation. Everyone has the right to the protection of the law against such interference or attacks.

Article 13

1. Everyone has the right to freedom of movement and residence within the borders of each State.
2. Everyone has the right to leave any country, including his own, and to return to his country.

Article 14

1. Everyone has the right to seek and to enjoy in other countries asylum from persecution.
2. This right may not be invoked in the case of prosecutions genuinely arising from nonpolitical crimes or from acts contrary to the purpose and principles of the United Nations.

Article 15

1. Everyone has the right to a nationality.
2. No one shall be arbitrarily deprived of his nationality nor denied the right to change his nationality.

Article 16

1. Men and women of full age, without any limitation due to race, nationality or religion, have the right to marry and to found a family. They are entitled to equal rights as to marriage, during marriage and at its dissolution.

2. Marriage shall be entered into only with the free and full consent of the intending spouses.

3. The family is the natural and fundamental group unit of society and is entitled to protection by society and the State.

Article 17

1. Everyone has the right to own property alone as well as in association with others.

2. No one shall be arbitrarily deprived of his property.

Article 18

Everyone has the right to freedom of thought, conscience and religion; this right includes freedom to change his religion or belief, and freedom, either alone or in community with others and in public or private, to manifest his religion or belief in teaching, practice, worship and observance.

Article 19

Everyone has the right to freedom of opinion and expression; this right includes freedom to hold opinions without interference and to seek, receive and impart information and ideas through any media and regardless of frontiers.

Article 20

1. Everyone has the right to freedom of peaceful assembly and association.

2. No one may be compelled to belong to an association.

Article 21

1. Everyone has the right to take part in the government of his country, directly or through freely chosen representatives.

2. Everyone has the right of equal access to public service in his country.

3. The will of the people shall be the basis of the authority of government; this will shall be expressed in periodic and genuine elections which shall be by universal and equal suffrage and shall be held by secret vote or equivalent free voting procedures.

Article 22

Everyone, as a member of society, has the right to social security and is entitled to the realisation, through national effort and international co-operation and in accordance with the organisation and resources of each State, of the economic, social and cultural rights indispensable for his dignity and the free development of his personality.

Article 23

1. Everyone has the right to work, to free choice of employment, to just and favourable conditions of work and to protection against unemployment.
2. Everyone, without any discrimination, has the right to equal pay for equal work.
3. Everyone who works has the right to just and favourable remuneration insuring for himself and his family an existence worthy of human dignity, and supplemented, if necessary, by other means of social protection.
4. Everyone has the right to form and to join trade unions for the protection of his interests.

Article 24

Everyone has the right to rest and leisure, including reasonable limitation of working hours and periodic holidays with pay.

Article 25

1. Everyone has the right to a standard of living adequate for the health and well-being of himself and of his family, including food, clothing, housing and medical care and necessary social services, and the right to security in the event of unemployment, sickness, disability, widowhood, old age or other lack of livelihood in circumstances beyond his control.
2. Motherhood and childhood are entitled to special care and assistance. All children, whether born in or out of wedlock, shall enjoy the same social protection.

Article 26

1. Everyone has the right to education. Education shall be free, at least in the elementary and fundamental stages. Elementary education shall be compulsory. Technical and professional education shall be made generally available and higher education shall be equally accessible to all on the basis of merit.
2. Education shall be directed to the full development of the human personality and to the strengthening of respect for human rights and fundamental freedoms. It shall promote understanding, tolerance and friendship among all nations, racial or religious groups, and shall further the activities of the United Nations for the maintenance of peace.

3. Parents have a prior right to choose the kind of education that shall be given to their children.

Article 27

1. Everyone has the right freely to participate in the cultural life of the community, to enjoy the arts and to share in scientific advancement and its benefits.

2. Everyone has the right to the protection of the moral and material interests resulting from any scientific, literary or artistic production of which he is the author.

Article 28

Everyone is entitled to a social and international order in which the rights and freedoms set forth in this Declaration can be fully realised.

Article 29

1. Everyone has duties to the community in which alone the free and full development of his personality is possible.

2. In the exercise of his rights and freedoms, everyone shall be subject only to such limitations as are determined by law solely for the purpose of securing due recognition and respect for the rights and freedoms of others and of meeting the just requirements of morality, public order and the general welfare in a democratic society.

3. These rights and freedoms may in no case be exercised contrary to the purposes and principles of the United Nations.

Article 30

Nothing in this Declaration may be interpreted as implying for any State, group or person any right to engage in any activity or to perform any act aimed at the destruction of any of the rights and freedoms set forth herein.

APPENDIX 2

[European] Convention for the Protection of Human Rights and Fundamental Freedoms*

Signed 4 November 1950,
Entered into force 3 September 1953

The Governments signatory hereto, being Members of the Council of Europe,

Considering the Universal Declaration of Human Rights proclaimed by the General Assembly of the United Nations on 10 December 1948;

Considering that this Declaration aims at securing the universal and effective recognition and observance of the Rights therein declared;

Considering that the aim of the Council of Europe is the achievement of greater unity between its Members and that one of the methods by which that aim is to be pursued is the maintenance and further realisation of Human Rights and Fundamental Freedoms;

Reaffirming their profound belief in those Fundamental Freedoms which are the foundation of justice and peace in the world and are best maintained on the one hand by an effective political democracy and on the other by a common understanding and observance of the Human Rights upon which they depend:

Being resolved, as the Governments of European countries which are likeminded and have a common heritage of political traditions, ideals, freedom and the rule of law to take the first steps for the collective enforcement of certain of the Rights stated in the Universal Declaration,

Have agreed as follows:

ARTICLE 1

The High Contracting Parties shall secure to everyone within their jurisdiction the rights and freedoms defined in Section 1 of this Convention.

---

*Only Section I, detailing substantive rights, has been reproduced here. The procedural sections of the convention have been omitted for reasons of space.

SECTION I

ARTICLE 2

1. Everyone's right to life shall be protected by law. No one shall be deprived of his life intentionally save in the execution of a sentence of a court following his conviction of a crime for which this penalty is provided by law.

2. Deprivation of life shall not be regarded as inflicted in contravention of this Article when it results from the use of force which is no more than absolutely necessary:

(a) in defence of any person from unlawful violence;
(b) in order to effect a lawful arrest or to prevent the escape of a person lawfully detained;
(c) in action lawfully taken for the purpose of quelling a riot or insurrection.

ARTICLE 3

No one shall be subjected to torture or to inhuman or degrading treatment or punishment.

ARTICLE 4

1. No one shall be held in slavery or servitude.

2. No one shall be required to perform forced or compulsory labour.

3. For the purpose of this Article the term "forced or compulsory labour" shall not include:

(a) any work required to be done in the ordinary course of detention imposed according to the provisions of Article 5 of this Convention or during conditional release from such detention;
(b) any service of a military character or, in case of conscientious objectors in countries where they are recognised, service exacted instead of compulsory military service;
(c) any service exacted in case of an emergency or calamity threatening the life or well-being of the community;
(d) any work or service which forms part of normal civic obligations.

ARTICLE 5

1. Everyone has the right to liberty and security of person.

No one shall be deprived of his liberty save in the following cases and in accordance with a procedure prescribed by law;

(a) the lawful detention of a person after conviction by a competent court;
(b) the lawful arrest or detention of a person for non-compliance with the lawful order of a court or in order to secure the fulfilment of any obligation prescribed by law;

(c) the lawful arrest or detention of a person effected for the purpose of bringing him before the competent legal authority on reasonable suspicion of having committed an offence or when it is reasonably considered necessary to prevent his committing an offence or fleeing after having done so;
(d) the detention of a minor by lawful order for the purpose of educational supervision or his lawful detention for the purpose of bringing him before the competent legal authority;
(e) the lawful detention of persons for the prevention of the spreading of infectious diseases, of persons of unsound mind, alcoholics or drug addicts or vagrants;
(f) the lawful arrest or detention of a person to prevent his effecting an unauthorised entry into the country or of a person against whom action is being taken with a view to deportation or extradition.

2. Everyone who is arrested shall be informed promptly, in a language which he understands, of the reasons for his arrest and of any charge against him.

3. Everyone arrested or detained in accordance with the provisions of paragraph 1(c) of this Article shall be brought promptly before a judge or other officer authorised by law to exercise judicial power and shall be entitled to trial within a reasonable time or to release pending trial. Release may be conditioned by guarantees to appear for trial.

4. Everyone who is deprived of his liberty by arrest or detention shall be entitled to take proceedings by which the lawfulness of his detention shall be decided speedily by a court and his release ordered if the detention is not lawful.

5. Everyone who has been the victim of arrest or detention in contravention of the provisions of this Article shall have an enforceable right to compensation.

Article 6

1. In the determination of his civil rights and obligations or of any criminal charge against him, everyone is entitled to a fair and public hearing within a reasonable time by an independent and impartial tribunal established by law. Judgment shall be pronounced publicly but the press and public may be excluded from all or part of the trial in the interest of morals, public order or national security in a democratic society, where the interests of juveniles or the protection of the private life of the parties so require, or to the extent strictly necessary in the opinion of the court in special circumstances where publicity would prejudice the interests of justice.

2. Everyone charged with a criminal offence shall be presumed innocent until proved guilty according to law.

3. Everyone charged with a criminal offence has the following minimum rights:

(a) to be informed promptly, in a language which he understands and in detail, of the nature and cause of the accusation against him;
(b) to have adequate time and facilities for the preparation of his defence;
(c) to defend himself in person or through legal assistance of his own choosing or, if he has not sufficient means to pay for legal assistance, to be given it free when the interests of justice so require;
(d) to examine or have examined witnesses against him and to obtain the attendance and examination of witnesses on his behalf under the same conditions as witnesses against him;
(e) to have the free assistance of an interpreter if he cannot understand or speak the language used in court.

Article 7

1. No one shall be held guilty of any criminal offence on account of any act or omission which did not constitute a criminal offence under national or international law at the time when it was committed.

2. This Article shall not prejudice the trial and punishment of any person for the act or omission which, at the time when it was committed, was criminal according to the general principles of law recognised by civilised nations.

Article 8

1. Everyone has the right to respect for his private and family life, his home and his correspondence.

2. There shall be no interference by a public authority with the exercise of this right except such as is in accordance with the law and is necessary in a democratic society in the interests of national security, public safety or the economic well-being of the country, for the prevention of disorder of crime, for the protection of health or morals, or for the protection of the rights and freedoms of others.

Article 9

1. Everyone has the right to freedom of thought, conscience and religion; this right includes freedom to change his religion or belief and freedom, either alone or in community with others and in public or private, to manifest his religion or belief, in worship, teaching, practice and observance.

2. Freedom to manifest one's religion or beliefs shall be subject only to such limitations as are prescribed by law and are necessary in a democratic society in the interests of public safety, for the protection of public order, health or morals, or for the protection of the rights and freedoms of others.

Article 10

1. Everyone has the right to freedom of expression. This right shall include freedom to hold opinions and to receive and impart information and ideas without interference by public authority and regardless of frontiers. This Article shall not prevent States from requiring the licensing of broadcasting, television or cinema enterprises.

2. The exercise of these freedoms, since it carries with it duties and responsibilities, may be subject to such formalities, conditions, restrictions or penalties as are prescribed by law and are necessary in a democratic society, in the interests of national security, territorial integrity or public safely, for the prevention of disorder or crime, for the protection of health or morals, for the protection of the reputation or rights of others, for preventing the disclosure of information received in confidence, or for maintaining the authority and impartiality of the judiciary.

Article 11

1. Everyone has the right to freedom of peaceful assembly and to freedom of association with others, including the right to form and to join trade unions for the protection of his interests.

2. No restrictions shall be placed on the exercise of these rights other than such as are prescribed by law and are necessary in a democratic society in the interests of national security or public safety, for the prevention of disorder or crime, for the protection of health or morals or for the protection of the rights and freedoms of others. This Article shall not prevent the imposition of lawful restrictions on the exercise of these rights by members of the armed forces, of the police or of the administration of the State.

Article 12

Men and women of marriageable age have the right to marry and to found a family, according to the national laws governing the exercise of this right.

Article 13

Everyone whose rights and freedoms as set forth in this Convention are violated shall have an effective remedy before a national authority notwithstanding that the violation has been committed by persons acting in an official capacity.

Article 14

The enjoyment of the rights and freedoms set forth in this Convention shall be secured without discrimination on any ground such as sex, race, colour, language, religion, political or other opinion, national or social origin, association with a national minority, property, birth or other status.

Article 15

1. In time of war or other public emergency threatening the life of the nation any High Contracting Party may take measures derogating from its obligations under this Convention to the extent strictly required by the exigencies of the situation, provided that such measures are not inconsistent with its other obligations under international law.

2. No derogation from Article 2, except in respect of deaths resulting from lawful acts of war, or from Articles 3, 4 (paragraph 1) and 7 shall be made under this provision.

3. Any High Contracting Party availing itself of this right of derogation shall keep the Secretary General of the Council of Europe fully informed of the measures which it has taken and the reasons therefor. It shall also inform the Secretary General of the Council of Europe when such measures have ceased to operate and the provisions of the Convention are again being fully executed.

Article 16

Nothing in Articles 10, 11 and 14 shall be regarded as preventing the High Contracting Parties from imposing restrictions on the political activity of aliens.

Article 17

Nothing in this Convention may be interpreted as implying for any State, group or person any right to engage in any activity or perform any act aimed at the destruction of any of the rights and freedoms set forth herein or at their limitation to a greater extent than is provided for in the Convention.

Article 18

The restrictions permitted under this Convention to the said rights and freedoms shall not be applied for any purpose other than those for which they have been prescribed.

First Protocol to the Convention

The Governments signatory hereto, being Members of the Council of Europe,

Being resolved to take steps to ensure the collective enforcement of certain rights and freedoms other than those already included in Section I of the Convention for the Protection of Human Rights and Fundamental Freedoms signed at Rome on 4 November 1950 (hereinafter referred to as "the Convention"),

Have agreed as follows:

Article 1

Every natural or legal person is entitled to the peaceful enjoyment of his possessions. No one shall be deprived of his possessions except in the public interest and subject to the conditions provided for by law and by the general principles of international law.

The preceding provisions shall not, however, in any way impair the right of a State to enforce such laws as it deems necessary to control the use of property in accordance with the general interest or to secure the payment of taxes or other contributions or penalties.

Article 2

No person shall be denied the right to education. In the exercise of any functions which it assumes in relation to education and to teaching, the State shall respect the right of parents to ensure such education and teaching in conformity with their own religious and philosophical convictions.

Article 3

The High Contracting Parties undertake to hold free elections at reasonable intervals by secret ballot, under conditions which will ensure the free expression of the opinion of the people in the choice of the legislature.

Article 4

Any High Contracting Party may at the time of signature or ratification or at any time thereafter communicate to the Secretary General of the Council of Europe a declaration stating the extent to which it undertakes that the provisions of the present Protocol shall apply to such of the territories for the international relations of which it is responsible as are named therein.

Any High Contracting Party which has communicated a declaration in virtue of the preceding paragraph may from time to time communicate a further declaration modifying the terms of any former declaration or terminating the application of the provisions of this Protocol in respect of any territory.

A declaration made in accordance with this Article shall be deemed to have been made in accordance with Paragraph (1) of Article 63 of the Convention.

Article 5

As between the High Contracting Parties the provisions of Articles 1, 2, 3 and 4 of this Protocol shall be regarded as additional Articles to the Convention and all the provisions of the Convention shall apply accordingly.

Article 6

This Protocol shall be open for signature by the Members of the Council of Europe, who are the signatories of the Convention; it shall be ratified at the same time as or after the ratification of the Convention. It shall enter into force after the deposit of ten instruments of ratification. As regards any signatory ratifying subsequently, the Protocol shall enter into force at the date of the deposit of its instrument of ratification.

The instruments of ratification shall be deposited with the Secretary General of the Council of Europe, who will notify all Members of the names of those who have ratified.

Done at Paris on the 20th day of March 1952, in English and French, both texts being equally authentic, in a single copy which shall remain deposited in the archives of the Council of Europe. The Secretary General shall transmit certified copies to each of the signatory Governments.

Fourth Protocol* Securing Certain Rights and Freedoms Other Than Those Already Included in the Convention and in the First Protocol Thereto

The Governments signatory hereto, being Members of the Council of Europe;

Being resolved to take steps to ensure the collective enforcement of certain rights and freedoms other than those already included in Section I of the Convention for the Protection of Human Rights and Fundamental Freedoms signed at Rome on 4 November 1950 (hereinafter referred to as "the Convention") and in Articles 1 to 3 of the First Protocol to the Convention, signed at Paris on 20 March 1952,

Have agreed as follows:

*Protocols not dealing with substantive rights have been omitted.

Article 1

No one shall be deprived of his liberty merely on the ground of inability to fulfil a contractual obligation.

Article 2

1. Everyone lawfully within the territory of a State shall, within that territory, have the right to liberty of movement and freedom to choose his residence.

2. Everyone shall be free to leave any country, including his own.

3. No restrictions shall be placed on the exercise of these rights other than such as are in accordance with law and are necessary in a democratic society in the interests of national security or public safety, for the maintenance of *ordre public,* for the prevention of crime, for the protection of health or morals, or for the protection of the rights and freedoms of others.

4. The rights set forth in paragraph 1 may also be subject, in particular areas, to restrictions imposed in accordance with law and justified by the public interest in a democratic society.

Article 3

1. No one shall be expelled, by means either of an individual or of a collective measure, from the territory of the State of which he is a national.

2. No one shall be deprived of the right to enter the territory of the State of which he is a national.

Article 4

Collective expulsion of aliens is prohibited.

Article 5

1. Any High Contracting Party may, at the time of signature or ratification of this Protocol, or at any time thereafter, communicate to the Secretary General of the Council of Europe a declaration stating the extent to which it undertakes that the provisions of this Protocol shall apply to such of the territories for the international relations of which it is responsible as are named therein.

2. Any High Contracting Party which has communicated a declaration in virtue of the preceding paragraph may, from time to time, communicate a further declaration modifying the terms of any former declaration or terminating the application of the provisions of this Protocol in respect of any territory.

3. A declaration made in accordance with the Article shall be deemed to have been made in accordance with paragraph 1 of Article 63 of the Convention.

4. The territory of any State to which this Protocol applies by virtue of ratification or acceptance by that State, and each territory to which this Protocol is applied by virtue of a declaration by that State under this Article, shall be treated as separate territories for the purpose of the references in Articles 2 and 3 to the territory of a State.

ARTICLE 6

1. As between the High Contracting Parties the provisions of Articles 1 to 5 of this Protocol shall be regarded as additional Articles to the Convention, and all the provisions of the Convention shall apply accordingly.

2. Nevertheless, the right of individual recourse recognised by a declaration made under Article 25 of the Convention, or the acceptance of the compulsory jurisdiction of the Court by a declaration made under Article 46 of the Convention, shall not be effective in relation to this Protocol unless the High Contracting Party concerned has made a statement recognising such right, or accepting such jurisdiction, in respect of all or any of Articles 1 to 4 of the Protocol.

ARTICLE 7

1. This Protocol shall be open for signature by the Members of the Council of Europe who are the signatories of the Convention; it shall be ratified at the same time as or after the ratification of the Convention. It shall enter into force after the deposit of five instruments of ratification. As regards any signatory ratifying subsequently, the Protocol shall enter into force at the date of the deposit of its instrument of ratification.

2. The instruments of ratification shall be deposited with the Secretary General of the Council of Europe, who will notify all Members of the names of those who have ratified.

In witness whereof, the undersigned, being duly authorised thereto, have signed this Protocol.

Done at Strasbourg, this 16th day of September 1963, in English and in French, both texts being equally authoritative, in a single copy which shall remain deposited in the archives of the Council of Europe. The Secretary General shall transmit certified copies to each of the signatory States.

Seventh Protocol*

The member States of the Council of Europe signatory hereto,

---

*Protocols not dealing with substantive rights have been omitted.

Being resolved to take further steps to ensure the collective enforcement of certain rights and freedoms by means of the Convention for the Protection of Human Rights and Fundamental Freedoms signed at Rome on 4 November 1950 (hereinafter referred to as "the Convention"):

Have agreed as follows:

Article 1

1. An alien lawfully resident in the territory of a State shall not be expelled therefrom except in pursuance of a decision reached in accordance with law and shall be allowed:
   (a) to submit reasons against his expulsion,
   (b) to have his case reviewed, and
   (c) to be represented for these purposes before the competent authority or a person or persons designated by that authority.

2. An alien may be expelled before the exercise of his rights under paragraph 1 (a), (b) and (c) of this Article, when such expulsion is necessary in the interests of public order or is grounded on reasons of national security.

Article 2

1. Everyone convicted of a criminal offence by a tribunal shall have the right to have conviction or sentence reviewed by a higher tribunal. The exercise of this right, including the grounds on which it may be exercised, shall be governed by law.

2. This right may be subject to exceptions in regard to offences of a minor character, as prescribed by law, or in cases in which the person concerned was tried in the first instance by the highest tribunal or was convicted following an appeal against acquittal.

Article 3

When a person has by a final decision been convicted of a criminal offence and when subsequently his conviction has been reversed, or he has been pardoned, on the ground that a new or newly discovered fact shows conclusively that there has been a miscarriage of justice, the person who has suffered punishment as a result of such conviction shall be compensated according to the law or the practice of the State concerned, unless it is proved that the non-disclosure of the unknown fact in time is wholly or partly attributable to him.

Article 4

1. No one shall be liable to be tried or punished again in criminal proceedings under the jurisdiction of the same State for an offence for which he has already been finally acquitted or convicted in accordance with the law and penal procedure of that State.

2. The provisions of the preceding paragraph shall not prevent the re-opening of the case in accordance with the law and penal procedure of the State concerned, if there is evidence of new or newly discovered facts, or if there has been a fundamental defect in the previous proceedings, which could affect the outcome of the case.

3. No derogation from this Article shall be made under Article 15 of the Convention.

Article 5

Spouses shall enjoy equality of rights and responsibilities of a private law character between them, and in their relations with their children, as to marriage, during marriage and in the event of its dissolution. This Article shall not prevent States from taking such measures as are necessary in the interests of the children.

Article 6

1. Any State may at the time of signature or when depositing its instrument of ratification, acceptance or approval, specify the territory or territories to which this Protocol shall apply and state the extent to which it undertakes that the provisions of this Protocol shall apply to this or these territories.

2. Any State may at any later date, by a declaration addressed to the Secretary General of the Council of Europe, extend the application of this Protocol to any other territory specified in the declaration. In respect of such territory the Protocol shall enter into force on the first day of the month following the expiration of a period of two months after the date of receipt by the Secretary General of such declaration.

3. Any declaration made under the two preceding paragraphs may, in respect of any territory specified in such declaration, be withdrawn or modified by a notification addressed to the Secretary General. The withdrawal or modification shall become effective on the first day of the month following the expiration of a period of two months after the date of receipt of such notification by the Secretary General.

4. A declaration made in accordance with this Article shall be deemed to have been made in accordance with paragraph 1 of Article 63 of the Convention.

5. The territory of any State to which this Protocol applies by virtue of ratification, acceptance or approval by that State, and each territory to which this Protocol is applied by virtue of a declaration by that State under this Article, may be treated as separate territories for the purpose of the reference in Article 1 to the territory of a State.

Article 7

1. As between the States Parties, the provisions of Articles 1 to 6 of this Protocol shall be regarded as additional Articles to the Convention, and all the provisions of the Convention shall apply accordingly.

2. Nevertheless, the right of individual recourse recognised by a declaration made under Article 25 of the Convention, or the acceptance of the compulsory jurisdiction of the Court by a declaration made under Article 46 of the Convention, shall not be effective in relation to this Protocol unless the State concerned has made a statement recognising such right, or accepting such jurisdiction in respect of Articles 1 to 5 of this Protocol.

Article 8

This Protocol shall be open for signature by member States of the Council of Europe which have signed the Convention. It is subject to ratification, acceptance or approval. A member State of the Council of Europe may not ratify, accept or approve this Protocol without previously or simultaneously ratifying the Convention. Instruments of ratification, acceptance or approval shall be deposited with the Secretary General of the Council of Europe.

Article 9

1. This Protocol shall enter into force on the first day of the month following the expiration of a period of two months after the date on which seven member States of the Council of Europe have expressed their consent to be bound by the Protocol in accordance with the provisions of Article 8.

2. In respect of any member State which subsequently expresses its consent to be bound by it, the Protocol shall enter into force on the first day of the month following the expiration of a period of two months after the date of the deposit of the instrument of ratification, acceptance or approval.

Article 10

The Secretary General of the Council of Europe shall notify all the member States of the Council of:

(a) any signature;

(b) the deposit of any instrument of ratification, acceptance or approval;

(c) any date of entry into force of this Protocol in accordance with Articles 6 and 9;

(d) any other act, notification or declaration, relating to this Protocol.

In witness whereof the undersigned, being duly authorised thereto, have signed this Protocol.

Done at Strasbourg, the twenty-two November one thousand nine hundred and eighty four, in English and French, both texts being equally authentic, in a single copy which shall be deposited in the archives of the Council of Europe. The Secretary General shall transmit certified copies to each member State of the Council.

APPENDIX 3A

American Declaration of the Rights and Duties of Man

O.A.S. Res. XXX *adopted* by the Ninth International Conference of American States, Bogotá, 1948. (Novena Conferencia Internacional Americana, *Actas y Documentos,* Vol. VI, pp. 297–302. Bogotá 1953.)

WHEREAS:

The American peoples have acknowledged the dignity of the individual, and their national constitutions recognize that juridical and political institutions, which regulate life in human society, have as their principal aim the protection of the essential rights of man and the creation of circumstances that will permit him to achieve spiritual and material progress and attain happiness;

The American states have on repeated occasions recognized that the essential rights of man are not derived from the fact that he is a national of certain state, but are based upon attributes of his human personality;

The international protection of the rights of man should be the principal guide of an evolving American law;

The affirmation of essential human rights by the American states together with the guarantees give by the internal regimes of the states establish the initial system of protection considered by the American states as being suited to the present social and juridical conditions not without a recognition on their part that they should increasingly strengthen that system in the international field as conditions become more favorable.

The Ninth International Conference of American States

AGREES:

To adopt the following:

American Declaration of the Rights and Duties of Man

Preamble

All men are born free and equal, in dignity and in rights, and, being endowed by nature with reason and conscience, they should conduct themselves as brothers one to another.

The fulfillment of duty by each individual is a prerequisite to the rights of all. Rights and duties are interrelated in every social and political activity of man. While rights exalt individual liberty, duties express the dignity of that liberty.

Duties of a juridical nature presuppose others of a moral nature which support them in principle and constitute their basis.

Inasmuch as spiritual development is the supreme end of human existence and the highest expression thereof, it is the duty of man to serve that end with all his strength and resources.

Since culture is the highest social and historical expression of that spiritual development, it is the duty of man to preserve, practice and foster culture by every means within his power.

And, since moral conduct constitutes the noblest flowering of culture, it is the duty of every man always to hold it in high respect.

Chapter One

Rights

ARTICLE I. Every human being has the right to life, liberty and the security of his person.

Right to life, liberty and personal security.

ARTICLE II. All persons are equal before the law and have the rights and duties established in this declaration, without distinction as to race, sex, language, creed or any other factor.

Right to equality before the law.

ARTICLE III. Every person has the right freely to profess a religious faith, and to manifest it both in public and in private.

Right to religious freedom and worship.

ARTICLE IV. Every person has the right to freedom of investigation, of opinion, and of the expression and dissemination of ideas, by any medium whatsoever.

Right to freedom of investigation, opinion, expression and dissemination.

ARTICLE V. Every person has the right to the protection of the law against abusive attacks upon his honor, his reputation, and his private and family life.

Right to protection of honor, personal reputation and private and family life.

ARTICLE VI. Every person has the right to establish a family, the basic element of society, and to receive protection therefor.

Rights to a family and to the protection thereof.

ARTICLE VII. All women during pregnancy and the nursing period, and all children have the right to special protection, care and aid.

Right to protection for mothers and children.

ARTICLE VIII. Every person has the right to fix his residence within the territory of the state of which he is a national, to move about freely within such territory, and not to leave it except by his own will.

Right to residence and movement.

ARTICLE IX. Every person has the right to the inviolability of his home.

Right to inviolability of the home.

ARTICLE X. Every person has the right to the inviolability and transmission of his correspondence.

Right to the inviolability and transmission of correspondence.

ARTICLE XI. Every person has the right to the preservation of his health through sanitary and social measures relating to food, clothing, housing and medical care, to the extent permitted by public and community resources.

Right to the preservation of health and to well-being.

ARTICLE XII. Every person has the right to an education, which should be based on the principles of liberty, morality and human solidarity.

Likewise every person has the right to an education that will prepare him to attain a decent life, to raise his standard of living and to be a useful member of society.

The right to an education includes the right to equality of opportunity in every case, in accordance with natural talents, merit and the desire to utilize the resources that the state or the community is in a position to provide.

Every person has the right to receive, free, at least a primary education.

Right to education.

ARTICLE XIII. Every person has the right to take part in the cultural

Right to the benefits of culture.

life of the community, to enjoy the arts, and to participate in the benefits that result from intellectual progress, especially scientific discoveries.

He likewise has the right to the protection of his moral and material interests as regards his inventions or any literary, scientific or artistic works of which he is the author.

ARTICLE XIV. Every person has the right to work, under proper conditions, and to follow his vocation freely, in so far as existing conditions of employment permit.

Right to work and to fair remuneration.

Every person who works has the right to receive such remuneration as will, in proportion to this [*sic*] capacity and skill, assure him a standard of living suitable for himself and for his family.

ARTICLE XV. Every person has the right to leisure time, to wholesome recreation and to the opportunity for advantageous use of his free time to his spiritual, cultural and physical benefit.

Right to leisure time and to the use thereof.

ARTICLE XVI. Every person has the right to social security which will protect him from the consequences of unemployment, old age, and disabilities arising from causes beyond his control that make it physically or mentally impossible for him to earn a living.

Right to social security.

ARTICLE XVII. Every person has the right to be recognized everywhere as a person having rights and obligations, and to enjoy the basic civil rights.

Right to recognition of juridical personality and of civil rights.

ARTICLE XVIII. Every person may resort to the courts to ensure respect for his legal rights. There

Right to a fair trial.

should likewise be available to him a simple, brief procedure whereby the courts will protect him from acts of authoriry [*sic*] that, to his prejudice, violate any fundamental constitutional rights.

ARTICLE XIX. Every person has the right to the nationality to which he is entitled by law and to change it, if he so wishes, for the nationality of any other country that is willing to grant it to him.

Right to nationality.

ARTICLE XX. Every person having legal capacity is entitled to participate in the government of his country, directly or through his representatives, and to take part in popular elections, which shall be by secret ballot, and shall be honest, periodic and free.

Right to vote and to participate in government.

ARTICLE XXI. Every person has the right to assemble peaceably with others in a formal public meeting or an informal gathering, in connection with matters of common interest of any nature.

Right of assembly.

ARTICLE XXII. Every person has the right to associate with others to promote, exercise and protect his legitimate interests of a political, economic, religious, social, cultural, professional, labor union or other nature.

Right of association.

ARTICLE XXIII. Every person has a right to own such private property as meets the essential needs of decent living and helps to maintain the dignity of the individual and of the home.

Right to property.

ARTICLE XXIV. Every person has the right to submit respectful petitions to any competent authority, for reasons of either general or private interest, and the right to obtain a prompt decision thereon.

Right of petition.

ARTICLE XXV. No person may be deprived of his liberty except in the cases and according to the procedures established by preexisting law.

Right to protection from arbitrary arrest.

No person may be deprived of liberty for nonfulfillment of obligations of a purely civil character.

Every individual who has been deprived of his liberty has the right to have the legality of his detention ascertained without delay by a court, and the right to be tried without undue delay, or, otherwise, to be released. He also has the right to humane treatment during the time he is in custody.

ARTICLE XXVI. Every accused person is presumed to be innocent until proved guilty.

Right to due process of law.

Every person accused of an offense has the right to be given an impartial and public hearing, and to be tried by courts previously established in accordance with preexisting laws, and not to receive cruel, infamous or unusual punishment.

ARTICLE XXVII. Every person has the right, in case of pursuit not resulting from ordinary crimes, to seek and receive asylum in foreign territory, in accordance with the laws of each country and with international agreements.

Right of asylum.

ARTICLE XXVIII. The rights of man are limited by the rights of others, by the security of all, and by the just demands of the general welfare and the advancement of democracy.

Scope of the rights of man.

Chapter Two

Duties

ARTICLE XXIX. It is the duty of the individual so to conduct himself in relation to others that each and every one may fully form and develop his personality.

Duties to society.

ARTICLE XXX. It is the duty of every person to aid, support, educate and protect his minor children, and it is the duty of children to honor their parents always and to aid, support and protect them when they need it.

Duties toward children and parents.

ARTICLE XXXI. It is the duty of every person to acquire at least an elementary education.

Duty to receive instruction.

ARTICLE XXXII. It is the duty of every person to vote in the popular elections of the country of which he is a national, when he is legally capable of doing so.

Duty of vote.

ARTICLE XXXIII. It is the duty of every person to obey the law and other legitimate commands of the authorities of his country and those of the country in which he may be.

Duty to serve the community and the nation.

ARTICLE XXXIV. It is the duty of every able-bodied person to render whatever civil and military service his country may require for its defense and preservation, and, in case of public disaster, to render such services as may be in his power.

It is likewise his duty to hold any public office to which he may be elected by popular vote in the state of which he is a national.

Duty to serve the community and the nation.

ARTICLE XXXV. It is the duty of every person to cooperate with the state and the community with

Duties with respect to social security and welfare.

respect to social security and welfare, in accordance with his ability and with existing circumstances.

ARTICLE XXXVI. It is the duty of every person to pay the taxes established by law for the support of public services.

Duty to pay taxes.

ARTICLE XXXVII. It is the duty of every person to work, as far as his capacity and possibilities permit, in order to obtain the means of livelihood or to benefit his community.

Duty to work.

ARTICLE XXXVIII. It is the duty of every person to refrain from taking part in political activities that, according to law, are reserved exclusively to the citizens of the state in which he is an alien.

Duty to refrain from political activities in a foreign country.

APPENDIX 3B

American Convention on Human Rights*

signed Nov. 22, 1969, *entered into force* July 18, 1978, O.A.S. Treaty Series No. 36, at 1, O.A.S. Off. Rec. OEA/Ser. L./V/II. 23 doc. rev. 2

PREAMBLE

The American states signatory to the present Convention,

Reaffirming their intention to consolidate in this hemisphere, within the framework of democratic institutions, a system of personal liberty and social justice based on respect for the essential rights of man;

Recognizing that the essential rights of man are not derived from one's being a national of a certain state, but are based upon attributes of the human personality and that they therefore justify international protection in the form of a convention reinforcing or complementing the protection provided by the domestic law of the American states;

Considering that these principles have been set forth in the Charter of the Organization of American States, in the American Declaration of the Rights and Duties of Man, and in the Universal Declaration of Human Rights, and that they have been reaffirmed and refined in other international instruments, worldwide as well as regional in scope;

Reiterating that, in accordance with the Universal Declaration of Human Rights, the ideal of free men enjoying freedom from fear and want can be achieved only if conditions are created whereby everyone may enjoy his economic, social, and cultural rights, as well as his civil and political rights; and

Considering that the Third Special Inter-American Conference (Buenos Aires, 1967) approved the incorporation into the Charter of the Organization itself of broader standards with respect to economic, social, and educational rights and resolved that an inter-American convention on human rights should determine the structure, competence, and procedure of the organs responsible for these matters, Have agreed upon the following:

---

*Only Part I, detailing substantive rights, has been reproduced here. The procedural parts of the convention have been omitted for reasons of space.

PART I
STATE OBLIGATIONS AND RIGHTS PROTECTED

Chapter I
General Obligations

Article 1
Obligation to Respect Rights

1. The States Parties to this Convention undertake to respect the rights and freedoms recognized herein and to ensure to all persons subject to their jurisdiction the free and full exercise of those rights and freedoms, without any discrimination for reasons of race, color, sex, language, religion, political or other opinion, national or social origin, economic status, birth, or any other social condition.

2. For the purposes of this Convention, "person" means every human being.

Article 2
Domestic Legal Effects

Where the exercise of any of the rights or freedoms referred to in Article 1 is not already ensured by legislative or other provisions, the States Parties undertake to adopt, in accordance with their constitutional processes and the provisions of this Convention, such legislative or other measures as may be necessary to give effect to those rights or freedoms.

Chapter II
Civil and Political Rights

Article 3
Right to Juridical Personality

Every person has the right to recognition as a person before the law.

Article 4
Right to Life

1. Every person has the right to have his life respected. This right shall be protected by law and, in general, from the moment of conception. No one shall be arbitrarily deprived of his life.

2. In countries that have not abolished the death penalty, it may be imposed only for the most serious crimes and pursuant to a final judgment rendered by a competent court and in accordance with a law establishing such punishment, enacted prior to the commission of the crime. The application of such punishment shall not be extended to crimes to which it does not presently apply.

3. The death penalty shall not be reestablished in states that have abolished it.

4. In no case shall capital punishment be inflicted for political offenses or related common crimes.

5. Capital punishment shall not be imposed upon persons who, at the time the crime was committed, were under 18 years of age or over 70 years of age; nor shall it be applied to pregnant women.

6. Every person condemned to death shall have the right to apply for amnesty, pardon, or commutation of sentence, which may be granted in all cases. Capital punishment shall not be imposed while such a petition is pending decision by the competent authority.

Article 5
Right to Humane Treatment

1. Every person has the right to have his physical, mental, and moral integrity respected.

2. No one shall be subjected to torture or to cruel, inhuman, or degrading punishment or treatment. All persons deprived of their liberty shall be treated with respect for the inherent dignity of the human person.

3. Punishment shall not be extended to any person other than the criminal.

4. Accused persons shall, save in exceptional circumstances, be segregated from convicted persons, and shall be subject to separate treatment appropriate to their status as unconvicted persons.

5. Minors while subject to criminal proceedings shall be separated from adults and brought before specialized tribunals, as speedily as possible, so that they may be treated in accordance with their status as minors.

6. Punishments consisting of deprivation of liberty shall have as an essential aim the reform and social readaptation of the prisoners.

Article 6
Freedom from Slavery

1. No one shall be subject to slavery or to involuntary servitude, which are prohibited in all their forms, as are the slave trade and traffic in women.

2. No one shall be required to perform forced or compulsory labor. This provision shall not be interpreted to mean that, in those countries in which the penalty established for certain crime is deprivation of liberty at forced labor, the carrying out of such a sentence imposed by a competent court is prohibited. Forced labor shall not adversely affect the dignity or the physical or intellectual capacity of the prisoner.

3. For the purposes of this article, the following do not constitute forced or compulsory labor:

a) work or service normally required of a person imprisoned in execution of a sentence or formal decision passed by the competent judicial authority. Such work or service shall be carried out under the supervision and control of public authorities, and any persons performing such work or service shall not be placed at the disposal of any private party, company, or juridical person;

b) military service and, in countries in which conscientious objectors are recognized, national service that the law may provide for in lieu of military service;

c) service exacted in time of danger or calamity that threatens the existence or the well-being of the community; or

d) work or service that forms part of normal civic obligations.

Article 7
Right to Personal Liberty

1. Every person has the right to personal liberty and security.

2. No one shall be deprived of his physical liberty except for the reasons and under the conditions established beforehand by the constitution of the State Party concerned or by a law established pursuant thereto.

3. No one shall be subject to arbitrary arrest or imprisonment.

4. Anyone who is detained shall be informed of the reasons for his detention and shall be promptly notified of the charge or charges against him.

5. Any person detained shall be brought promptly before a judge or other officer authorized by law to exercise judicial power and shall be entitled to trial within a reasonable time or to be released without prejudice to the continuation of the proceedings. His release may be subject to guarantees to assure his appearance for trial.

6. Anyone who is deprived of his liberty shall be entitled to recourse to a competent court, in order that the court may decide without delay on the lawfulness of his arrest or detention and order his release if the arrest or detention is unlawful. In States Parties whose laws provide that anyone who believes himself to be threatened with deprivation of his liberty is entitled to recourse to a competent court in order that it may decide on the lawfulness of such threat, this remedy may not be restricted or abolished. The interested party or another person in his behalf is entitled to seek these remedies.

7. No one shall be detained for debt. This principle shall not limit the orders of a competent judicial authority issued for nonfulfillment of duties of support.

Article 8
Right to a Fair Trial

1. Every person has the right to a hearing, with due guarantees and within a reasonable time, by a competent, independent, and impartial

tribunal, previously established by law, in the substantiation of any accusation of a criminal nature made against him or for the determination of his rights and obligations of a civil, labor, fiscal, or any other nature.

2. Every person accused of a criminal offense has the right to be presumed innocent so long as his guilt has not been proven according to law. During the proceedings, every person is entitled, with full equality, to the following minimum guarantees:

a) the right of the accused to be assisted without charge by a translator or interpreter, if he does not understand or does not speak the language of the tribunal or court;

b) prior notification in detail to the accused of the charges against him;

c) adequate time and means for the preparation of his defense;

d) the right of the accused to defend himself personally or to be assisted by legal counsel of his own choosing, and to communicate freely and privately with his counsel;

e) the inalienable right to be assisted by counsel provided by the state, paid or not as the domestic law provides, if the accused does not defend himself personally or engage his own counsel within the time period established by law;

f) the right of the defense to examine witnesses present in the court and to obtain the appearance, as witnesses, of experts or other persons who may throw light on the facts;

g) the right not to be compelled to be a witness against himself or to plead guilty; and

h) the right to appeal the judgment to a higher court.

3. A confession of a guilt by the accused shall be valid only if it is made without coercion of any kind.

4. An accused person acquitted by a nonappealable judgment shall not be subjected to a new trial for the same cause.

5. Criminal proceedings shall be public, except insofar as may be necessary to protect the interests of justice.

Article 9
Freedom from Ex Post Facto Laws

No one shall be convicted of any act or omission that did not constitute a criminal offense, under the applicable law, at the time it was committed. A heavier penalty shall not be imposed than the one that was applicable at the time the criminal offense was committed. If subsequent to the commission of the offense the law provides for the imposition of a lighter punishment, the guilty person shall benefit therefrom.

Article 10
Right to Compensation

Every person has the right to be compensated in accordance with the law in the final event he has been sentenced by a final judgment through a miscarriage of justice.

Article 11
Right to Privacy

1. Everyone has the right to have his honor respected and his dignity recognized.

2. No one may be the object of arbitrary or abusive interference with his private life, his family, his home, or his correspondence, or of unlawful attacks on his honor or reputation.

3. Everyone has the right to the protection of the law against such interference or attacks.

Article 12
Freedom of Conscience and Religion

1. Everyone has the right to freedom of conscience and of religion. This right includes freedom to maintain or to change one's religion or beliefs, and freedom to profess or disseminate one's religion or beliefs, either individually or together with other, in public or in private.

2. No one shall be subject to restrictions that might impair his freedom to maintain or to change his religion or beliefs.

3. Freedom to manifest one's religion and beliefs may be subject only to the limitations prescribed by law that are necessary to protect public safety, order, health, or morals, or the rights or freedoms of others.

4. Parents or guardians, as the case may be, have the right to provide for the religious and moral education of their children or wards that is in accord with their own convictions.

Article 13
Freedom of Thought and Expression

1. Everyone has the right to freedom of thought and expression. This right includes freedom to seek, receive, and impart information and ideas of all kinds, regardless of frontiers, either orally, in writing, in print, in the form of art, or through any other medium of one's choice.

2. The exercise of the right provided for in the foregoing paragraph shall not be subject to prior censorship but shall be subject to subsequent imposition of liability, which shall be expressly established by law to the extent necessary to ensure:

a) respect for the rights or reputations of others; or

b) the protection of national security, public order, or public health or morals.

3. The right of expression may not be restricted by indirect methods or means, such as the abuse of government or private controls over newsprint, radio broadcasting frequencies, or equipment used in the dissemination of information, or by any other means tending to impede the communication and circulation of ideas and opinions.

4. Notwithstanding the provisions of paragraph 2 above, public entertainments may be subject by law to prior censorship for the sole purpose of regulating access to them for the moral protection of childhood and adolescence.

5. Any propaganda for war and any advocacy of national, racial, or religious hatred that constitute incitements to lawless violence or to any other similar illegal action against any person or group of persons on any grounds including those of race, color, religion, language, or national origin shall be considered as offenses punishable by law.

Article 14
Right of Reply

1. Anyone injured by inaccurate or offensive statements or ideas disseminated to the public in general by a legally regulated medium of communication has the right to reply or to make a correction using the same communications outlet, under such conditions as the law may establish.

2. The correction or reply shall not in any case remit other legal liabilities that may have been incurred.

3. For the effective protection of honor and reputation, every publisher, and every newspaper, motion picture, radio, and television company, shall have a person responsible who is not protected by immunities or special privileges.

Article 15
Right of Assembly

The right of peaceful assembly, without arms, is recognized. No restrictions may be placed on the exercise of this right other than those imposed in conformity with the law and necessary in a democratic society in the interest of national security, public safety or public order, or to protect public health or morals or the rights or freedoms of others.

Article 16
Freedom of Association

1. Everyone has the right to associate freely for ideological, religious, political, economic, labor, social, cultural, sports, or other purposes.

2. The exercise of this right shall be subject only to such restrictions established by law as may be necessary in a democratic society, in the interest of national security, public safety or public order, or to protect public health or morals or the rights and freedoms of others.

3. The provisions of this article do not bar the imposition of legal restrictions, including even deprivation of the exercise of the right of association, on members of the armed forces and the police.

Article 17
Rights of the Family

1. The family is the natural and fundamental group unit of society and is entitled to protection by society and the state.

2. The right of men and women of marriageable age to marry and to raise a family shall be recognized, if they meet the conditions required by domestic laws, insofar as such conditions do not affect the principle of nondiscrimination established in the Convention.

3. No marriage shall be entered into without the free and full consent of the intending spouses.

4. The States Parties shall take appropriate steps to ensure the equality of rights and the adequate balancing of responsibilities of the spouses as to marriage, during marriage, and in the event of its dissolution. In case of dissolution, provision shall be made for the necessary protection of any children solely on the basis of their own best interests.

5. The law shall recognize equal rights for children born out of wedlock and those born in wedlock.

Article 18
Right to a Name

Every person has the right to a given name and to the surnames of his parents or that of one of them. The law shall regulate the manner in which the right shall be ensured for all, by the use of assumed names if necessary.

Article 19
Rights of the Child

Every minor child has the right to the measures of protection required by his condition as a minor on the part of his family, society, and the state.

Article 20
Right to Nationality

1. Every person has the right to a nationality.

2. Every person has the right to the nationality of the state in whose territory he was born if he does not have the right to any other nationality.

3. No one shall be arbitrarily deprived of his nationality or of the right to change it.

Article 21
Right to Property

1. Everyone has the right to the use and enjoyment of his property. The law may subordinate such use and enjoyment to the interest of society.

2. No one shall be deprived of his property except upon payment of just compensation, for reasons of public utility or social interest, and in the cases and according to the forms established by law.

3. Usury and any other form of exploitation of man by man shall be prohibited by law.

Article 22
Freedom of Movement and Residence

1. Every person lawfully in the territory of a State Party has the right to move about in it, and to reside in it subject to the provisions of the law.

2. Every person has the right to leave any country freely, including his own.

3. The exercise of the foregoing rights may be restricted only pursuant to a law to the extent necessary in a democratic society to prevent crime or to protect national security, public safety, public order, public morals, public health, or the rights or freedoms of others.

4. The exercise of the rights recognized in paragraph 1 may also be restricted by law in designated zones for reasons of public interest.

5. No one can be expelled from the territory of the state of which he is a national or be deprived of the right to enter it.

6. An alien lawfully in the territory of a State Party to this Convention may be expelled from it only pursuant to a decision reached in accordance with law.

7. Every person has the right to seek and be granted asylum in a foreign territory, in accordance with the legislation of the state and international conventions, in the event he is being pursued for political offenses or related common crimes.

8. In no case may an alien be deported or returned to a country, regardless of whether or not it is his country of origin, if in that country his right to life or personal freedom is in danger of being violated because of his race, nationality, religion, social status, or political opinions.

9. The collective expulsion of aliens is prohibited.

Article 23
Right to Participate in Government

1. Every citizen shall enjoy the following rights and opportunities:

a) to take part in the conduct of public affairs, directly or through freely chosen representatives:

b) to vote and to be elected in genuine periodic elections, which shall be by universal and equal suffrage and by secret ballot that guarantees the free expression of the will of the voters; and

c) to have access, under general conditions of equality, to the public service of his country.

2. The law may regulate the exercise of the rights and opportunities referred to in the preceding paragraph only on the basis of age, nationality, residence, language, education, civil and mental capacity, or sentencing by a competent court in criminal proceedings.

Article 24
Right to Equal Protection

All persons are equal before the law. Consequently, they are entitled, without discrimination, to equal protection of the law.

Article 25
Right to Judicial Protection

1. Everyone has the right to simple and prompt recourse, or any other effective recourse, to a competent court or tribunal for protection against acts that violate his fundamental rights recognized by the constitution or laws of the state concerned or by this Convention, even though such violation may have been committed by persons acting in the course of their official duties.

2. The States Parties undertake:

a) to ensure that any person claiming such remedy shall have his rights determined by the competent authority provided for by the legal system of the state;

b) to develop the possibilities of judicial remedy; and

c) to ensure that the competent authorities shall enforce such remedies when granted.

Chapter III
Economic, Social, and Cultural Rights

Article 26
Progressive Development

The States Parties undertake to adopt measures, both internally and through international cooperation, especially those of an economic and technical nature, with a view to achieving progressively, by legislation or other appropriate means, the full realization of the rights implicit in the economic, social, education, scientific, and cultural standards set forth in the Charter of the Organization of American States as amended by the Protocol of Buenos Aires.

Chapter IV
Suspension of Guarantees, Interpretation and Application

Article 27
Suspension of Guarantees

1. In time of war, public danger, or other emergency that threatens the independence or security of a State Party, it may take measures derogating from its obligations under the present Convention to the extent and for the period of time strictly required by the exigencies of the situation, provided that such measures are not inconsistent with its other obligations under international law and do not involve discrimination on the ground of race, color, sex, language, religion, or social origin.

2. The foregoing provision does not authorize any suspension of the following articles: Article 3 (Right to Juridical Personality), Article 4 (Right to Life), Article 5 (Right to Humane Treatment), Article 6 (Freedom from Slavery), Article 9 (Freedom from *Ex Post Facto* Laws), Article 12 (Freedom of Conscience and Religion), Article 17 (Rights of the Family), Article 18 (Right to a Name), Article 19 (Rights of the Child), Article 20 (Right to Nationality), and Article 23 (Right to Participate in Government), or of the judicial guarantees essential for the protection of such rights.

3. Any State Party availing itself of the right of suspension shall immediately inform the other States Parties, through the Secretary General of the Organization of American States, of the provisions the application of which it has suspended, the reasons that gave rise to the suspension, and the date set for the termination of such suspension.

Article 28
Federal Clause

1. Where a State Party is constituted as a federal state, the national government of such State Party shall implement all the provisions of the Convention over whose subject matter it exercises legislative and judicial jurisdiction.

2. With respect to the provisions over whose subject matter the constituent units of the federal state have jurisdiction, the national government shall immediately take suitable measures, in accordance with its constitution and its laws, to the end that the competent authorities of the constituent units may adopt appropriate provisions for the fulfillment of this Convention.

3. Whenever two or more States Parties agree to form a federation or other type of association, they shall take care that the resulting federal or other compact contains the provisions necessary for continuing and rendering effective the standards of this Convention in the new state that is organized.

Article 29
Restrictions Regarding Interpretation

No provision of this Convention shall be interpreted as:

a) permitting any State Party, group, or person to suppress the enjoyment or exercise of the rights and freedoms recognized in this Convention or to restrict them to a greater extent than is provided for herein;

b) restricting the enjoyment or exercise of any right or freedom recognized by virtue of the laws of any State Party or by virtue of another convention to which one of the said states is a party;

c) precluding other rights or guarantees that are inherent in the human personality or derived from representative democracy as a form of government; or

d) excluding or limiting the effect that the American Declaration of the Rights and Duties of Man and other international acts of the same nature may have.

Article 30
Scope of Restrictions

The restrictions that, pursuant to this Convention, may be placed on the enjoyment or exercise of the rights and freedoms recognized herein may be applied except in accordance with laws enacted for reasons of general interest and in accordance with the purpose for which such restrictions have been established.

Article 31
Recognition of Other Rights

Other rights and freedoms recognized in accordance with the procedures established in Articles 76 and 77 may be included in the system of protection of the Convention.

Chapter V
Personal Responsibilities

Article 32
Relationship Between Duties and Rights

1. Every person has responsibilities to his family, his community, and mankind.

2. The rights of each person are limited by the rights of others, by the security of all, and by the just demands of the general welfare, in a democratic society.

APPENDIX 4

Ratifications of Selected Human Rights Instruments*

Adopted under UN Auspices

International Covenant on Civil and Political Rights: Ratifications (as of 31 Dec. 1982)

Australia, Austria[a], Barbados[b], Bolivia[b], Bulgaria, Byelorussian S.S.R., Canada[a,b], Central African Republic[b], Chile, Colombia[b], Costa Rica[b], Cyprus, Czechoslovakia, Denmark[a,b], Dominican Republic[b], Ecuador[b], Egypt, El Salvador, Finland[a,b], France, Gambia, German Democratic Republic, Federal Republic of Germany[a], Guinea, Guyana, Hungary, Iceland[a,b], India, Iran, Iraq, Italy[a,b], Jamaica[b], Japan, Jordan, Kenya, Democratic People's Republic of Korea, Lebanon, Libya, Madagascar[b], Mali, Mauritius[b], Mexico, Mongolia, Morocco, Netherlands[a,b], New Zealand[a], Nicaragua[b], Norway[a,b], Panama[b], Peru[b], Poland, Portugal, Romania, Rwanda, Saint Vincent and the Grenadines[b], Senegal[a,b], Spain, Sri Lanka[a], Suriname[b], Sweden[a,b], Syria, Tanzania, Trinidad and Tobago[b], Tunisia, Ukrainian S.S.R., Union of Soviet Socialist Republics, United Kingdom[a], Uruguay[b], Venezuela[b], Vietnam, Yugoslavia, Zaire[b]

[a]Also has recognized the competence of the Human Rights Committee to hear interstate complaints under article 41.

[b]Also has ratified the Optional Protocol.

International Covenant on Economic, Social and Cultural Rights: Ratifications (as of 31 December 1982)

Australia, Austria, Barbados, Bolivia, Bulgaria, Byelorussian S.S.R., Canada, Central African Republic, Chile, Colombia, Costa Rica, Cyprus, Czechoslovakia, Denmark, Dominican Republic, Ecuador, Egypt, El Salvador, Finland, France, Gambia, German Democratic Republic, Federal Republic of Germany, Guinea, Guyana, Honduras, Hungary, Iceland, India, Iran, Iraq, Italy, Jamaica, Japan, Jordan, Kenya, Democratic People's Republic of Korea, Lebanon, Libya, Madagascar, Mali, Mauritius, Mexico, Mongolia, Morocco, Netherlands, New Zealand, Nicaragua, Norway, Panama, Peru, Philippines, Poland, Portugal, Romania, Rwanda, Saint Vincent and the Grenadines, Senegal, Solomon Islands, Spain, Sri Lanka, Suriname, Sweden, Syria, Tanzania, Trinidad and Tobago, Tunisia, Ukrainian S.S.R., Union of Soviet Socialist Republics, United Kingdom, Uruguay, Venezuela, Vietnam, Yugoslavia, Zaire

*Reproduced from: *Guide to International Human Rights Practice,* ed. Hurst Hannum (London: Macmillan, 1984), pp. 297–301.

International Convention on the Elimination of All Forms of Racial Discrimination: Ratifications (as of July 1982)

Algeria, Argentina, Australia, Austria, Bahamas, Bangladesh, Barbados, Belgium, Bolivia, Botswana, Brazil, Bulgaria, Burundi, Byelorussian S.S.R., Cameroon, Canada, Cape Verde, Central African Republic, Chad, Chile, China, Colombia, Costa Rica[a], Cuba, Cyprus, Czechoslovakia, Denmark, Ecuador[a], Egypt, El Salvador, Ethiopia, Fiji, Finland, France[a], Gabon, Gambia, German Democratic Republic, Federal Republic of Germany, Ghana, Greece, Guinea, Guyana, Haiti, Holy See, Hungary, Iceland[a], India, Iran, Iraq, Israel, Italy[a], Ivory Coast, Jamaica, Jordan, Republic of Korea, Kuwait, Laos, Lebanon, Lesotho, Liberia, Libya, Luxembourg, Madagascar, Mali, Malta, Mauritius, Mexico, Mongolia, Morocco, Nepal, Netherlands[a], New Zealand, Nicaragua, Niger, Nigeria, Norway[a], Pakistan, Panama, Papua New Guinea, Peru, Philippines, Poland, Qatar, Romania, Rwanda, Saint Vincent and the Grenadines, Senegal[a], Seychelles, Sierra Leone, Solomon Islands, Somalia, Spain, Sri Lanka, Sudan, Swaziland, Sweden[a], Syria, Tanzania, Togo, Tonga, Trinidad and Tobago, Tunisia, Uganda, Ukrainian S.S.R., Union of Soviet Socialist Republics, United Arab Emirates, United Kingdom, Upper Volta, Uruguay[a], Venezuela, Vietnam, Democratic Yemen, Yugoslavia, Zaire, Zambia

[a]Has recognized the right of the Committee to receive individual complaints under article 14.

Convention on the Prevention and Punishment of the Crime of Genocide: Ratifications (as of 1 July 1982)

Afghanistan, Albania, Algeria, Argentina, Australia, Austria, Bahamas, Barbados, Belgium, Brazil, Bulgaria, Burma, Byelorussian S.S.R., Canada, Chile, Colombia, Costa Rica, Cuba, Cyprus, Czechoslovakia, Denmark, Ecuador, Egypt, El Salvador, Ethiopia, Fiji, Finland, France, Gambia, German Democratic Republic, Federal Republic of Germany, Ghana, Greece, Guatemala, Haiti, Honduras, Hungary, Iceland, India, Iran, Iraq, Ireland, Israel, Italy, Jamaica, Jordan, Democratic Kampuchea, Republic of Korea, Laos, Lebanon, Lesotho, Liberia, Luxembourg, Mali, Mexico, Monaco, Mongolia, Morocco, Nepal, Netherlands, New Zealand, Nicaragua, Norway, Pakistan, Panama, Papua New Guinea, Peru, Philippines, Poland, Romania, Rwanda, Saint Vincent and the Grenadines, Saudi Arabia, Spain, Sri Lanka, Sweden, Syria, Tonga, Tunisia, Turkey, Ukrainian S.S.R., Union of Soviet Socialist Republics, United Kingdom, Upper Volta, Uruguay, Venezuela, Vietnam, Yugoslavia, Zaire

International Convention on the Suppression and Punishment of the Crime of Apartheid: Ratifications (as of 1 July 1982)

Algeria, Bahamas, Barbados, Benin, Bulgaria, Burundi, Byelorussian S.S.R., Cameroon, Cape Verde, Central African Republic, Chad, Cuba,

Czechoslovakia, Ecuador, Egypt, El Salvador, Ethiopia, Gabon, Gambia, German Democratic Republic, Ghana, Guinea, Guyana, Haiti, Hungary, India, Iraq, Jamaica, Democratic Kampuchea, Kuwait, Laos, Liberia, Libya, Madagascar, Mali, Mexico, Mongolia, Nepal, Nicaragua, Niger, Nigeria, Panama, Peru, Philippines, Poland, Qatar, Romania, Rwanda, Saint Vincent and the Grenadines, São Tomé and Príncipe, Senegal, Seychelles, Somalia, Sri Lanka, Sudan, Suriname, Syria, Tanzania, Trinidad and Tobago, Tunisia, Ukranian S.S.R., Union of Soviet Socialist Republics, United Arab Emirates, Upper Volta, Vietnam, Yugoslavia, Zaire

Convention on the Elimination of All Forms of Discrimination against Women: Ratifications (as of 1 July 1982[a])

Austria, Barbados, Bhutan, Bulgaria, Byelorussian S.S.R., Canada, Cape Verde, China, Colombia, Cuba, Czechoslovakia, Dominica, Ecuador, Egypt, El Salvador, Ethiopia, German Democratic Republic, Guyana, Haiti, Hungary, Laos, Mexico, Mongolia, Nicaragua, Norway, Panama, Philippines, Poland, Portugal, Romania, Rwanda, Saint Vincent and the Grenadines, Sri Lanka, Sweden, Ukrainian S.S.R., Union of Soviet Socialist Republics, Uruguay, Vietnam, Yugoslavia

[a]The Convention was adopted only in 1979 and entered into force in 1981; fifty-one additional states have signed but not yet ratified it.

Convention and Protocol Relating to the Status of Refugees: Ratifications (as of 1 July 1982)

Algeria, Angola, Argentina, Australia, Austria, Belgium, Benin, Bolivia, Botswana, Brazil, Burundi, Cameroon, Canada, Central African Republic, Chad, Chile, Colombia, Congo, Costa Rica, Cyprus, Denmark, Djibouti, Dominican Republic, Ecuador, Egypt, Ethiopia, Fiji, Finland, France, Gabon, Gambia, Federal Republic of Germany, Ghana, Greece, Guinea, Guinea-Bissau, Holy See, Iceland, Iran, Ireland, Israel, Italy, Ivory Coast, Jamaica, Japan[b], Jordan[a], Kenya, Lesotho, Liberia, Liechtenstein, Luxembourg, Madagascar[a], Mali, Malta, Monaco[a], Morocco, Netherlands, New Zealand, Nicaragua, Niger, Nigeria, Norway, Panama, Paraguay, Peru[a], Philippines, Portugal, Rwanda, São Tomé and Príncipe, Senegal, Seychelles, Sierra Leone, Somalia, Spain, Sudan, Suriname, Swaziland[b], Sweden, Switzerland, Tanzania, Togo, Tunisia, Turkey, Uganda, United Kingdom, United States of America[b], Upper Volta, Uruguay, Yemen, Yugoslavia, Zaire, Zambia, Zimbabwe

[a]Ratified the Convention only.
[b]Ratified the Protocol only, which incorporates the Convention by reference.

Convention for the Suppression of the Traffic in Persons and of the Exploitation of the Prostitution of Others: Ratifications (as of 1 July 1982)

Albania, Algeria, Argentina, Belgium, Brazil, Bulgaria, Byelorussian S.S.R., Cameroon, Central African Republic, Congo, Cuba, Czechoslovakia, Djibouti, Ecuador, Egypt, Ethiopia, Finland, France, German Democratic Republic, Guinea, Haiti, Hungary, India, Iraq, Israel, Italy, Japan, Jordan, Republic of Korea, Kuwait, Laos, Libya, Malawi, Mali, Mexico, Morocco, Niger, Norway, Pakistan, Philippines, Poland, Romania, Senegal, Singapore, South Africa, Spain, Sri Lanka, Syria, Ukranian S.S.R., Union of Soviet Socialist Republics, Upper Volta, Venezuela, Yugoslavia

Adopted under the Auspices of the Organization of American States: Ratifications (as of Jan. 1983)

American Convention on Human Rights

Barbados[c], Bolivia, Colombia, Costa Rica[a,b], Dominican Republic[c], Ecuador[c], El Salvador[c], Grenada[c], Guatemala[c], Haiti, Honduras[b], Jamaica[a,c], Mexico[c], Nicaragua, Panama, Peru[b], Venezuela[a,b,c]

[a]Filed declaration accepting interstate complaints.
[b]Filed declaration accepting jurisdiction of the Inter-American Court.
[c]With a declaration or reservation.

OAS Charter

Antigua and Barbuda, Argentina, Bahamas, Barbados, Bolivia, Brazil, Chile, Colombia, Costa Rica, Cuba, Dominica, Dominican Republic, Ecuador, El Salvador, Grenada, Guatemala, Haiti, Honduras, Jamaica, Mexico, Nicaragua, Panama, Paraguay, Peru, Saint Lucia, Saint Vincent and the Grenadines, Suriname, Trinidad and Tobago, United States of America, Uruguay, Venezuela

Adopted under the Auspices of the Council of Europe: Ratifications (as of 31 Dec. 1982)

The European Convention on Human Rights

Austria[a], Belgium[a], Cyprus, Denmark[a], France[a], Federal Republic of Germany[a], Greece, Iceland[a], Ireland[a], Italy[a], Liechtenstein[a], Luxembourg[a], Malta, Netherlands[a], Norway[a], Portugal[a], Spain[a], Sweden[a], Switzerland[a], Turkey, United Kingdom[a]

[a]Accepted right of individual petition under article 25. [On 20 November 1985, Greece accepted the right of individual petition—*Editor*.]

Protocol No. 1

Austria, Belgium, Cyprus, Denmark, Federal Republic of Germany, Greece, Iceland, Ireland, Italy, Luxembourg, Malta, Netherlands, Norway, Portugal, Sweden, Switzerland, Turkey, United Kingdom

Protocol No. 4

Austria, Belgium, Denmark, France, Federal Republic of Germany, Iceland, Ireland, Italy, Luxembourg, Malta, Netherlands, Norway, Portugal, Sweden, Switzerland, United Kingdom

European Agreement Relating to Persons Participating in Proceedings of the European Commission and Court of Human Rights

Belgium, Cyprus, Federal Republic of Germany, Ireland, Italy, Luxembourg, Malta, Netherlands, Norway, Portugal, Sweden, Switzerland, United Kingdom

APPENDIX 5

Checklist to Help Select the Most Appropriate Forum*

The following series of questions is designed to elicit the basic information that one needs in order to decide what courses of action might be most appropriate to redress a particular human rights violation.

I. In *which country* did the violations occur?
   A. Is it a *party to* any human rights or other relevant *treaties*?
      1. Universal—International Covenant on Civil and Political Rights and Optional Protocol? International Covenant on Economic, Social and Cultural Rights? International Labor Organization conventions? Convention on the Elimination of All Forms of Racial Discrimination? Apartheid Convention? Convention and Protocol on the Status of Refugees?
      2. Regional—European Convention on Human Rights (including acceptance of the right of individual petition under article 25)? American Convention on Human Rights?
   B. Is it a country of *special interest to international bodies*?
      1. South Africa?
      2. Israel-occupied territories?
      3. Bolivia?
      4. Chile?
      5. El Salvador?
      6. Guatemala?
      7. Subject of a current study by the Inter-American Commission on Human Rights?
   C. To which *international organizations* does the country belong?
      1. United Nations?
      2. UNESCO?
      3. International Labor Organization?
      4. Organization of American States?
      5. European Economic Community
   D. If not a party to any relevant conventions, a state may still be held responsible under such procedures as ECOSOC Resolution 1503 for violations of rights set forth in the Universal Declaration of Human Rights or other widely accepted norms such as prohibitions against torture, genocide, slavery, apartheid, or discrimination.

---

*Reproduced from: *Guide to International Human Rights Practice*, ed. Hurst Hannum (London: Macmillan, 1984), pp. 288–90.

II. *What rights* have been violated? Are they the subjects of specialized conventions, agencies, or procedures?
   A. Trade union rights or freedom of association? (ILO)
   B. Cultural, educational, social, or scientific freedom? (UNESCO)
   C. Racial discrimination? (Committee on Racial Discrimination)
   D. Disappearance of the victim? (Human Rights Commission Working Group)
   E. Slaverylike practices? (Sub-Commission Working Group)
   F. Prison conditions? (Standard Minimum Rules)

III. Is the victim a victim of an *individual violation* or of a widespread *pattern of violations*?
   A. If an *individual* violation, who is complaining?
      1. Victim himself or herself?
      2. Relative or legal representative?
      3. Nongovernmental organization or person unconnected to the victim?
      4. If not connected to the victim, what is the basis for the complaint on his or her behalf?
      5. Does the NGO have direct and/or reliable knowledge of the alleged violations?
   B. If a *widespread* violation, there may be no requirement to exhaust domestic remedies (see below), but communications which seek to raise broad issues rather than to redress individual complaints can be raised by individuals or NGOs (as opposed to governments) only under ECOSOC Resolution 1503 ("consistent pattern of gross violations"), the relevant ILO conventions (available only to recognized employers' or employees' groups), the procedures of the Inter-American Commission on Human Rights, or submitted to specialized UN bodies such as the working group on disappearances of the Human Rights Commission, the working group on slavery of the Sub-Commission on Prevention of Discrimination and Protection of Minorities, and the special rapporteurs or committees concerned with Bolivia, Chile, El Salvador, Guatemala, the Israeli-occupied territories, and southern Africa.

IV. What steps have been taken to obtain *redress at the domestic* (national) *level*?
   A. Are there effective administrative or judicial procedures available?
   B. If so, have they been fully exhausted?
      1. As noted (question III), those procedures which address country situations involving large-scale violations, as well as noncomplaint procedures such as UN rapporteurs or working groups, do *not* generally require prior exhaustion of domestic remedies.

2. Individual complaint procedures—e.g., under the European Convention on Human Rights—*do* generally require exhaustion.

V. What *remedy* is sought?
   A. Publicity only?
   B. Investigation?
   C. Changes in national legislation?
   D. Individual remedies?
      1. Protection, release from detention?
      2. Specific redress—e.g., compensation, granting of exit permit or visa, change in civil status?
   E. Even confidential procedures may create diplomatic pressure on a responsive government, and they may have a greater chance of resolving individual cases than more public procedures. In the case of widespread violations, however, maximum publicity may be more important than the quiet or partial resolution of only a few individual cases.

VI. Can *more than one procedure* be utilized at the same time? Is the same situation appropriate for treatment as both an individual complaint and an investigation into a pattern or practice of violations?

VII. What *resources* are available to the complainant?
   A. Are the procedures so complex or the violations so massive that the assistance of a lawyer, NGO, or even a government is essential?
   B. What actual costs (research, photocopying, travel, etc.) are involved?
   C. What political (in a broad sense) resources are available—e.g., help from a friendly government, sympathetic trade union, church group, domestic political groups, journalists, parallel interest groups?

APPENDIX 6

Strasbourg: The Capital of Human Values*

The summer of 1979 marked the end of the first decade of what has become the most sophisticated human rights teaching program in the world. Throughout the month of July, in the Alsatian city of Strasbourg, on the Rhine river where France and Germany meet, over 200 law students, practicing lawyers, jurists and specialists in related disciplines from more than 40 different countries heard lectures by some of the foremost living authorities in the human rights field. They examined in depth the case law of contemporary human rights, and probed the intricacies of international humanitarian law.

The International Institute of Human Rights (or, to use the other official language, L'Institut International des Droits de l'Homme) was created in 1969 by French jurist René Cassin, who devoted his Nobel Peace Prize to that purpose. Cassin's career had been a dynamic one: president of the Federal Union of World War I Veterans, French delegate to the League of Nations, associate of De Gaulle in London during the Nazi occupation, vice-president of the French Council of State and president of the Constitutional Council after the war, active participant in the creation of UNESCO and—most important—the virtual father of the Universal Declaration of Human Rights.

As his life neared its close (he died at age 88 in 1976), Cassin determined to found an Institute which, independent of all government influence, could maximally promote human rights by sensitizing students and teachers to the vital importance of that discipline. The International Institute of Human Rights would constitute, Cassin envisaged, "an international center of thought and education which has heretofore not existed anywhere."

His focus was on the educational side of human rights—as contrasted, for example, with the "activistic" emphasis of such organizations as Amnesty International. "The goal of my Institute," he said, "is to influence the universities. Aside from religions, the university is the sole permanent element in a country. The presence of numerous courses on human rights in the universities could profoundly modify the development of peoples everywhere."

Along the same line, Cassin said: "If, in the years I have left, I am given the happy privilege of seeing, thanks to the International Institute,

---

*Originally published in *Human Rights* 9 (1) (Spring, 1980), and reprinted by permission of the Section of Individual Rights and Responsibilities of the American Bar Association. Mme René Cassin was so kind as to send the author a note of appreciation on the publication of the article.

that the universities and educators in general have become more fully aware of their task relative to human rights, thereby influencing the young to promote and guarantee such rights, a step will have been taken toward peace, and I will be able to step off the stage without regret, like a builder who has gotten the materials together and started to construct a refuge for mankind."[439]

Since Cassin's death, the Institute has operated with this same philosophy under the distinguished presidency of Edgar Faure, president of the French National Assembly.

No more appropriate city could have been chosen for the Institute's headquarters and summer teaching sessions than Strasbourg. Seat of the European Court of Human Rights, as well as of the Council of Europe (now including the largest elective parliamentary assembly in the world), Strasbourg has become a veritable capital of Europe and a center from which fundamental human rights law emanates.

Historically, perhaps no other major city has learned internationalism so deeply and so well. Founded by Roman legions as a military camp on the Rhine, Strasbourg became a mercantile and trade center in the middle ages (etymologically, "Strasbourg" means "crossroad city"). It was one of the so-called "free cities" of the Holy Roman Empire, meaning that, except for the direct supervision of the Emperor (who invariably had too much else on his mind to pay attention to its affairs), it could go its own way, independent of local territorial lords. The city became a refuge of the oppressed, such as Jews, and still boasts a large and active community of Jewish people.

Strasbourg was one of the chief cities of the Protestant Reformation, and the return to classical and biblical sources was typified there by the foundation of the University by the Reformers Calvin and Bucer. After the Thirty Years' War, the city became French. From 1870 to 1918 it was forced to submit to germanization by the Kaiser, in flagrant disregard of the desires and rights of its Alsatian citizenry. During the Second World War, Strasbourg was treated even more cruelly; many of its young men were deported to fight for the Third Reich on the Russian front.

The Strasbourger has thus learned his lessons in human rights in a long and hard school. An inheritor of two cultures, he is a born internationalist. Living in a city where whole sections such as the Petite France have changed imperceptibly since Calvin's time, with the Black Forest and the Vosges mountains offering a vista of eternal permanence, he takes—as did Alsatian Albert Schweitzer—the long view. Human rights need the best efforts of the present, founded on the most stable values of the past.

In line with René Cassin's educational objectives, the International Institute of Human Rights has devoted the month of July to human rights teaching for the past 10 years. Each summer, students, scholars and practitioners of law and related disciplines are invited, mainly by posters sent to law faculties throughout the world, to spend four weeks at the Institute's Study Session at the Faculty of Law of the University of Strasbourg. Costs are nominal, for the French government in effect subsidizes attendance by permitting registrants to live in the university dormitories and eat in the student cafeterias on the same basis as French nationals.

The pattern of the Study Sessions has remained essentially the same since the beginning. In the mornings, major lecture courses (what the French call "cours magistraux") are scheduled. The afternoons are devoted primarily to seminars on the case law of the European Convention on Human Rights, the Inter-American Commission on Human Rights, the UN system, and international humanitarian law.

The Institute publishes case books on the European and American systems (edited by H. Petzold of the European Court of Human Rights and T. McCarthy of the Division of Human Rights of the United Nations), and the seminars on humanitarian law are conducted by legal specialists from the International Committee of the Red Cross in Geneva (Veuthey, Gasser, Sandoz, *et al.*) An effort is made in the afternoon seminars to employ a bit of the American "case method," while the morning sessions follow the European instructional pattern of formal lectures by world-renowned authorities.

Each major professor generally gives a course consisting of five one-hour lectures, and—to make certain that the participants are able to interact with the lecturers—a free-for-all discussion hour is given as well. Lectures are grouped into weekly units with a theme for each week, so that students benefit from four different lecturers in the same general field each week: a total of at least 16 lecturers over the entire month.

Since 1970, the Institute's Study Sessions have thus exposed participants to the entire spectrum of the world's professorial and professional human rights community. The first (1970) session included René Cassin himself; A. C. Kiss, director of research at the French National Center for Scientific Research; Frank Newman, then on the faculty of Boalt Hall, now a judge of the California Supreme Court; and Professor Thomas Buergenthal, well known to American law students as the author (with Louis Sohn) of the most comprehensive casebook in any language on human rights law.

In the intervening years the same high standards have consistently prevailed, with a conscious effort to balance lecturers from north (Europe and North America) and south (Africa and South America), as well as the geographical and ideological east and west. In 1978, to take one example, Professor Mochvan of the Institute of State and Law in Moscow gave a major lecture series; Mochvan is distinguished as the first scholar in the U.S.S.R. to have published a general work on the law of human rights.

The 1979 Study Session fully maintained, and indeed extended, past tradition. For the first time, the number of registered participants exceeded the 200 mark. The weekly themes were, first, the "international dimensions of human rights" (a wide-angled effort to deal with larger, especially jurisprudential, issues); second, the American Convention on Human Rights (which entered into force less than a year previously, on July 18, 1978); third, the so-called "new" or "third generation" human rights (the right to peace, to development, environmental rights, etc.); and, lastly, human rights during armed conflicts and during periods of alleged "exception." Here is a sampling of the major professors who treated these themes:

- Professor Lung-chu Chen of the New York Law School, editor of *Human Rights:* "Human Rights and World Public Order." Dr. Chen offered insights into the application of the McDougal-Lasswell-Chen "policy-oriented" jurisprudence to the human rights field, drawing on their forthcoming work, *Human Rights and World Public Order: The Basic Policies of an International Law of Human Dignity* (Yale University Press, February, 1980).
- Z. Resich, dean of the School of Law at the University of Warsaw, Poland: "The International Protection of the Rights of the Child." Participants could hardly maintain, on the basis of these lectures, that the International Year of the Child is a Communist plot to undermine the family! Resich asserted, inter alia: "The most general need, aside from the organization of the school system, is that the state reinforce, protect and sustain the family, which still remains the primary and indispensable milieu for the education of children."
- T. McCarthy of the United Nations: "Transnational Corporations and Human Rights." McCarthy offered a sobering analysis of the ways in which not a few transnationals have contributed to human rights violations in developing and developed countries.
- T. Buergenthal of the University of Texas Law School: "The American Convention in Light of the European Convention on Human Rights." This trenchant comparative analysis was presented by the only American appointed to the bench of the Inter-American Court of Human Rights, an appointment which speaks eloquently of Buergenthal's personal stature, since the U.S. has still not ratified the American Convention.

The week devoted to "new" human rights elicited some valuable differences in emphasis. Karel Vasak, director of UNESCO's Division of Human Rights, had offered a strong apologia for a "third generation" of human rights in his inaugural lecture for the Tenth Study Session. Professor Jean Rivero of the University of Paris, however, warned the participants against "diluting" existing, recognized human rights by too readily stressing new rights having no legal remedies. This advice was not to be taken lightly, coming from the foremost French authority on "libertes publiques" (what we common lawyers would call "civil rights"). Concrete analyses of "new" human rights were, however, persuasively carried out by V. Kartashkin of the Institute of State and Law, Moscow (the right to peace, as embodied in the UN Covenants), and A. C. Kiss (environmental rights).

The final week, devoted primarily to humanitarian law, featured two spellbinders: trilingual Thomas Fleiner of the Swiss University of Fribourg's Law Faculty, discussing "The Application of Humanitarian Law to Conflicts Within a State," and Richard Baxter, professor at the Harvard Law School and judge of the International Court of Justice, treating what he rightly regarded as "human rights subjected to the greatest possible pressure": "Means and Methods of Combat in the Light of Recent Developments of International Humanitarian Law and of International Human Rights."

At the final ceremony of the Session, six two-time participants (among 12 candidates) received the Institute's coveted Diplôme in the International and Comparative Law of Human Rights, having passed, in French or English, gruelling written and oral examinations and having successfully argued the pros and cons of a case of admissibility actually presented to the European Commission on Human Rights.

Another major aspect of the Institute's summer program is the "CIFREDH," an acronym for the French equivalent of "International Training Center for Human Rights Teaching in Universities," which operates with the financial assistance of UNESCO. Participation is strictly limited to persons who already hold teaching posts, who will shortly enter on academic careers or who can otherwise justify their attendance by a recommendation from the dean of their law faculty. The object of the CIFREDH meetings (they are scheduled late each day to permit participants to attend the regular Study Session lectures and seminars as well) is to "teach teachers how to teach human rights." After the Study Session ends, a number of students in the CIFREDH are given the opportunity to spend the first two weeks of August as interns ("stagiaires") in European human rights organizations (the European Commission on Human Rights, UNESCO's Human Rights Division, the International Committee of the Red Cross, etc.).

The CIFREDH is under the direction of one of the foremost living authorities in the field: A. H. Robertson, professeur-associé at the University of Paris, secretary-general of the Institute, and author of such classics as *Human Rights in Europe*. Assisting Dr. Robertson was Jean-Bernard Marie, dynamic and prolific scholar on the staff of the National Center for Scientific Research. The tone of the CIFREDH is suggested by mentioning just one of its registrants in 1979: Dean Mehedi of the Faculty of Law of the University of Oran, Algeria, who obtained the Institute's Diplôme and introduced a proposal which will soon bring into existence an International Association of Human Rights Teachers.

Marc Agi, recent French biographer of René Cassin, takes pains to emphasize how concerned Cassin was to interrelate religion and human rights. At the 1970 meeting of the Decalogue Lawyers Society in Chicago, Cassin maintained that a direct and powerful relationship existed between the Ten Commandments and the Universal Declaration of Human Rights.[440]

Appropriately, therefore, in 1979, the first annual International Seminar in Theology and Law was organized by this author as an independent but coordinated program in conjunction with the regular Study Session of the International Institute of Human Rights. Some 30 students, including lawyers, clergy, and social workers enrolled in three courses tailor-made for them: "Law and Gospel: The Interrelations of Theology and Law"; "Legal Evidence and Ultimate Commitment"; and "The Theological Basis of Human Rights." The Seminar's motto—*John 1:17:* "The law was given through Moses; grace and truth came through Jesus Christ."

Out of the annual Study Sessions of the International Institute of Human Rights come opportunities and challenges for the U.S. attorney. The American attorney needs to gain an international perspective on human rights, instead of narrowly focusing on domestic U.S. civil rights. The legal profession in America is sadly balkanized, with attorneys often concerned only with the narrow jurisprudence of the state in which they are admitted to practice. With some exceptions, our human rights concerns seem hardly ever to rise above the level of national civil rights (except to flay nations which are our ideological opponents for their human rights violations!). The U.S. has the worst record of any major nation in the world today in the non-ratification of international human rights conventions.

One remedy might be for more American attorneys to think seriously about spending a July in Strasbourg, not only sampling some of the best cuisine known to gastronomy, but more especially developing a taste for human rights based on the only sound recipe: a supranational one whose essential ingredient is respect for the rule of law in general and for people wherever they live.

For information on enrolling in the International Institute of Human Rights Summer Study Session and conjoint programs, write:

Institut International des Droits de l'Homme
1, quai Lezay-Marnésia
67000 Strasbourg, France

(or)

The Simon Greenleaf School of Law
3855 E. LaPalma Avenue
Anaheim, CA 92807, U.S.A.

References

A herculean—and not entirely successful—effort has been made to restrict bibliographical citations to the most essential and accessible materials. Foreign language publications (especially French works) cannot be avoided, owing to the international nature of the human rights field.

[1] R. G. Frey, *Rights, Killing, and Suffering* (Oxford: Basil Blackwell, 1983), pp. 43–44.

[2] Puig Rosado, *72 dessins d'observation faits comme des rats* (Grenoble: Editions Jacques Glénat, 1975), cover illustration.

[3] *The [London] Times,* 13 November 1984. Far more serious was the Animal Liberation Front's scare tactic the weekend of November 17 (the claim to have poisoned Mars candy bars in the British Isles); David Mellor, Under Secretary of State, Home Office, spoke for many when he declared in the House of Commons: "It is a little hard to be lectured about animal rights by people who are plainly so contemptuous about human rights" (*The [London] Times,* 20 November 1984).

[4] John Aspinall, "Man's Place in Nature," in *Animals' Rights—A Symposium,* ed. David Peterson and Richard D. Ryder (London: Centaur, 1979), pp. 20–21. The book is "a record of the proceedings of the Symposium held under the auspices of the R.S.P.C.A. at Trinity College, Cambridge, on the Ethical Aspects of Man's Relationships with Animals, 18th and 19th August, 1977"; Aspinall's speech was "spontaneous."

[5] Michel Villey, *Le droit et les droits de l'homme* (Paris: Presses Universitaires de France, 1983), pp. 136–53.

[6] T. Robert Ingram, *What's Wrong with Human Rights* (Houston: St. Thomas, 1978).

[7] John W. Whitehead, *The Second American Revolution* (Elgin, Ill.: David C. Cook, 1982), p. 116. For my review of this book, see *Simon Greenleaf Law Review* 2 (1982–83): 156–58.

[8] Marc Lienhard, "Protestantism and Human Rights," *Human Rights Teaching* [UNESCO] 2:1 (1981): 31. This journal is published in a French language edition as well, and the French text of Lienhard's important article also appears in *Christianisme et droits de l'homme,* ed. Emmanuel Hirsch (Paris: Librairie des Libertés, 1984).

[9] Robert H. Jackson, "Closing Address in the Nuremberg Trial," in *Proceedings in the Trial of the Major War Criminals Before the International Military Tribunal* 19 (1948): 397.

[10] A. H. Robertson, "The European Convention on Human Rights," in *The International Protection of Human Rights,* ed. Evan Luard (London: Thames and Hudson, 1967), pp. 99–100.

[11] John Warwick Montgomery, "The Marxist Approach to Human Rights: Analysis & Critique," *Simon Greenleaf Law Review* 3 (1983–84): 106–19.

[12] See, for example, John Dugard, "Using the Law to Pervert Justice," *Human Rights* [American Bar Association] 11:2 (Summer 1983): 22–25, 50–54; and his book, *Human Rights and the South African Legal Order* (1978); also, Odette Guitard, *L'Apartheid* (Paris: Presses Universitaires de France, 1983). At the 10 December 1984, White House Human Rights Day ceremony, President Reagan called South African apartheid "repugnant" and signed a proclamation that included South Africa among countries whose human rights policies are "affronts to the human conscience."

[13] *Case Studies on Human Rights and Fundamental Freedoms: A World Survey,* ed. Willem A. Veenhoven, 5 vols. (The Hague: Martinus Nijhoff, 1975–76).

[14] *Torture in the Eighties* (New York: Amnesty International, 1984).

[15] Joel Feinberg, "Duties, Rights and Claims," *American Philosophical Quarterly* 3:2 (1966): 8.

[16] Richard Pierre Claude, Review of *The International Dimensions of Human Rights* ed. Karel Vasak, *Human Rights Quarterly* 5:4 (November 1983): 536.

[17] The most helpful general documentary surveys of the entire field in English and in French are: *The International Dimensions of Human Rights,* ed. Karel Vasak (Paris: UNESCO, 1979 [also available in a French edition], English rev. ed. by Philip Alston, 1982); Maurice Torrelli and Renée Baudouin, *Les droits de l'homme et les libertés publiques* (Montréal: Les Presses de l'Université du Québec, 1972); *Basic Documents on Human Rights,* ed. Ian Brownlie, 2d ed. (Oxford: Clarendon, 1981); *The Human Rights Reader,* ed. Walter Laqueur and Barry Rubin (New York: New American Library Meridian Books, 1979); *Teaching Human Rights,* ed. Julian R. Friedman and Laurie S. Wiseberg (Washington, D.C.: Human Rights Internet, 1981). In Spanish, the indispensable work is José Castán Tobeñas, *Los derechos del hombre,* ed. Luisa Marín Castán, 3d ed. (Madrid: Reus, 1985).

[18] Cf. John Warwick Montgomery, *The Shape of the Past,* rev. ed. (Minneapolis: Bethany, 1975), pp. 77–78, 149.

[19] Signed by 159 nations and organizations by the deadline date for signature (11 December 1984). The United States, the United Kingdom, and West Germany did not sign it. To enter into force, the Treaty must be ratified by sixty signatories (fourteen have ratified to date).

[20] Responsible literature on "third-generation" rights includes: W. Paul Gormley, *Human Rights and Environment: The Need for International Cooperation* (Leyden, Netherlands: A. W. Sijthoff, 1976); Jean-François Guilhaudis, *Le droit des peuples à disposer d'eux-mêmes* (Grenoble: Presses Universitaires de Grenoble, 1976); International Commission of Jurists, *Development, Human Rights and the Rule of Law* (Oxford and New York: Pergamon, 1981); Mario Bettati, *Le nouvel ordre économique international* (Paris: Presses Universitaires de France, 1983).

[21] See, e.g., Jean Rivero, "Le problème des 'nouveaux' droits de l'homme," *Résumés des Cours*[10] (Strasbourg, France: International Institute of Human Rights, 1979).

[22] Donne, incidentally, served as a clergyman to lawyers (barristers) before he became dean of St. Paul's: he was preacher to the Honourable Society of Lincoln's Inn from 1616 to 1622, and in 1623 preached the dedication sermon for the Lincoln's Inn Chapel, where the bell is still tolled on the death of Masters of the Bench of that learned society.

[23] René Cassin, "From the Ten Commandments to the Rights of Man," in *Of Law and Man: Essays in Honor of Haim H. Cohn*, ed. Shlomo Shoham (New York and Tel Aviv: Sabra Books, 1971), pp. 13–25. For the text of the Universal Declaration, see appendix 1. Johannes Morsink certainly goes too far in maintaining that "the U.N. representatives . . . replace eighteenth-century deism with a twentieth-century secular humanism" ("The Philosophy of the Universal Declaration," *Human Rights Quarterly* 6 [3] [August 1984]: 333-34). The absence of reference in the Declaration to "nature and nature's God" is hardly the equivalent of "turning down any suggestion of a normative source transcendent to human nature." The Commission of Human Rights, which drafted the Declaration (chiefly drawing on Cassin's labors) and the Third Committee which revised it (one of its most influential members was Lebanese Christian Charles Malik) avoided for political and pragmatic reasons the question of the ultimate origin of human rights—leaving each signatory and reader to supply the lacuna (hopefully with transcendence, as Cassin and Malik surely did).

[24] John P. Humphrey, "The Universal Declaration of Human Rights: Its History, Impact and Juridical Character," in *Human Rights: Thirty Years After the Universal Declaration,* ed. B. G. Ramcharan (The Hague, Netherlands: Martinus Nijhoff, 1979), p. 37.

[25] See Evan Luard, "Promotion of Human Rights by UN Political Bodies," in *International Protection of Human Rights* (op. cit. in n. 10 above), pp. 132–59.

[26] See appendix 4 ("Ratifications of Selected Human Rights Instruments").

[27] Louis B. Sohn, "Human Rights: Their Implementation and Supervision by the United Nations," in *Human Rights in International Law: Legal and Policy Issues,* vol. 2, ed. Theodor Meron (Oxford: Clarendon, 1984), p. 391. See also Marc J. Bossuyt, "Recent Developments in the United Nations Human Rights Procedures," *Recueil des Cours* 16 (Strasbourg, France: International Institute of Human Rights, 1985).

[28] Cf. Dana D. Fischer, "International Reporting Procedures," in *Guide to International Human Rights Practice,* ed. Hurst Hannum (London: Macmillan, 1984), pp. 165–85.

[29] See the excellent survey by Theo C. Van Boven, "Protection of Human Rights through the United Nations System," ibid., pp. 46–56.

[30] Sohn, op. cit. (in n. 27 above), p. 386.

[31] See appendix 4 ("Ratifications of Selected Human Rights Instruments"). For the reasons behind and rationalizations for nonratification, see Louis Henkin, "International Human Rights and Rights in the United States," in Meron (op. cit. in n. 27 above), 1:50–55. Ratification of the Genocide treaty on 19 February 1986 was due chiefly to the efforts of Senator Proxmire; unhappily, emasculating provisos, designed by those of a more nationalistic bent, greatly

marred the victory—e.g., that the submission of any treaty dispute involving the U.S. to the World Court will necessitate the prior consent of the U.S. government, and that extradition is mandatory only if the act concerned is a criminal offense under the laws of both the United States and the nation requesting extradition.

32 The reporting system of the (admittedly politicized) Committee on the Elimination of Racial Discrimination has been much strengthened by the procedural innovation of 1972, originally proposed by the Committee's distinguished, long-time member Prof. Dr. Karl Josef Partsch, providing for the presence and questioning of a state's representative when the Committee considers that state's report: Karl Josef Partsch, "The United Nations Committee for the Elimination of Racial Discrimination: Structure and Working Methods," unpublished lecture delivered 29 March 1985 at the Simon Greenleaf School of Law, Orange, California. On fact-finding in general, see *International Law and Fact-Finding in the Field of Human Rights,* ed. B. G. Ramcharan (The Hague, Netherlands: Martinus Nijhoff, 1982).

33 The Secretary-General of the UN has also accomplished much through the exercise of good offices: B. G. Ramcharan, *Humanitarian Good Offices in International Law: The Good Offices of the United Nations Secretary-General in the Field of Human Rights* (The Hague, Netherlands: Martinus Nijhoff, 1983).

34 Stephen Marks, "The Complaint Procedure of the United Nations Educational, Scientific and Cultural Organization (UNESCO)," in Hannum (op. cit. in n. 28 above), p. 105.

35 Francis Wolf, "Human Rights and the International Labour Organisation," in Meron, *Human Rights in International Law* (op. cit. in n. 27 above), 2:286n.48. See also Lee Swepston, "Human Rights Complaint Procedures of the International Labor Organization," in Hannum (op. cit. in n. 28 above), pp. 74–93.

36 For Hartling's background and philosophy of life, see Alfred E. Pedersen, "Hartling Talks about Refugees," *Scanorama* [SAS], March 1982, pp. 37–41.

37 David Carliner, "Domestic and International Protection of Refugees," in Hannum (op. cit. in n. 28 above), p. 248. See also Gilbert Jaeger, "Status and International Protection of Refugees," *Résumés des Cours* 9 (Strasbourg, France: International Institute of Human Rights, 1978); Guy S. Goodwin-Gill, *The Refugee in International Law* (Oxford: Clarendon, 1983); and Richard B. Lillich, *The Human Rights of Aliens in Contemporary International Law* (Manchester: Manchester University Press, 1985).

38 See Montgomery, "Marxist Approach to Human Rights" (op. cit. in n. 11 above), *passim*.

39 Cf. William Korey, "Human Rights at the U.N.: Illusion and Reality," in Shoham (op. cit. in n. 23 above), pp. 27–45.

40 For the text of the European Convention's articles detailing substantive rights, see appendix 2.

[41] See Rosalyn Higgins, "Damages for Violation of One's Human Rights," in *Explorations in Ethics and International Relations,* ed. Nicholas A. Sims (London: Croom Helm, 1981), pp. 45–67.

[42] This chart appears in *What Is the Council of Europe Doing to Protect Human Rights?* (Strasbourg: Council of Europe, 1977), p. 29. The two most useful book-length treatments of the European system of human rights protection are A. H. Robertson, *Human Rights in Europe,* 2d ed. (Manchester: Manchester University Press, 1977), and Francis G. Jacobs, *The European Convention on Human Rights* (Oxford: Clarendon, 1975).

[43] [1979] Yearbook of the European Convention on Human Rights 402 (European Court of Human Rights).

[44] To avoid a judgment against them by the European Court of Human Rights, the Greek colonels' junta denounced the Convention on 12 December 1969. After the restoration of democracy, Greece ratified the Convention again on 28 November 1974.

[45] See M. Evans, "The European Social Charter," in *Fundamental Rights,* ed. J. W. Bridge, D. Lasok, et al. (London: Sweet & Maxwell, 1973), pp. 278–90.

[46] Leading cases are *Stauder v. City of Ulm,* 29/69 [1969] ECR 419, [1970] CMLR 112; *Nold v. Commission,* 4/73 [1974] ECR 491, [1974] 2 CMLR 338; and *Rutili v. Minister for the Interior,* 36/75 [1975] ECR 1219, [1976] 1 CMLR 140. Even if T. C. Hartley is correct that expediency rather than principle infuses these cases, it is still of great importance that the Luxembourg Court declared that fundamental human rights are part of the "general principles of law" of the Communities; see Hartley, *The Foundations of European Community Law* (Oxford: Clarendon, 1981), pp. 122–28. Cf. L. Neville Brown and Francis G. Jacobs, *The Court of Justice of the European Communities* (London: Sweet & Maxwell, 1977), pp. 223–28, and D. Lasok and J. W. Bridge, *An Introduction to the Law and Institutions of the European Communities*, 3d ed. (London: Butterworths, 1982), pp. 139–42.

[47] See *Costa v. ENEL*, 6/64 [1964] ECR 585, [1964] CMLR 425, and cf. Lawrence Collins, *European Community Law in the United Kingdom,* 2d ed. (London: Butterworths, 1980), pp. 1–6.

[48] On Marxist views, see Montgomery, "Marxist Approach to Human Rights" (op. cit. in n. 11 above), pp. 92, 166. Newman's evaluation appears under the title, "The Convention and World-Wide Human Rights: Some Iconoclastic Inquiries," in *Privacy and Human Rights,* ed. A. H. Robertson (Manchester: Manchester University Press, 1973), pp. 413–24. On problems of admissibility in general, see Laurids Mikaelsen, *European Protection of Human Rights: The Practice and Procedure of the European Commission of Human Rights on the Admissibility of Applications from Individuals and States* (Alphen aan den Rijn, Netherlands: Sijthoff & Noordhoff, 1980).

[49] "In 1969, I wrote in *The Late Great Planet Earth* that I, along with many other Bible students, believed that the European Economic Community (EEC or "Common Market") was the beginning of the revised form of the Roman Empire predicted in the Bible. . . . The 'anti-Christ' will drive the 10-nation confederacy [sic.] to its place as the world's greatest power"—Hal Lindsey,

The 1980's: Countdown to Armageddon (New York: Bantam, 1982), pp. 103–5.

[50] Robertson, *Human Rights in Europe* (op. cit. in n. 42 above), p. 278.

[51] Robert E. Norris, "The Individual Petition Procedure of the Inter-American System for the Protection of Human Rights," in Hannum (op. cit. in n. 28 above), pp. 108–9.

[52] Thomas Buergenthal, "The Revised OAS Charter and the Protection of Human Rights," *American Journal of International Law* 69 (1975): 832.

[53] For the list of ratifications, see appendix 4.

[54] The texts of both (excluding purely procedural articles of the American Convention) are reproduced in appendix 3.

[55] Montgomery, "Marxist Approach to Human Rights" (op. cit. in n. 11 above), pp. 100–101, 149.

[56] John Warwick Montgomery, *Slaughter of the Innocents: Abortion, Birth Control and Divorce in Light of Science, Law and Theology* (Westchester, Ill.: Crossway, 1981), pp. 118–19; see also John Warwick Montgomery, "The Rights of Unborn Children," *Simon Greenleaf Law Review* 5 (1985–86).

[57] See Thomas Buergenthal, "The Inter-American Court of Human Rights," *American Journal of International Law* 76 (1982): 231.

[58] Thomas Buergenthal, "The Inter-American System for the Protection of Human Rights," in Meron (op. cit. in n. 27 above), 2:487.

[59] Cf. the final chapter, on "The Effectiveness of the Inter-American System," in *Protecting Human Rights in the Americas: Selected Problems*, ed. Thomas Buergenthal, Robert Norris, and Dinah Shelton (Kehl, West Germany: N. P. Engel Publisher, 1982), pp. 230–69.

[60] Richard Gittleman, "The African Commission on Human and Peoples' Rights: Prospects and Procedures," in Hannum (op. cit. in n. 28 above), p. 161.

[61] Ibid., p. 154.

[62] *Human Rights Quarterly* 5:4 (November 1983): 467–90.

[63] Henkin, op. cit. (in n. 31 above), p. 45. By far the most important domestic U.S. human rights instrument is the Bill of Rights (Amendments I–X to the federal Constitution); on it, see especially *The Great Rights,* ed. Edmond Cahn (New York: Macmillan, 1963), and Bernard Schwartz, *The Great Rights of Mankind: A History of the American Bill of Rights* (New York: Oxford University Press, 1977).

[64] Robert E. Jonas and John D. Gorby, "West German Abortion Decision: A Contrast to *Roe* v. *Wade*—with Commentaries," *John Marshall Journal of Practice & Procedure* 9 (1976): 551–695; Harold O. J. Brown, "Abortion: Rights or Technicalities? A Comparison of *Roe* v. *Wade* with the Abortion Decision of the German Federal Constitutional Court," *Human Life Review,* Summer 1975, pp. 60–85; D. P. Kommers, "Abortion and Constitution: United States and West Germany," *American Journal of Comparative Law* 25 (1977): 255–85. See also the citations in n. 56 above.

[65] See Janet LaRue, "Abortion: Justice Harry A. Blackmun and the *Roe* v. *Wade* Decision," *Simon Greenleaf Law Review* 2 (1982–83): 122–45.

66 Montgomery, "Marxist Approach to Human Rights" (op. cit. in n. 11 above), especially pp. 99ff. Cf. Louis Henkin, *The Rights of Man Today* (London: Stevens, 1979), pp. 55–88.

67 See John C. H. Wu, *Fountain of Justice* (London: Sheed and Ward, 1959), pp. 63–70; and *Jurisprudence: A Book of Readings,* ed. John Warwick Montgomery (Strasbourg, France: International Scholarly Publishers; Orange, Calif.: Simon Greenleaf School of Law, 1980), pp. 277–85, 331–38.

68 See Kenneth Roberts-Wray, *Commonwealth and Colonial Law* (London: Stevens, 1966), especially the Foreword by Lord Denning. The 1982 Canadian Charter of Rights and Freedoms, which begins with the great line, "Canada is founded upon principles that recognize the supremacy of God and the rule of law," is a further testimony to the continuing influence of the unwritten English Constitution on human rights in the Commonwealth. Cf. Walter S. Tarnopolsky, "The New Canadian Charter of Rights and Freedoms As Compared and Contrasted with the American Bill of Rights," *Human Rights Quarterly* 5:3 (August 1983): 227–74.

69 Leading advocates are: Lord Scarman in his 1974 Hamlyn lectures (*English Law—The New Dimension*), Professor Wade in his Hamlyn lectures of 1980, and Lord Chancellor Hailsham in his *Elective Dictatorship* (1976), *The Dilemma of Democracy* (1978), and his Hamlyn lectures of 1983. Cf. *Do We Need a Bill of Rights?* ed. Colin M. Campbell (London: Temple Smith, 1980). On Lord Hailsham's Christian world-view, see *Simon Greenleaf Law Review* 4 (1984–85).

70 See Hans-Peter Gasser, "Introduction to Humanitarian Law," *Résumés des Cours* 14 (Strasbourg, France: International Institute of Human Rights, 1983).

71 Reprinted from the *International Review of the Red Cross,* September–October 1978, p. 247. See also Jean Pictet, *The Principles of International Humanitarian Law* (Geneva: International Committee of the Red Cross, n.d.)—originally published as a series of articles in the *International Review of the Red Cross,* September, October, and November 1966.

72 Yoram Dinstein, "Human Rights in Armed Conflict: International Humanitarian Law," in Meron (op. cit. in n. 27 above), 2:360. See also *Documents on the Laws of War,* ed. Adam Roberts and Richard Guelff (Oxford: Clarendon, 1982), especially pp. 391ff.

73 For an excellent survey, see Jonathan Power, *Amnesty International: The Human Rights Story* (New York: McGraw-Hill, 1981).

74 "Warsaw 14 Set Up New Rights Group," *The [London] Times,* 13 November 1984. On NGO's in general, see David Weissbrodt, "The Contribution of International Nongovernmental Organizations to the Protection of Human Rights," in Meron (op. cit. in n. 27 above), 2:403–38.

75 See the biannual *Review* and the quarterly *Newsletter* of the International Commission of Jurists.

76 Jean-Yves Calvez, *Droits de l'homme, justice, évangile* (Paris: Le Centurion, 1985); Michel Simon, *Les droits de l'homme: guide d'informations et de réflexion* (Lyon: Chronique Sociale, 1985); René Coste, *L'Eglise et les droits de l'homme* (Tournai, Belgium: Desclée, 1983); John Langan, "Human Rights in Roman Catholicism," *Journal of Ecumenical Studies* 19:3 (Summer

1982); 25–39; Michel Schooyans, "Catholicism and Human Rights," *Human Rights Teaching* [UNESCO] 2:1 (1981): 20–24 (this journal is published in a French language edition as well, and the French text of Schooyans's article also appears in Hirsch [op. cit. in n. 8 above]).

77 Otfried Höffe, et al., *Jean Paul II et les droits de l'homme* (Fribourg, Switzerland: Editions Universitaires Fribourg, 1980); and Philippe-I. André-Vincent, *Les droits de l'homme dans l'enseignement de Jean Paul II* (Paris: Librairie Générale de Droit et de Jurisprudence, 1983).

78 See Lienhard, op. cit. (in n. 8 above), pp. 27–30. Examples are: *How Christian Are Human Rights? Report on an Interconfessional Consultation, Geneva, April 30–May 3, 1980,* ed. Eckehart Lorenz (Geneva: Lutheran World Federation, 1981), with excellent bibliography (also available in German); *A Christian Declaration on Human Rights: Theological Studies of the World Alliance of Reformed Churches,* ed. Allen O. Miller (Grand Rapids: Eerdmans, 1977); *Church and Nation: Theological Conference Papers* (Grand Rapids: Reformed Ecumenical Synod, 1981); *RES Testimony on Human Rights* (Grand Rapids: Reformed Ecumenical Synod, 1983). See also Gordon Spykman's annotated "Human Rights: A Selective Bibliography," *Transformation* 1:3 July–September 1984): 16–18. (My personal thanks to Professor Spykman for his courtesy and kindness in putting a number of valuable publications at my disposal.)

79 See John Warwick Montgomery, *The Shaping of America* (Minneapolis: Bethany, 1976), *passim*; and John Warwick Montgomery, "Evangelical Social Responsibility in Theological Perspective," in *Our Society in Turmoil*, ed. Gary R. Collins (Carol Stream, Ill.: Creation House, 1970), pp. 11–23, 281–82.

80 Guy Aurenche (former president of ACAT), *L'Aujourd'hui des droits de l'homme*, new ed. (Paris: Nouvelle Cité, 1980); also Francis Schaeffer, "Christian Faith and Human Rights," *Simon Greenleaf Law Review* 2 (1982–83): 3–12; John Stott, "Human Rights," in his *Issues Facing Christians Today* (Basingstoke, Hants, England: Marshall, Morgan & Scott, 1984), pp. 139–52; also, the citations in n. 56 above. Mention should be made of two Canadian Calvinist organizations (the Institute of Christian Studies and the Christian Labour Association of Canada) which, though not engaged primarily in human rights activity, have produced useful position papers and essays in the field, such as: Paul Marshall, *Human Rights Theories in Christian Perspective* (Toronto: Institute for Christian Studies, 1983); Paul Marshall and Ed Vanderkloet, *Foundations of Human Rights* (Rexdale, Ontario: Christian Labour Association of Canada, 1981); Richard Forbes, *Humanism & Human Rights: A Christian View* (Rexdale, Ontario: Christian Labour Association of Canada, 1968).

81 M. C. Bassiouni, "The 'Human Rights Program': The Veneer of Civilization Thickens," *DePaul Law Review* 21:2 (Winter 1971): 271–85.

82 Eberhard Welty, *A Handbook of Christian Social Ethics,* vol. 1, trans. G. Kirstein and J. Fitzsimons (Freiburg, West Germany: Herder; Edinburgh-London: Nelson, 1960), pp. 267–68.

[83] Alan S. Rosenbaum, "Introduction: The Editor's Perspectives on the Philosophy of Human Rights," in his *The Philosophy of Human Rights: International Perspectives* (Westport, Conn.: Greenwood, 1980), p. 24.

[84] Felix S. Cohen, *The Legal Conscience: Selected Papers,* ed. Lucy Kramer Cohen (New Haven, Conn.: Yale University Press, 1960), p. 172. Cohen's essay, "Human Rights: An Appeal to Philosophers," appeared originally in *The Review of Metaphysics* 6 (June 1953): 617–22.

[85] Alan R. White, *Rights* (Oxford: Clarendon, 1984), pp. 2, 173.

[86] Henry D. Aiken, "Rights, Human and Otherwise," *The Monist* 52:4 (October 1968): 515.

[87] Albert Ellis, "Rational-Emotive Therapy," in *Four Psychotherapies,* ed. Leonard Hersher (New York: Appleton-Century-Crofts, 1970), pp. 47–83; Albert Ellis, *Humanistic Psychotherapy: The Rational-Emotive Approach* (New York: McGraw-Hill, 1974).

[88] Cohen, *loc. cit.* (in n. 84 above).

[89] Joel Feinberg, "The Nature and Value of Rights," in *Rights, Justice and the Bounds of Liberty* (Princeton, N.J.: Princeton University Press, 1980), p. 153. Feinberg's essay earlier appeared in *The Journal of Value Inquiry* 14 (1970): 243–57.

[90] M. D. A. Freeman, *The Rights and Wrongs of Children* (London, England, and Dover, N.H.: Frances Pinter, 1983), p. 37.

[91] White, op. cit. (in n. 85 above), pp. 105–6.

[92] Rosenbaum, op. cit. (in n. 83 above), p. 27.

[93] Wesley N. Hohfeld, "Some Fundamental Legal Conceptions As Applied in Judicial Reasoning," *Yale Law Journal* 23:1 (November 1913): 30. This seminal essay was posthumously reprinted in Hohfeld's collected papers under the title, *Fundamental Legal Conceptions* (1919). For an excellent discussion of Hohfeldian analysis, see J. W. Harris, *Legal Philosophies* (London: Butterworths, 1980), pp. 76–86. Lawrence C. Becker makes an interesting attempt to extend Hohfeld's method in his essay, "Three Types of Rights," *Georgia Law Review* 13:4 (Summer 1979): 1197–1220.

[94] Jerome J. Shestack, "The Jurisprudence of Human Rights," in Meron (op. cit. in n. 27 above), 1:72.

[95] Vilhelm Aubert, *In Search of Law: Sociological Approaches to Law* (Oxford: Martin Robertson, 1983), p. 170. Aubert's entire chapter on "Human Rights and the Promotional Function of Law" bears on the comparative meaning and significance of first- and second-generation rights (pp. 152–73). The author is professor of sociology at the University of Oslo.

[96] Maurice Cranston, "Human Rights, Real and Supposed," in *Political Theory and the Rights of Man,* ed. D. D. Raphael (London: Macmillan, 1967), pp. 96ff. See also Cranston's *What Are Human Rights?* (London: Bodley Head, 1973), especially chap. 8.

[97] Robert Nozick, *Anarchy, State, and Utopia* (Oxford: Basil Blackwell, 1974), pp. 149ff.; and cf. his discussion of rights in his *Philosophical Explanations* (Oxford: Clarendon, 1984), pp. 498–504. On Nozick, see the critical reviews of *Anarchy, State, and Utopia* by Thomas Nagel (*Yale Law Journal* 85:1 [November 1975]: 136–49) and by Michael Teitelman (*Columbia Law Review*

77 [1977]: 495–509); Shestack, op. cit. (in n. 94 above), pp. 94–95; and *Reading Nozick: Essays on "Anarchy, State, and Utopia,"* ed. Jeffrey Paul (Oxford: Basil Blackwell, 1982).

[98] Antony Flew, "What Is a Right?" *Georgia Law Review* 13:4 (Summer 1979): 1134–41. Cf. Flew's credo in *What I Believe: 13 Eminent People of Our Time Argue for Their Philosophy of Life,* ed. Mark Booth (New York: Crossroad; London: Waterstone, 1984), pp. 29–38.

[99] R. S. Downie, "Social Equality," in *The Philosophy of Human Rights: International Perspectives,* ed. Rosenbaum (op. cit. in n. 83 above), pp. 127–35; cf. also Downie's *Roles and Values: An Introduction to Social Ethics* (London: Methuen, 1971), p. 49. For Richard Wasserstrom's position, see his "Rights, Human Rights, and Racial Discrimination," in *Human Rights,* ed. A. I. Melden (Belmont, Calif.: Wadsworth, 1970), pp. 96–101; this essay originally appeared in *The Journal of Philosophy* 61 (1964): 628–41.

[100] Alan Gewirth, "The Basis and Content of Human Rights," in his *Human Rights: Essays on Justification and Applications* (Chicago: University of Chicago Press, 1982), pp. 64ff.; and cf. his *Reason and Morality* (Chicago: University of Chicago Press, 1978), *passim.*

[101] David Watson, "Welfare Rights and Human Rights," *Journal of Social Policy* 6:1 (1977): 31–46.

[102] Rosenbaum, op. cit. (in n. 83 above), pp. 30–31.

[103] Freeman, op. cit. (in n. 90 above), p. 38.

[104] White, op. cit. (in n. 85 above), p. 172.

[105] H. L. A. Hart, "Bentham," *Proceedings of the British Academy* 48 (1962): 297, 315. Cf. his fundamental essay, "Are There Any Natural Rights?" *Philosophical Review* 64:2 (April 1955): 175–91.

[106] White, op. cit. (in n. 85 above), p. 107.

[107] Ibid., p. 108.

[108] Flew, op. cit. (in n. 98 above), p. 1133.

[109] Martin P. Golding, "Towards a Theory of Human Rights," *The Monist* 52:4 (October 1968): 548–49.

[110] White, op. cit. (in n. 85 above), pp. 128–29, 132.

[111] Neil MacCormick, "Children's Rights: A Test-case for Theories of Right," in his *Legal Right and Social Democracy* (Oxford: Clarendon, 1982), pp. 154–66. On fetal rights and interest theory, see Montgomery, "The Rights of Unborn Children," *loc. cit.* (in n. 56 above).

[112] Christopher Stone, *Should Trees Have Standing? Toward Legal Rights for Natural Objects* (New York: Avon, 1975), especially chap. 2.

[113] Frey, op. cit. (in n. 1 above), p. 143.

[114] Ibid., p. 144.

[115] Ibid., pp. 150–51. Frey's already powerful argument could have been much strengthened had he substituted French Citroën automobiles in his illustration.

[116] Michael Tooley, *Abortion and Infanticide* (Oxford: Clarendon, 1983), p. 419. For a detailed review of this work, see *Simon Greenleaf Law Review* 5 (1985–86).

[117] A. I. Melden, *Rights and Persons* (Berkeley and Los Angeles: University of California Press, 1980), p. 192. See also his *Rights and Right Conduct* (Oxford: Basil Blackwell, 1959).

[118] Geoffrey Marshall, "Rights, Options, and Entitlements," in *Oxford Essays in Jurisprudence*, 2d ser., ed. A. W. B. Simpson (Oxford: Clarendon, 1973), p. 228.

[119] Melden, *Rights and Persons* (op. cit. in n. 117 above), p. 185. To be sure, Melden is here arguing against any simple derivation of human rights from the will of God; Antony Flew characteristically argues in the same vein (op. cit. [in n. 98 above], pp. 1118–20). We shall return to the point in chap. 5.

[120] White, op. cit. (in n. 85 above), pp. 173–74.

[121] Ibid., p. 93.

[122] See, for example, Ruth Benedict's *Patterns of Culture*. Not so incidentally, the scientific objectivity of Ruth Benedict's early work, upon which her reputation was established, has been thoroughly undermined by the publication of Judith S. Modell's *Ruth Benedict: Patterns of a Life* (Philadelphia: University of Pennsylvania Press, 1983). On nineteenth-century secularization as a phenomenon in the history of ideas, see Montgomery, *The Shaping of America* (op. cit. in n. 79 above), pp. 69–87.

[123] Though attempts are frequently made to distinguish legal positivism from legal realism, we use the two terms synonymously. "Realism" is the more common expression for this school of thought in common-law countries (England, America, etc.), "positivism" in civil-law areas (the European continent especially). Professor Summers designates the position of Austin, Hart, and Kelsen as "analytical positivism," while using the expression "American pragmatic instrumentalism" for the views of John Chipman Gray and Oliver Wendell Holmes, Jr., and includes in the latter category (with indifferent success, in my opinion) Roscoe Pound, Jerome Frank, Karl Llewellyn, and Felix Cohen (Robert Samuel Summers, *Instrumentalism and American Legal Theory* [Ithaca, N.Y.: Cornell University Press, 1982], pp. 22–25).

[124] Jeremy Bentham, *A Comment on the Commentaries: A Criticism of William Blackstone's Commentaries on the Laws of England,* ed. Charles Warren Everett (Oxford: Clarendon, 1928).

[125] These memorable phrases appear in Bentham's *Anarchical Fallacies:* see the older standard edition of his *Works,* vol. 2, ed. John Bowring (Edinburgh, 1838–43), pp. 501–2. Cf. Professor Twining's "The Contemporary Significance of Bentham's Anarchical Fallacies," *Archiv für Rechts- und Sozialphilosophie* 41 (1975): 315; and the essays on utilitarianism and human rights by John Gray, Allan Gibbard, and James Fishkin in *Human Rights,* ed. Ellen Frankel Paul, Jeffrey Paul, and Fred D. Miller, Jr. (Oxford: Basil Blackwell, 1984), pp. 73–107.

[126] See H. L. A. Hart, "Natural Rights: Bentham and John Stuart Mill," in Hart's *Essays on Bentham: Studies in Jurisprudence and Political Theory* (Oxford: Clarendon, 1982), pp. 79–104. Hart has been much involved in the production of the new University of London-Athlone Press edition of *The Collected Works of Jeremy Bentham* (1968 to date).

[127] Hart has presented his philosophy of law systematically in *The Concept of Law* (Oxford: Clarendon, 1961). Harris, (op. cit. [in n. 93 above], pp. 105–14) offers a helpful interpretation of Hart's ideas, with good bibliography.

[128] Hart, "Are There Any Natural Rights?" (op. cit. in n. 105 above).

[129] Rosenbaum, op. cit. (in n. 83 above), p. 33.

[130] Hart, *Concept of Law* (op. cit. in n. 127 above), pp. 105–6.

[131] Hans Kelsen, *The Law of the United Nations* (London: Stevens; New York: Praeger, 1951).

[132] Kelsen's philosophy of law is set forth in such works as his *General Theory of Law and State* (1945), *What Is Justice?* (1957), and *The Pure Theory of Law* (rev. ed., 1960). For a useful overview of his thought, see Harris, op. cit. (in n. 93 above), pp. 59–75.

[133] Lecture delivered by Hans Kelsen at the University of California, 20 November 1962 (tape at Boalt Hall Library); cf. R. G. Decker, "The Secularization of Anglo-American Law: 1800–1970," *Thought* 49 (1974): 292–93.

[134] Ronald Dworkin, *Taking Rights Seriously* (London: Duckworth, 1977), pp. 22–25.

[135] Ibid., p. 29. Harris (op. cit. [in n. 93 above], pp. 172–92) surveys Dworkin's position and provides secondary bibliography.

[136] Dworkin, op. cit. (in n. 134 above), p. xii.

[137] On the miseries of presuppositionalism, philosophical and theological, see John Warwick Montgomery, *Faith Founded on Fact* (Nashville and New York: Thomas Nelson, 1978), especially pp. 107–27.

[138] Frey, op. cit. (in n. 1 above), p. 55. Hart has severely criticized Dworkin's rights thesis—along with Robert Nozick's—in his essay, "Between Utility and Rights," *Columbia Law Review* 79 (1979): 828–46; this essay is reprinted in *The Idea of Freedom,* ed. A. Ryan (Oxford: Clarendon, 1979). For Neil MacCormick's objections to Dworkin's philosophy of human rights, see MacCormick, op. cit. (in n. 111 above), pp. 126–53. The best collection of critical opinion on Dworkin's views (it includes the Hart and MacCormick critiques just cited, together with many others and a fifty-three-page reply by Dworkin) is *Ronald Dworkin and Contemporary Jurisprudence,* ed. Marshall Cohen (London: Duckworth, 1984).

[139] Ch. Perelman, "Can the Rights of Man Be Founded?" in *The Philosophy of Human Rights,* ed. Rosenbaum (op. cit. in n. 83 above), p. 47. See also M. J. Detmold, *The Unity of Law and Morality: A Refutation of Legal Positivism* (London: Routledge & Kegan Paul, 1984), *passim.*

[140] Cf. C. G. Haines, *The Revival of Natural Law Concepts* (Cambridge: Harvard University Press, 1958).

[141] John Finnis, *Natural Law and Natural Rights* (Oxford: Clarendon, 1980), p. 3. Finnis's list of human goods is based upon Germain Grisez, "The First Principle of Practical Reason," *Natural Law Forum* 10 (1965): 168–96.

[142] Henry B. Veatch, review of *Natural Law and Natural Rights* by John Finnis, *American Journal of Jurisprudence* 26 (1981): 253.

[143] Z. K. Bankowski, review of *Natural Law and Natural Rights* by John Finnis, *Law Quarterly Review* 98 (July 1982): 474.

[144] Veatch, op. cit. (in n. 142 above), p. 250.

[145] G. E. Moore, *Principia Ethica* (Cambridge: Cambridge University Press, 1903), chap. i.

[146] Martin P. Golding, "Philosophy of Law, History of," *The Encyclopedia of Philosophy,* vol. 6, ed. Paul Edwards (New York: Macmillan & The Free Press, 1967), pp. 262–63.

[147] Roscoe Pound, *Jurisprudence*, 5 vols. (St. Paul, Minn.: West, 1959).

[148] Shestack, op. cit. (in n. 94 above), p. 85.

[149] Julius Stone, *The Province and Function of Law* (Sydney, Australia, 1946); cf. also Stone's article, "Roscoe Pound and Sociological Jurisprudence," *Harvard Law Review* 78 (1965): 1578–84.

[150] Julius Stone, *Human Law and Human Justice* (London: Stevens, 1965), p. 341.

[151] See John Rawls, *A Theory of Justice* (Oxford: Oxford University Press, 1973), and the works of Alan Gewirth cited in n. 100 above.

[152] David A. J. Richards, "Human Rights and the Moral Foundations of the Substantive Criminal Law," *Georgia Law Review* 13:4 (Summer 1979): 1411–12.

[153] Gewirth, *Human Rights* (op. cit. in n. 100 above), especially pp. 52–53, 68–76; and cf. his essay in the same volume, "The 'Is-Ought' Problem Resolved" (pp. 100–127). A detailed treatment of Gewirth's principle of generic consistency is included in Roger Pilon's essay, "Ordering Rights Consistently," *Georgia Law Review* 13:4 (Summer 1979): 1171–96.

[154] Cf. Harris, op. cit. (in n. 93 above), pp. 268–71.

[155] Robert Paul Wolff, *Understanding Rawls: A Reconstruction and Critique of "A Theory of Justice"* (Princeton, N.J.: Princeton University Press, 1977), pp. 207–10.

[156] D. P. Chattopadhyaya, "Human Rights, Justice, and Social Context," in *The Philosophy of Human Rights: International Perspectives,* ed. Rosenbaum (op. cit. in n. 83 above), pp. 179–81.

[157] Flew, op. cit. (in n. 98 above), pp. 1129, 1132.

[158] Nozick, op. cit. (in n. 97 above), p. 206.

[159] D. J. Bentley, "John Rawls: A Theory of Justice," *University of Pennsylvania Law Review* 121:5 (May 1973): 1074. Gewirth (*Human Rights* [op. cit. in n. 100 above], p. 44) maintains that Rawls' veil-of-ignorance doctrine suffers from complete circularity: "The argument attains its egalitarian conclusion only by putting into its premises the egalitarianism of persons' universal equal ignorance of all their particular qualities. This ignorance has no independent rational justification, since humans are not in fact ignorant of all their particular qualities. Hence, apart from an initial egalitarian moral outlook, why should any actual rational informed persons accept the principle about equal moral rights that stems from such ignorance?"

[160] Thomas M. Scanlon, Jr., "Rawls' Theory of Justice," *University of Pennsylvania Law Review* 121:5 (May 1973): 1069.

[161] Wolff, op. cit. (in n. 155 above), p. 20.

[162] Anthony D'Amato, "Rawls' Theory of Justice and International Society," in D'Amato's *Jurisprudence: A Descriptive and Normative Analysis of Law* (Dordrecht, Netherlands: Martinus Nijhoff, 1984), p. 274.

[163] Jack Donnelly, review of *Human Rights: Essays on Justification and Applications* by Alan Gewirth, *Human Rights Quarterly* 5:3 (August 1983): 377. See also the recent exchange between Gewirth and Arthur C. Danto in *Human Rights,* ed. Paul, Paul, and Miller, pp. 1–34.

[164] Wolff, op. cit. (in n. 155 above), p. 111.

[165] Montgomery, "Marxist Approach to Human Rights" (op. cit. in n. 11 above). See this book-length treatment for the primary and secondary sources supporting my discussion of Marxism in the present work.

[166] Lung-chu Chen, "Human Rights and World Public Order," *Résumés des Cours* 10 (Strasbourg, France: International Institute of Human Rights, 1979): 6.

[167] Published by Yale University Press; 1016 pages.

[168] Shestack, op. cit. (in n. 94 above), p. 96. We have silently corrected "(5) health" to "(5) wealth": a most unfortunate and misleading typographical error. As Chen expresses it, "The peoples of the world . . . in relation to wealth . . . seek access to the production and sharing of goods and services."

[169] Jordan J. Paust, "Authority: from a Human Rights Perspective," *American Journal of Jurisprudence* 28 (1983): 75.

[170] Shestack, op. cit. (in n. 94 above), p. 96.

[171] Chen, op. cit. (in n. 166 above), p. 8.

[172] Cf. Higgins's essay, "Policy Considerations and the International Judicial Process," *International and Comparative Law Quarterly* 17 (1968): 58.

[173] Chen, op. cit. (in n. 166 above), p. 14.

[174] Ibid., p. 13.

[175] White, op. cit. (in n. 85 above), pp. 172–73. One is left with the same conclusion on reading the essays by Vlastos, Hart, Gewirth, Dworkin, Raz, and others collected in *Theories of Rights,* ed. Jeremy Waldron (Oxford: Oxford University Press, 1984).

[176] Frey, op. cit. (in n. 1 above), p. 47.

[177] Ibid., pp. 48–49.

[178] See above, chap. 1, the text corresponding to n. 9.

[179] Gregory Vlastos, "Justice and Equality," in *Human Rights,* ed. Melden (op. cit. in n. 99 above), especially pp. 82–83.

[180] Rosenbaum, op. cit. (in n. 83 above), p. 32; and cf. Kai Nielsen, "Scepticism and Human Rights," *The Monist* 52:4 (October 1968): 573.

[181] See whole number 370 of the *Philosophical Review* (64:2 [April 1955]), containing "Are There Any Natural Rights?" (H. L. A. Hart), "Inalienable Rights" (Stuart M. Brown, Jr.), and "Natural and Inalienable Rights" (William K. Frankena). Frankena, after criticizing the views of Hart and Brown, concludes weakly: "We all agree that there are natural and inalienable rights, at least hypothetically. But I have wanted to say that there are other natural or inalienable rights besides Hart's equal right to be free or Brown's right to governmental protection, as traditional theory held, and that they are prima facie rights, not actual ones" (p. 232).

[182] See Montgomery, "Marxist Approach to Human Rights" (op. cit. in n. 11 above), pp. 77–79, 177. I there point out that the Marxist cannot in fact have his cake and eat it too.

183 Ludwig Wittgenstein, *Tractatus Logico-Philosophicus,* paras, 6.41–6.421; and see Wittgenstein's posthumously published, "A Lecture on Ethics," *Philosophical Review* 74 (January 1965). Contemporary evangelical relegation of Wittgenstein to the enemy's camp (e.g., John S. Feinberg, "Noncognitivism: Wittgenstein," in *Biblical Errancy: An Analysis of Its Philosophical Roots,* ed. Norman L. Geisler [Grand Rapids: Zondervan, 1981], pp. 161–201) fails to appreciate the unity of Wittgenstein's thought or the high importance of the verification principle for Christian apologetics—and reflects the negativism and separation characteristic of the fundamentalist mindset; contrast Montgomery, *The Suicide of Christian Theology* (Minneapolis: Bethany, 1971), pp. 267–313, 325–41, 363–70; and Montgomery, *Where Is History Going? Essays in Support of the Historical Truth of the Christian Revelation* (Minneapolis: Bethany, 1972), pp. 133–40.

184 Kurt Baier, *The Moral Point of View* (New York: Random House, 1965), p. 157.

185 Doubtless this aphorism was developed (or reflected) in Archimedes' lost work Πεπὶ ζυγῶν (*On Balances or Levers*). "Archimedes (287–212) is very generally regarded not only as the greatest mathematician but as the greatest mechanist or engineer of antiquity"—Benjamin Farrington, *Greek Science,* rev. ed. (Harmondsworth, Middlesex: Penguin, 1961), p. 214.

186 Jean-Jacques Rousseau, *Contrat social,* bk. 2, chap. 7.

187 Schaeffer, op. cit. (in n. 80 above), p. 11.

188 Flew, op. cit. (in n. 98 above), p. 1119. That this issue is by no means closed in contemporary philosophy is plain from the symposium volume, *Divine Commands and Morality,* ed. Paul Helm (New York: Oxford University Press, 1981).

189 See *Jurisprudence: A Book of Readings,* ed. Montgomery (op. cit. in n. 67 above), pp. 317–30; and cf. John Warwick Montgomery, *The Law Above the Law* (Minneapolis: Bethany, 1975), p. 43.

190 Rosenbaum, op. cit. (in n. 83 above), p. 33.

191 Peter K. Y. Woo, "A Metaphysical Approach to Human Rights from a Chinese Point of View," in *Philosophy of Human Rights*, ed. Rosenbaum (op. cit. in n. 83 above), p. 122.

192 Ibid., pp. 115–16.

193 Elaine Pagels, "The Roots and Origins of Human Rights," in *Human Dignity: The Internationalization of Human Rights; Essays Based on an Aspen Institute Workshop,* ed. Robert B. McKay and Harlan Cleveland (Dobbs Ferry, N.Y.: Oceana, 1979), p. 3. Cf. Kana Mitra, "Human Rights in Hinduism," *Journal of Ecumenical Studies* 19:3 (Summer 1982): 77–87.

194 Arthur Koestler, *The Lotus and the Robot* (New York: Macmillan, 1961), especially pp. 236–41, 268–75.

195 Schaeffer, op. cit. (in n. 80 above), p. 5. Cf. S. R. Mohan Das, "Discrimination in India," in *Case Studies on Human Rights and Fundamental Freedoms,* ed. Veenhoven (op. cit. in n. 13 above), 2:157–77.

196 For examples, see Aspinall, "Man's Place in Nature," in *Animals' Rights—A Symposium,* ed. Peterson and Ryder (op. cit. in n. 4 above), pp. 19–20; and Jack Austin, "Buddhist Attitudes Towards Animal Life," ibid., pp. 25–33.

[197] Saneh Chamarik, "Buddhism and Human Rights," *Human Rights Teaching* [UNESCO] 2:1 (1981): 18–19. This journal is also published in a French language edition.

[198] Ibid., pp. 18–20. Cf. Kenneth K. Inada, "The Buddhist Perspective on Human Rights," *Journal of Ecumenical Studies* 19:3 (Summer 1982): 66–76.

[199] There is also the mystic Sufi tradition of "inner spiritual freedom" in Islam; this is emphasized by Seyyed Hossein Nasr in his short essay, "The Concept and Reality of Freedom in Islam and Islamic Civilization," in *Philosophy of Human Rights: International Perspectives*, ed. Rosenbaum (op. cit. in n. 83 above), pp. 95–101. On Islamic jurisprudence in general and its derivation from the Koran and from Islamic religious tradition, see in particular Joseph Schacht, *The Origins of Muhammadan Jurisprudence* (Oxford: Clarendon, 1979); Noel J. Coulson, *A History of Islamic Law* (Edinburgh: Edinburgh University Press, 1964); Noel J. Coulson, *Conflicts and Tensions in Islamic Jurisprudence* (Chicago: University of Chicago Press, 1969); Louis Milliot, *Introduction à l'étude du droit musulman* (Paris: Recueil Sirey, 1953); and D. F. Mulla, *Principles of Mahomedan Law,* 17th ed. by M. Hidayatullah (Bombay: N. M. Tripathi Private Ltd., 1972).

[200] A discussion of these principles is to be found in Ihsan Hamid Al-Mafregy, "l'Islam et les droits de l'homme," in *Islam et droits de l'homme,* ed. Emmanuel Hirsch (Paris: Librairie des Libertés, 1984), pp. 11–49; Dr. Al-Mafregy gave a short summary of his paper in English in *Human Rights Teaching* [UNESCO] 2:1 (1981): 11–14. See also Riffat Hassan, "On Human Rights and the Qur'anic Perspective," *Journal of Ecumenical Studies* 19:3 (Summer 1982): 51–65.

[201] These words are from A. K. Brohi's keyn. address, "The Nature of Islamic Law and the Concept of Human Rights," in *Human Rights in Islam: Report of a Seminar Held in Kuwait, December 1980* (Geneva: International Commission of Jurists, 1982), p. 51.

[202] The papers from the several Saudi Arabia colloquia have been published in French as a series of pamphlets, and also bound together (as a single volume) under the cover title, *Colloques de Riyad, de Paris, du Vatican, de Genève et de Strasbourg sur le dogme musulman et les droits de l'homme en Islam entre juristes de l'Arabie Saoudite et emminents juristes et intellectuels européens* (Beirut, Lebanon: Dar Al-Kitab Allubnani, n.d.).

[203] The French text of the Islamic Declaration, with introduction by M. A. SiNaceur, head of UNESCO's Philosophy Division, appears in *Droits de l'homme, droits des peuples,* ed. Alain Fenet (Paris: Presses Universitaires de France, 1982), pp. 221–38; it is reprinted in *Islam et droits de l'homme,* ed. Hirsch (op. cit. in n. 200 above), pp. 209–36.

[204] See above, chap. 2, the text paragraph corresponding to n. 33.

[205] Amadou Mahtar M'Bow, "La lumière de l'Islam," in *Islam et droits de l'homme,* ed. Hirsch (op. cit. in n. 200 above), pp. 91–94.

[206] Sir Norman Anderson, "Islam," in *The World's Religions,* ed. Sir Norman Anderson, 3d ed. (London: Inter-Varsity, 1955), pp. 82, 88–90, 93–94. See also Anderson's *Islamic Law in the Modern World* (New York: New York University Press, 1959) and *Law Reform in the Muslim World* (London:

University of London/Athlone Press, 1976). For the Koranic texts to which Anderson refers, see Robert Roberts, *The Social Laws of the Qorân, Considered, and Compared with Those of the Hebrew and Other Ancient Codes,* new ed. (London: Curzon, 1971). Cf. Professor Robert Ernest Hume's enumeration of the "elements of weakness in Islam" in his *The World's Living Religions,* rev. ed. (New York: Scribner, 1950), pp. 232–33.

207 The late President Sadat made his religious position in this respect entirely plain when I spoke with him at his home at Aswan on 14 April 1978: see my articles, "Open Doors in the Middle East," *Christianity Today,* 2 March 1979, p. 69, and "Presenting the Prince of Peace," *Christianity Today,* 23 March 1979, pp. 62, 66.

208 See also in this connection Khomeini's bizarre and disturbing "Green Book": Ayatollah Khomeiny, *Principes politiques, philosophiques, sociaux et religieux extraits de trois ouvrages majeurs de l'Ayatollah,* ed. and trans. Jean-Marie Xavière (Paris: Editions Libres-Hallier, 1979). Khomeini's *Resaleh Towzih al-Masael* has now been translated into English in its entirety under the title, *A Clarification of Questions* (London: Westview/Bowker, 1984); in it we are told that apostasy is a capital offense and that the children of apostates (for example, Baha'is) should be killed if they will not recant.

209 Joseph Albright, "Why Sudan Cuts Off Thieves' Hands," *The London Times,* 26 September 1984. Cf. Costa Luca, "Discrimination in the Arab Middle East," in *Case Studies on Human Rights and Fundamental Freedoms,* ed. Veenhoven (op. cit. in n. 13 above), 1:211–40; Clemens Amelunxen, "Marriage and Woman in Islamic Countries," ibid., 2:83–99; and John Laffin, "The Arabs as Slavers," ibid., 4:431–59.

210 John Warwick Montgomery, "How Muslims Do Apologetics," in his *Faith Founded on Fact* (op. cit. in n. 137 above), pp. 81–99. This essay originally appeared in *Muslim World* 51:2 (April 1961), with author's "Corrigendum" in the July 1961 *Muslim World.*

211 Sir Norman Anderson, *The Evidence for the Resurrection* (London: Inter-Varsity, 1966).

212 Abraham Kaplan, "Human Relations and Human Rights in Judaism," in *Philosophy of Human Rights: International Perspectives,* ed. Rosenbaum (op. cit. in n. 83 above), pp. 84–85. See also the essays collected in *Judaïsme et les droits de l'homme,* ed. Emmanuel Hirsch (Paris: Librairie des Libertés, 1984); Daniel F. Polish, "Judaism and Human Rights," *Journal of Ecumenical Studies* 19:3 (Summer 1982): 40–50; Louis Henkin, "Judaism and Human Rights," *Judaism: A Quarterly Journal of Jewish Life and Thought* 25:4 (1976): 436–37; and the *Israel Yearbook on Human Rights* [Tel Aviv University Faculty of Law], vol. 1 (1971) to date. On Jewish jurisprudence in general, see Ze'ev W. Falk, "Jewish Law," in *An Introduction to Legal Systems,* ed. J. Duncan M. Derrett (New York: Praeger, 1968), pp. 28–53.

213 See Roberts, op. cit. (in n. 206 above), *passim.* On the oft-criticized—and seriously misunderstood—law of "an eye for an eye and a tooth for a tooth," see Marvyn Tower, "Popular Misconceptions: A Note on the *Lex Talionis,*" *Law & Justice* [England], No. 80/81 (Hilary/Easter 1984): 25–31. Even in the matter of slavery one should n. that "already in the Hebrew Bible we find

that legislation regarding slavery is of a nature to undermine and erode the institution as such. . . . Biblical and rabbinic legislation concerning slaves actually turns slavery into a kind of hired labour. The slave gains total freedom in the 'sabbatical' (seventh) year or at the latest in the Jubilee Year. He becomes free automatically if his master causes him bodily injury"—R. J. Zwi Werblosky, "Judaism and Human Rights," *Human Rights Teaching* [UNESCO] 2:1 (1981): 8. Concerning the alleged "racism" and "genocide" practiced by the Israelites of the Old Testament, Professor Herbert Chanan Brichto of Hebrew Union College is worth quoting *in extenso* ("The Hebrew Bible on Human Rights," in *Essays on Human Rights: Contemporary Issues and Jewish Perspectives,* ed. David Sidorsky [Philadelphia: Jewish Publication Society of America, 1979], p. 221):

> What is noteworthy in Scripture as concerns the program of war against the populations which Israel is to supplant in the Promised Land is that the victims are not regarded as less than human or as inferior racial stock. Self-serving as the justification may be, Israel's predecessors on the land are seen as having defaulted on their right to territory and survival by reason of a long history of inveterate immorality. By contrast, the divine Landlord who brings Israel to populate the territory to be vacated warns his new tenants against encroaching upon neighboring peoples who had in earlier times, by God's fiat, also supplanted elements of the original sinful stock.
>
> The clue to a people's essential incompatibility with Israel is the injunction against intermarriage. The noteworthy point is that except for the Amorites, who are "sinful," this injunction is extended to only two peoples, the Ammonites and the Moabites, *both of whom are Israel's kindred.* The injunction against intermarriage is grounded on an historic trespass of kinship obligations. The Edomites and the Egyptians are explicitly excluded from this prohibition, which applied to no other of the many peoples with whom Israel had contact.
>
> Accordingly, concepts of racism derived from modern experience fail to explain the relationships prevalent in the culture of the biblical Middle East. The patterns of group and ethnic conflict are real, but they are complexly woven and do not fit by any means into a modern framework of racist interpretation.

214 See, e.g., United Nations Commission on Human Rights Resolution of 13 March 1973 "deploring Israel's persistent defiance of the relevant resolutions of the United Nations and its continued policy of violating the basic human rights of the population in the occupied Arab territories" (cf. the similar UN Commission on Human Rights Resolution of 23 March 1972); Michael Adams, "Israel's Treatment of the Arabs in the Occupied Areas," *Journal of Palestine Studies,* Winter 1977; and Georges R. Tamarin, "Israeli Society: Authoritarian Traditionalism versus Pluralist Democracy," in *Case Studies on Human Rights and Fundamental Freedoms*, ed. Veenhoven (op. cit. in n. 13 above), 2:101–36. I have critiqued the Israeli Penal Law Amendment (Enticement To Change Religion) Law, 5738–1977 (Hebrew text in the

Knesset Gazette, No. 1313) in my article, "Israel vs. the 'Religious Enticers,' " *Inspiration* 1:4 (September–October 1978): 24–25, 79–80 (*Inspiration* is no longer published, but photocopies of this article can be obtained from Petersen Publishing Co., Photo and Research Library, 8490 Sunset Blvd., Los Angeles, CA 90069).

215 In *What I Believe,* ed. Booth (op. cit. in n. 98 above), p. 73 (italics mine).

216 G. Ernest Wright, *The Old Testament Against Its Environment* (London: SCM, 1950).

217 Jeanne Hersch, *Birthright of Man* (Paris: UNESCO, 1969).

218 C. S. Lewis, *The Abolition of Man* (New York: Macmillan, 1947), pp. 51–61.

219 Werblosky, op. cit. (in n. 213 above), p. 7.

220 See R. E. Hume, op. cit. (in n. 206 above), *passim*, and Bruce A. Demarest, *General Revelation* (Grand Rapids: Zondervan, 1982), pp. 255–59.

221 René Cassin, "Religions et droits de l'homme," in *Jura Hominis ac civis. René Cassin: Amicorum discipulorumque liber,* vol. 4, ed. International Institute of Human Rights (Paris: Editions A. Pedone, 1972), p. 99.

222 See, e.g., Ephesians 2:8–9; Romans 1–3; and the entire Book of Galatians.

223 D. L. Perrott, "The Logic of Fundamental Rights," in *Fundamental Rights* , ed. Bridge, Lasok, et al. (op. cit. in n. 45 above), p. 13.

224 On contemporary Marxist interest in natural law and the diverse styles of modern secular natural rights theory, see W. Suchecki (Faculty of Law, University of Warsaw), "The Quest for Value-Oriented Jurisprudence," in *Anglo-Polish Legal Essays,* ed. W. E. Butler (Dobbs Ferry, N.Y.: Transnational Publishers, 1982), pp. 33–53.

225 Cf. H. Lauterpacht's excellent treatment of "The Law of Nature, the Law of Nations, and the Rights of Man" in his *An International Bill of the Rights of Man* (New York: Columbia University Press, 1945), pp. 1–65.

226 Marcus Tullius Cicero, *De legibus,* bk. 2, chap. 4. On the world view of Stoicism, see Eduard Zeller, *Outlines of the History of Greek Philosophy,* ed. Wilhelm Nestle, trans. L. R. Palmer, 13th rev. ed. (London: Routledge & Kegan Paul, 1950), pp. 209–27; and Johnny Christensen, *An Essay on the Unity of Stoic Philosophy* (Copenhagen: Munksgaard/Scandinavian University Books, 1962).

227 Cf. A. P. d'Entrèves, *Natural Law,* 2d ed. (London: Hutchinson University Library, 1970), pp. 22–36.

228 Thomas Aquinas, *Summa Theologica,* bks. I–II, QQ 90–97. See Elmer Gelinas, "The Natural Law According to Thomas Aquinas," *Simon Greenleaf Law Review* 2 (1982–83): 13–36; and Jean-Marie Aubert, *Loi de Dieu, Lois des hommes* (Tournai, Belgium: Desclée, 1964).

229 Jacques Maritain, *The Rights of Man and Natural Law,* trans. Doris C. Anson (New York: Scribner, 1943), p. 66. Cf. Louis Lachance, *Le droit et les droits de l'homme* (Paris: Presses Universitaires de France, 1959).

230 Rosenbaum, op. cit. (in n. 83 above), p. 25.

231 On Luther, see Philip S. Watson, *Let God Be God! An Interpretation of the Theology of Martin Luther* (London: Epworth, 1947), pp. 73–85, 105–16; and Marc Lienhard, "Luther et les droits de l'homme," *Revue d'Histoire et de Philosophie Religieuses* 54:1 (1974): 15–29 (English translation in *A Lutheran*

Reader on Human Rights, ed. Jørgen Lissner and Arne Sovik: *LWF Report* 1–2 [September 1978]: 66–80). Paul Helm of the University of Liverpool's Department of Philosophy, in delivering the Third Finlayson Lecture, provides an excellent overview of "Calvin and Natural Law": *The Scottish Bulletin of Evangelical Theology* 2 (1984): 5–22.

232 See the celebrated debate between Barth and Brunner, *Natural Theology: Comprising "Nature and Grace" by Professor Dr. Emil Brunner and the Reply "No!" by Dr. Karl Barth,* trans. Peter Fraenkel (London: Geoffrey Bles, 1946).

233 John Warwick Montgomery, "Karl Barth and Contemporary Theology of History," in his *Where Is History Going? Essays in Support of the Historical Truth of the Christian Revelation,* (reprint, Minneapolis: Bethany, 1972), pp. 104–5; and Montgomery, "A Critical Examination of Emil Brunner's *The Divine Imperative,* Bk. III," in his *Shape of the Past* (op. cit. in n. 18 above), pp. 358–74.

234 See, for example, Alan F. Johnson, "Is There a Biblical Warrant for Natural-Law Theories?" *Journal of the Evangelical Theological Society* 25:2 (June 1982): 185–99; and Demarest, *General Revelation* (op. cit. in n. 220 above). Professor Demarest (p. 244) rejects on biblical grounds the entire—predominately Dutch hyper-Calvinist—tradition that maintains that "no knowledge is mediated by general revelation in nature and providence" (Demarest refers specifically to Abraham Kuyper, G. C. Berkouwer, Cornelius Van Til, Gordon Clark, T. F. Torrance, and Donald Bloesch—as well as Karl Barth). Jacques Ellul, as one would expect, follows Barth in unqualifiedly rejecting natural theology: see his *Theological Foundation of Law,* trans. Marguerite Wieser (New York: Seabury, 1969); and cf. John Warwick Montgomery, "Technology and Eschatology," in his *Faith Founded on Fact* (op. cit. in n. 137 above), pp. 155–59.

235 Quoted in Lienhard, "Protestantism and Human Rights" (op. cit. in n. 8 above), p. 30.

236 Perrott, op. cit. (in n. 223 above), pp. 13–15.

237 Carl J. Friedrich, *The Philosophy of Law in Historical Perspective,* 2d ed. (Chicago: University of Chicago Press, Phoenix Books, 1963), p. 33. See also Montgomery, *The Law Above the Law* (op. cit. in n. 189 above), pp. 38–40.

238 C. S. Lewis, *The Case for Christianity* (New York: Macmillan, 1943), reprinted in his *Mere Christianity* (New York: Macmillan, 1953).

239 Cf. Alan Gewirth, "The Golden Rule Rationalized," in his *Human Rights* (op. cit. in n. 100 above), pp. 128–42, and see my discussion of contemporary neo-Kantian moral philosophies in the previous chapter.

240 Daniel Vidal, "Examining the European Commission's Theses," in *A Christian Declaration on Human Rights,* ed. Miller (op. cit. in n. 78 above), p. 42.

241 Perrott, op. cit. (in n. 223 above), p. 12.

242 Shestack, op. cit. (in n. 94 above), pp. 76–77.

243 Kai Nielsen, "Can Faith Validate God-Talk?" in *New Theology No. 1,* ed. Martin E. Marty and Dean G. Peerman (New York: Macmillan, 1964), especially p. 147; C. B. Martin, "A Religious Way of Knowing," in *New*

Essays in Philosophical Theology, ed. Antony Flew and Alasdair MacIntyre (London: SCM, 1955), pp. 76–95; Frederick Ferré, *Language, Logic and God* (New York: Harper, 1961), pp. 94–104.

244 Acts 17:18–19, 22–23, 30–31. The late classical scholar E. M. Blaiklock of the University of Auckland, New Zealand, in delivering the Annual Wheaton College Graduate School Lectures, 21–22 October 1964, on the subject of Paul's Areopagus address, noted that Paul ignored the Epicureans ("the Sadducees of the Greeks"), doubtless because of the intellectual dishonesty into which their movement had fallen, and concentrated on the Stoics, who continued to hold a high view of natural law.

245 In Acts 17:28 Paul quoted Cleanthes (300 B.C.), *Hymn to Zeus* 5, and/or Aratus (270 B.C.), *Phoenom.* 5. Cf. J. B. Lightfoot's essay, "St. Paul and Seneca," in his *St. Paul's Epistle to the Philippians* (reprint, Grand Rapids: Zondervan, 1953); F. W. Farrar, *Seekers After God* (London: Macmillan, 1906); N. B. Stonehouse, *Paul Before the Areopagus, and Other New Testament Studies* (Grand Rapids: Eerdmans, 1957); B. Gärtner, *The Areopagus Speech and Natural Revelation* (Lund, 1955); and J. Sevenster, *Paul and Seneca* (Leiden: Brill, 1961).

246 John Warwick Montgomery, "Jesus Christ and History," in his *Where is History Going?* (op. cit. in n. 233 above), pp. 37–74.

247 Cf. John Warwick Montgomery, "Legal Reasoning and Christian Apologetics," in his *Law Above the Law* (op. cit. in n. 189 above), pp. 84–90; and John Warwick Montgomery, *Law & Gospel: A Study in Jurisprudence* (Oak Park, Ill.: Christian Legal Society, 1978), pp. 34–37.

248 Stephen E. Toulmin, *The Uses of Argument* (Cambridge: Cambridge University Press, 1958), p. 7.

249 Mortimer J. Adler, *How To Think About God* (New York: Macmillan, 1980), p. 150.

250 Jerome Hall, "Religion, Law and Ethics—A Call for Dialogue," *Hastings Law Journal* 29 (July 1978): 1273. We are not persuaded that Job's faith was quite as firm—or as irrational—as Hall suggests, but the reference to Job is in any case an *obiter dictum*!

251 Montgomery, "Jesus Christ and History," loc. cit. (in n. 246 above), pp. 37–74; F. F. Bruce, *The New Testament Documents: Are They Reliable?* 5th rev. ed. (London: Inter-Varsity, 1960); John Warwick Montgomery, "The Fourth Gospel Yesterday and Today," in his *Suicide of Christian Theology* (op. cit. in n. 183 above), pp. 428–65. On the extrabiblical evidence, see C. R. Haines, *Heathen Contact with Christianity During Its First Century and a Half; Being All References to Christianity Recorded in Pagan Writings During That Period* (Cambridge, England: Deighton, Bell, 1923), and Gary R. Habermas, *Ancient Evidence for the Life of Jesus* (Nashville: Thomas Nelson, 1984).

252 Simon Greenleaf, *The Testimony of the Evangelists, Examined by the Rules of Evidence Administered in Courts of Justice,* reprinted in Montgomery, *The Law Above the Law* (op. cit. in n. 189 above), pp. 91ff.

253 Lord Hailsham, *The Door Wherein I Went* (London: Collins, 1975), pp. 32–33; the theological and apologetic portion of Lord Hailsham's autobiography has been photolithographically reproduced in *Simon Greenleaf Law Review* 4 (1984–85): 1–67, with editorial introduction by John Warwick Montgomery.

254 C. S. Lewis, "Modern Theology and Biblical Criticism," in his *Christian Reflections,* ed. Walter Hooper (Grand Rapids: Eerdmans, 1967), pp. 152–66; Gerhard Maier, *The End of the Historical-Critical Method,* trans. E. W. Leverenz and R. F. Norden (St. Louis: Concordia, 1977); and cf. John Warwick Montgomery, "Why Has God Incarnate Suddenly Become Mythical?" in *Perspectives on Evangelical Theology,* ed. Kenneth S. Kantzer and Stanley N. Gundry (Grand Rapids: Baker, 1979), pp. 57–65.

255 A. N. Sherwin-White, *Roman Society and Roman Law in the New Testament* (Oxford: Clarendon, 1963), p. 187.

256 My lectures and Professor Stroll's are published in Montgomery, *Where Is History Going?* (op. cit. in n. 233 above), pp. 37–74 and 207–21.

257 Alan Saltzman, "Criminal Law: How to Expose Perjury Through Cross-Examination," *Los Angeles Daily Journal,* 4 November 1982.

258 Patrick L. McCloskey and Ronald L. Schoenberg, *Criminal Law Advocacy,* vol. 5 (New York: Matthew Bender, 1984), para. 12.01[b].

259 Second Peter 1:16. In vv. 17–18, Peter states expressly that he was with Jesus when he was transfigured (Matt. 17:2; Mark 9:2; Luke 9:29).

260 McCloskey and Schoenberg, op. cit. (in n. 258 above), vol. 5, para. 12.03.

261 A point made as early as the fourth century by the historian Eusebius of Caesarea, and reiterated by such classical apologists as Hugo Grotius ("the father of international law"), in his *The Truth of the Christian Religion,* trans. John Clarke, new ed. (London: William Baynes, 1825), bk. 2, sec. 6 ("The resurrection of Christ proved from credible testimony"), pp. 85–88; this section of Grotius's work is photolithographically reproduced in *Jurisprudence: A Book of Readings,* ed. Montgomery (op. cit. in n. 67 above), pp. 327–30.

262 John 8:44; et al.

263 "People just do not see things in an identical way when their positions and chances for observation vary. [If so,] the case is a frame-up"—F. Lee Bailey and Henry B. Rothblatt, *Fundamentals of Criminal Advocacy* (Rochester, N.Y.: Lawyers Co-operative Publishing Co.; San Francisco: Bancroft-Whitney, 1974), para. 500, p. 420.

264 John 20:30–31; 21:25. See Edmund H. Bennett (late dean of the Boston University School of Law), *The Four Gospels from a Lawyer's Standpoint* (Boston: Houghton, Mifflin, 1899), photolithographically reproduced with editorial introduction by John Warwick Montgomery in *Simon Greenleaf Law Review* 1 (1981–82).

265 Luke 24:25.

266 J. B. Phillips, *Ring of Truth: A Translator's Testimony* (New York: Macmillan, 1967).

267 See John Warwick Montgomery, *Myth, Allegory and Gospel* (Minneapolis: Bethany, 1974), pp. 11–31, 116–18.

268 Luke 3:1–3.

269 See, for example, E. M. Blaiklock, *The Archaeology of the New Testament* (Grand Rapids: Zondervan, 1970), and Edwin M. Yamauchi, *The Stones and the Scriptures* (reprint, Grand Rapids: Baker, 1981).

270 Richard A. Givens, *Advocacy* (New York: McGraw-Hill, 1980), pp. 13–14.

[271] Ibid., p. 12.

[272] Bruce, op. cit. (in n. 251 above), pp. 45–46.

[273] Peter Murphy, *A Practical Approach to Evidence* (London: Financial Training, 1982), pp. 123–24. Cf. George B. Johnston, "The Development of Civil Trial by Jury in England and the United States," *Simon Greenleaf Law Review* 4 (1984–85): 69–92.

[274] Greenleaf, *Testimony of the Evangelists* (op. cit. in n. 252 above), pp. 132–33.

[275] Matthew 12:38–40; 16:4; Luke 11:29; John 2:18–22.

[276] I.e., did the Resurrection occur in *ordinary* history? We do not deal here with the unverifiable vagaries of "hyper-history" or "supra-history" (as in the thought of Karl Barth and certain of his neo-orthodox followers), or with "existential" resurrections (Rudolf Bultmann and the post-Bultmannians). I have discussed elsewhere these modern theological attempts to have one's cake and eat it too: Montgomery, "Karl Barth and Contemporary Theology of History," in his *Where Is History Going?* (op. cit. in n. 233 above), pp. 100–117; cf. pp. 225–39 ("Faith, History and the Resurrection"); and Montgomery, "Luther's Hermeneutic vs. the New Hermeneutic," in his *In Defense of Martin Luther* (Milwaukee: Northwestern, 1970), pp. 40–85.

[277] Concerning the historical and evidential value of these appearances, see Merrill Tenney, *The Reality of the Resurrection* (New York: Harper, 1963); Josh McDowell, *The Resurrection Factor* (San Bernardino, Calif.: Here's Life, 1981); Richard Riss, *The Evidence for the Resurrection of Jesus Christ* (Minneapolis: Bethany, 1977); and Sir Norman Anderson, *The Evidence for the Resurrection* (op. cit. in n. 211 above).

[278] David Hume, *Enquiry Concerning Human Understanding,* sec. 10 ("Of Miracles"). For critique, see C. S. Lewis, *Miracles* (New York: Macmillan, 1947), especially chaps. 8 and 13; and Montgomery, *The Shape of the Past* (op. cit. in n. 18 above), pp. 289–93.

[279] Frank Morison [Albert Henry Ross], *Who Moved the Stone?* new ed. (London: Faber & Faber, 1944).

[280] Cf. Matthew 27:62–66.

[281] John Warwick Montgomery, "Science, Theology, and the Miraculous," in his *Faith Founded on Fact* (op. cit. in n. 137 above), pp. 43–73, especially p. 54.

[282] See Edwin M. Yamauchi, "Passover Plot or Easter Triumph? A Critical Review of H. Schonfield's Recent Theory," in *Christianity for the Tough Minded,* ed. John Warwick Montgomery (Minneapolis: Bethany, 1973), pp. 261–71.

[283] Von Daniken had "obtained the money [over $130,000 in debts] by misrepresentation of his financial situation, falsifying the hotel's books to make it appear solvent. A court psychiatrist examined von Daniken and found him a prestige-seeker, a liar and an unstable and criminal psychopath with a hysterical character, yet fully accountable for his acts"—Richard R. Lingeman, "Erich von Daniken's Genesis," *New York Times Book Review,* 31 March 1974, p. 6.

[284] Probability reasoning is virtually universal in the law: it operates both in common law and in noncommon law systems of jurisprudence, and in "civilized" and "primitive" legal systems indiscriminately. See Montgomery, *Law & Gospel* (op. cit. in n. 247 above), pp. 35–36.

[285] *Fed. R. Evid.* 401. This definition was derived from Professor Thayer's classic *Preliminary Treatise on Evidence* (1898).

[286] Thomas Sherlock, *The Tryal of the Witnesses of the Resurrection of Jesus* (London: J. Roberts, 1729), p. 62; Sherlock's book is photolithographically reproduced in *Jurisprudence: A Book of Readings,* ed. Montgomery (op. cit. in n. 67 above), and the quoted passage appears there on p. 400.

[287] See Luke 24:36–43.

[288] I have applied proof by *res ipsa loquitur* to the Resurrection in my *Law & Gospel* (op. cit. in n. 247 above), p. 35.

[289] Elizabeth F. Loftus, *Eyewitness Testimony* (Cambridge: Harvard University Press, 1979); cf. her popular article on this subject in *Psychology Today* 18:2 (February 1984): 22–26.

[290] Edward B. Arnolds, William K. Carroll, Melvin B. Lewis, and Michael P. Seng, *Eyewitness Testimony: Strategies and Tactics* (New York: McGraw-Hill, 1984), pp. 400–401. See also the invaluable work by Scots Advocate Marcus Stone, *Proof of Fact in Criminal Trials* (Edinburgh: W. Green, 1984), *passim.*

[291] John 20:19–28.

[292] Carl F. H. Henry, *God, Revelation and Authority* (Waco, Tex.: Word, 1976), vol. 1, pp. 220–23, 230–38, 256–63; vol. 2, pp. 313–34. Ronald H. Nash, "The Use and Abuse of History in Christian Apologetics," *Christian Scholar's Review* 1:3 (Spring 1971): 217–26; Ronald H. Nash, *Christian Faith and Historical Understanding* (Grand Rapids: Zondervan; Dallas: Probe, 1984). I have responded to Carl Henry in my book, *Faith Founded on Fact* (op. cit. in n. 137 above), pp. xvii-xxv. Paul D. Feinberg wrote a devastating critique of Nash's *Christian Scholar's Review* article in the next issue of that journal: "History: Public or Private? A Defense of John Warwick Montgomery's Philosophy of History," *Christian Scholar's Review* 1:4 (Summer 1971): 325–31; it is reprinted in my *Shape of the Past* (op. cit. in n. 18 above), pp. 375–82. Nash's book *Christian Faith and Historical Understanding* (which, sadly, does not seem to have benefitted in any way from Feinberg's insights) has been critically reviewed by Francis J. Beckwith: "Does Evidence Matter?" *Simon Greenleaf Law Review* 4 (1984–85): 231–35.

[293] R. C. Sproul, John Gerstner, and Arthur Lindsley, *Classical Apologetics* (Grand Rapids: Zondervan, 1984). Norman L. Geisler, *Miracles and Modern Thought,* with a response by R. C. Sproul (Grand Rapids: Zondervan; Dallas: Probe, 1982).

[294] John Warwick Montgomery, "Gordon Clark's Historical Philosophy," in Montgomery, *Where Is History Going?* (op. cit. in n. 233 above), especially p. 164.

[295] Feinberg, "History: Public or Private?" in Montgomery, *The Shape of the Past* (op. cit. in n. 18 above), p. 379.

[296] *Williams* v. *North Carolina,* 325 U.S. 226, 65 Sup. Ct. 1092, 157 A.L.P. 1366 (italics mine).

[297] Geisler, *Miracles and Modern Thought* (op. cit. in n. 293 above), p. 66. Remarkably, Geisler seems entirely unacquainted with my detailed treatment of this issue in my book *Faith Founded on Fact* (op. cit. in n. 137 above), pp. 43–73—even though my book was published four years before his.

[298] Ibid., p. 61.

[299] See, for example, *State* v. *Elliott,* 45 Iowa 486.

[300] Montgomery, *Faith Founded on Fact* (op. cit. in n. 137 above), p. 61.

[301] John 10:30; 14:8–9. Cf. Mark 2:5–7; 14:61–64.

[302] E.g., Matthew 4:4; 5:17–19; John 5:39; 10:35.

[303] E.g., Matthew 12:38–42; 19:3-6; 24:37–39; Luke 24:25–27.

[304] John 14:26; 16:12–15. Swiss theologian Oscar Cullmann has made much of the apostolic memory as the inspired link between Jesus' ministry and the New Testament Scriptures.

[305] Acts 1:21–26; 9:26–27; Galatians 2:11–13; 2 Peter 3:15–16.

[306] See *God's Inerrant Word: An International Symposium on the Trustworthiness of Scripture,* ed. John Warwick Montgomery (Minneapolis: Bethany, 1974); John Warwick Montgomery, *Crisis in Lutheran Theology,* 2d ed. (Minneapolis: Bethany, 1973), 2 vols.; Montgomery, *The Shape of the Past* (op. cit. in n. 18 above), pp. 138–45.

[307] From the Greek noun *kenosis,* whose verb form (= "empty oneself/divest oneself of privileges") is applied to Christ in Philippians 2:6–8. However, biblical teaching on Incarnation has no resemblance to the liberal theological theory of Jesus' fallibility. Theological liberals—typically—developed the theory to have their cake (a divine Jesus) and eat it too (simultaneous rejection of Jesus' conservative view of scriptural authority). Cf. Montgomery, *Crisis in Lutheran Theology* (op. cit. in n. 306 above), 1:91–93. It is perhaps worth noting that the well-known passage in the Gospels in which Jesus states that he does not know the hour of His Second Coming (Mark 13:32) is no confirmation of Kenotic theory, for (1) only a single, eschatological item of knowledge is involved, and (2) Jesus' disclaimer of knowledge on this point shows that in His incarnate state He was nonetheless fully aware of the boundaries of His knowledge, and being in control of His knowledge He would not have advertently or inadvertently given false or misleading information when He did make positive assertions (e.g., on the reliability of the Bible).

[308] Montgomery, "Marxist Approach to Human Rights" (op. cit. in n. 11 above), pp. 51–53, 138–41. The principle of the end justifying the means is also central to Fletcherian situation ethics; see Joseph Fletcher and John Warwick Montgomery, *Situation Ethics—True or False: A Dialogue Between Joseph Fletcher and John Warwick Montgomery* (Minneapolis: Bethany, Dimension Books, 1972), especially pp. 25–26, 31–35.

[309] Wittgenstein, "A Lecture on Ethics" (op. cit. in n. 183 above), p. 7.

[310] Acts 1:3.

[311] John Warwick Montgomery, *How Do We Know There Is a God? and Other Questions Inappropriate in Polite Society* (Minneapolis: Bethany, 1973), pp. 28–29.

[312] Martin Luther, *De servo arbitrio, WA* [the standard, critical *Weimarer Ausgabe* of the Reformer's writings] 18, 606. Cf. Montgomery, "Luther's Hermeneutic vs. the New Hermeneutic" (op. cit. in n. 276 above), especially pp. 69–76.

[313] Alec McCowen, *Personal Mark* (London: Hamish Hamilton, 1984).

[314] Rousas John Rushdoony, *The Institutes of Biblical Law* (Nutley, N.J.: Craig, 1973), p. 399. This mammoth work nonetheless contains many valuable insights.

[315] Romans 4, Galatians 3, Hebrews 11.

[316] See Montgomery, *The Shaping of America* (op. cit. in n. 79 above), p. 44.

[317] See C. F. W. Walther's classic, *The Proper Distinction between Law and Gospel,* trans. W. H. T. Dau (St. Louis: Concordia, 1929), *passim.*

[318] H. B. Clark, *Biblical Law,* 2d ed. (Portland, Ore.: Binfords & Mort, 1944), para. 53, p. 32.

[319] Remarkably, Rushdoony and his associate Gary North recognize the folly of strict sabbatarianism; North writes, *inter alia,* of what such judaizing would do to contemporary life: "An obvious example is the steel industry. The costs involved in shutting down a steel plant and then restarting it are prohibitive. Steel could not be manufactured under such conditions"—Gary North, "The Economics of Sabbath-Keeping," appendix 4 to Rushdoony, *The Institutes of Biblical Law* (op. cit. in n. 314 above), p. 836, n. 16.

[320] The woman-taken-in-adultery pericope is not always found in the early manuscripts of the Gospel of John, but, if not, it invariably appears elsewhere in the Gospels (e.g., in Luke). Thus, its genuineness seems indisputable.

[321] Cf. Clark, op. cit. (in n. 318 above), paras. 455–59, pp. 295–97.

[322] Walter Harrelson, *The Ten Commandments and Human Rights* (Philadelphia: Fortress, 1980), pp. 192, 130. Professor Harrelson and I were colleagues on the faculty of the Divinity School of the University of Chicago in 1959–1960; in spite of his catastrophic theology, he is a most charming and courtly gentleman.

[323] Matthew 5:17, 21–22, 27–28.

[324] For another kind of list, based more directly on the Universal Declaration, see *The Rule of Law and Human Rights: Principles and Definitions* (Geneva: International Commission of Jurists, 1966), pp. 52–60.

[325] Declared Lord Diplock, one of the very greatest English Christian judges of our time: "The fundamental human right is not to a legal system that is infallible but to one that is fair" (*Maharaj* v. *Attorney-General of Trinidad and Tobago* (No. 2) [1978] 1 W.L.R. 902, 911).

[326] "The maxim *nemo bis in idipsum vexari,* grounded upon the scriptural injunction 'affliction shall not rise up the second time' (Nah. 1:9), is the most ancient guaranty in the bill of rights. Its origin in English law is prehistoric and its application has been continuous"—George W. Dalzell, *Benefit of Clergy in America* (Winston-Salem, N.C.: John F. Blair, 1955), p. 12. Cf. in general, John Marshall Gest, *The Influence of Biblical Texts upon English Law: Address before the Phi Beta Kappa and Sigma Xi Societies* (Philadelphia: George H. Buchanan, 1910), and Gary J. Edles, "Biblical Parallels in American Law," *New York State Bar Journal* 49:8 (December 1977): 644–47, 697–99.

327 See Montgomery, *Slaughter of the Innocents* (op. cit. in n. 56 above), *passim*.

328 Brichto, op. cit. (in n. 213 above), pp. 229–30. See also Francis A. Schaeffer, *Pollution and the Death of Man: The Christian View of Ecology* (Wheaton: Tyndale, 1970), reprinted in his *Complete Works: A Christian Worldview*, vol. 5 (Westchester, Ill.: Crossway, 1982), pp. 1–76; and John Stott, "Our Human Environment," in his *Issues Facing Christians Today* (op. cit. in n. 80 above), pp. 109–21.

329 Daniel John Meador, *Habeas Corpus and Magna Carta* (Charlottesville, Va.: University Press of Virginia, 1966), p. 7.

330 Wu, op. cit. (in n. 67 above), pp. 69–70.

331 Edward S. Corwin, *The "Higher Law" Background of American Constitutional Law* (Ithaca, N.Y.: Cornell University Press, Great Seal Books, 1955). Also: Carl J. Friedrich, *Transcendent Justice: The Religious Dimension of Constitutionalism* (Durham, N.C.: Duke University Press, 1964); Edwin Vieira, Jr., "Rights and the United States Constitution: The Declension from Natural Law to Legal Positivism," *Georgia Law Review* 13:4 (Summer 1979): 1447–1500.

332 See Carl L. Becker, *The Declaration of Independence: A Study in the History of Political Ideas* (New York: Vintage, 1958), and Montgomery, *The Shaping of America* (op. cit. in n. 79 above), pp. 61–68. Locke's *Reasonableness of Christianity* is available edited and abridged by I. T. Ramsey (Stanford: Stanford University Press, 1958). The hyper-Calvinist reconstructionists (Hebden Taylor, Gregg Singer, et al.), in their campaign to replace constitutional contract theory by theocracy, try to turn Locke into an eighteenth-century pagan—conveniently forgetting that he was an apologist for revealed Christianity!

333 Montgomery, *Law & Gospel* (op. cit. in n. 247 above), pp. 39–40.

334 Jellinek's thesis was set forth in his work, *The Declaration of the Rights of Man and of Citizens: A Contribution to Modern Constitutional History*, trans. Max Farrand (1901; reprint, New York: H. Holt, 1982); Troeltsch's reputation rests especially on his *The Social Teaching of the Christian Churches*, trans. Olive Wyon (New York: Harper Torchbooks, 1960), 2 vols. Cf. Yves Madiot, *Droits de l'homme et libertés publiques* (Paris: Masson, 1976), p. 43, n. 2; Lienhard, "Protestantism and Human Rights" (op. cit. in n. 8 above), pp. 25–27; Roger Mehl, "La tradition protestante et les droits de l'homme," *Revue d'Histoire et de Philosophie Religieuses* 58:4 (1978): 367–77; U. Scheuner, "Les droits de l'homme à l'intérieur des Eglises protestantes," ibid., pp. 379–97; Montgomery, *The Shaping of America* (op. cit. in n. 79 above), pp. 37ff.

335 Quoted in a personal interview with Gerald Kaufman, "When Evil Invokes the Bible," *The [London] Times*, 24 January 1985. Contrast John Warwick Montgomery, "Freedom and the Gospel," in his *Suicide of Christian Theology* (op. cit. in n. 183 above), pp. 213–16.

336 These are the words of Art. 52 of the new Soviet Constitution; see *Constitution (Fundamental Law). Adopted . . . on October 7, 1977* (Moscow: Novosti Press Agency Publishing House, 1980). Cf. Montgomery, "Marxist Approach to Human Rights" (op. cit. in n. 11 above), pp. 101–2, 107–8.

337 See especially *Reynolds v. U.S.*, 98 U.S. 145 (1878).

338 St. John A. Robilliard, *Religion and the Law: Religious Liberty in Modern English Law* (Manchester: Manchester University Press, 1984).

339 Lienhard, "Protestantism and Human Rights" (op. cit. in n. 8 above), p. 36. Cf. Commission of the Churches on International Affairs, *Study Paper on Religious Liberty* (Geneva: World Council of Churches, 1981).

340 See above, chap. 3, text at nn. 90–91.

341 Concretely, the absence of national medical and dental insurance coverage in the United States is a scandal, viewed in revelational terms: lives are ruined economically every day by astronomical hospital and doctors' bills.

342 Cf. Nathan Söderblom's Nobel Lecture of 11 December 1930 on "The Role of the Church in Promoting Peace," in *Nobel Lectures: Peace, 1926–1950*, vol. 2, ed. Frederick W. Haberman (Amsterdam: Elsevier, 1972), pp. 91–122. On the weaknesses of Söderblom's ecumenical theology, see John Warwick Montgomery, *Ecumenicity, Evangelicals, and Rome* (Grand Rapids: Zondervan, 1969), pp. 105–7.

343 Cf. Shestack, op. cit. (in n. 94 above), pp. 104–5. On the NIEO in general, see Thomas M. Franck and Mark M. Munansangu, *The New International Economic Order: International Law in the Making?* (New York: United Nations Institute for Training and Research, 1982).

344 Henkin, "International Human Rights and Rights in the United States" (op. cit. in n. 31 above), p. 49.

345 Stephen P. Marks, "Principles and Norms of Human Rights Applicable in Emergency Situations," in *The International Dimensions of Human Rights* (op. cit. in n. 17 above), pt. 1, chap. 5, p. 217 (1979 ed.).

346 Norman L. Geisler, *Ethics: Alternatives and Issues* (Grand Rapids: Zondervan, 1971), especially pp. 130–32. Geisler updates and defends his original position, denominating it "graded absolutism," in his *Options in Contemporary Christian Ethics* (Grand Rapids: Baker, 1981), pp. 81–101.

347 Cf. Adolf Köerle, *The Quest for Holiness*, trans. John C. Mattes (Minneapolis: Augsburg, 1938). My present book is not an ethics text, but to obviate misunderstandings I shall reply to Geisler's three major objections to Reformation ethics (which he terms "ideal absolutism" or "conflicting absolutism" or "the lesser-evil view"). (1) "It holds the individual guilty for doing his best in an unavoidably bad situation." But this is precisely God's judgment against every generation of mankind since Adam fell: "When you shall have done all those things which are commanded you, say, We are unprofitable servants" (Luke 17:10). (2) "There is always at least one right thing to do"—1 Corinthians 10:13. But (a) in "hiding place" situations (Nazi demanding to know if Corrie ten Boom has Jews hidden in the house), neither lying nor sacrificing human life is the "right thing to do" (remember that Jesus classifies lying as devilish—John 8:44), and (b) the temptation which we need never give in to (1 Cor. 10:13) is the temptation of *irresponsibility*—of not bothering to go through the agonizing process of choosing the lesser of evils. (3) Reformation ethics "would render the sinlessness of Christ either impossible or meaningless." But to be true man, Christ neither had to have every particular human experience (He never experienced old age, for

example) nor had to experience every particular human temptation (He was never in the military, nor was He apparently ever presented with the "hiding place" situation). To be "touched with the feeling of our infirmities" and "tempted in all points like as we are, yet without sin" (Heb. 4:15) requires *qualitative*, not quantitative, identification with fallen mankind. God was incarnate "in the fullness of time" (Gal. 4:4): doubtless one aspect of God's choice of time and place was to insure that during His sojourn on earth He would not have to choose even a lesser evil; and His omniscience (except as to the hour of the Second Coming) while in the earthly state gave Him the knowledge totally to avoid ethically compromising choices. See Erwin Lutzer, *The Morality Gap* (Chicago: Moody, 1972), especially pp. 111–12; and cf. below, n. 376.

348 Montgomery, in *Situation Ethics—True or False* (op. cit. in n. 308 above), p. 83.

349 See chap. 3, my discussion of the problems involved in defining human rights.

350 Shestack, op. cit. (in n. 94 above), p. 76, n. 24. Note that biblical revelation achieves the link-up between morals and rights which is so vital to any philosophy of human rights, but which necessarily eludes secular thinking in the field (see Frey's position, as discussed above in chap. 5, text at nn. 176–77).

351 See the citations in n. 87 above.

352 Montgomery, *The Shaping of America* (op. cit. in n. 79 above), p. 154 (see the entire discussion of this issue on pp. 152–58).

353 Cf. Nelson Keener's unfortunate article title, "To Obey Is Better Than to Evangelize," *Fundamentalist Journal* 3:4 (April 1984): 66.

354 Montgomery, *The Shaping of America* (op. cit. in n. 79 above), p. 157.

355 Roland de Pury, *Evangile et droits de l'homme* (Geneva: Labor et Fides, 1981), p. 266. De Pury here paraphrases Matthew 25:31–46.

356 Archibald Cox, *The Role of the Supreme Court in American Government* (New York: Oxford University Press, 1976), p. 61.

357 Wu, op. cit. (in n. 67 above), p. 63.

358 Anthony D'Amato, "The Conflict between Legal and Moral Obligation: The 'Bad Samaritan' Paradigm," in his *Jurisprudence: A Descriptive and Normative Analysis of Law* (op. cit. in n. 162 above), pp. 287–303.

359 See above, chap. 2, text at n. 56, and the citations in that note.

360 Hugo Grotius, *The Law of War and Peace,* trans. Francis W. Kelsey, reprint ed. (Indianapolis: Bobbs-Merrill, 1925), Prolegomena, para. 42, p. 24.

361 This is the thesis of the two volumes edited by Dominican Robert Campbell: *Spectrum of Protestant Beliefs* (Milwaukee: Bruce, 1968), to which the present writer was a major contributor; and *Spectrum of Catholic Attitudes* (Milwaukee: Bruce, 1969).

362 See above, chap. 7, text at n. 322.

363 *Ecumenical Review* 27:2 (April 1975): 93–146; the essay by David Jenkins is particularly agonizing.

364 John B. Cobb, Jr., *A Christian Natural Theology: Based on the Thought of Alfred North Whitehead* (Philadelphia: Westminster, 1965); Norman Pitten-

ger, *Process Thought and Christian Faith* (New York: Macmillan, 1968); and cf. Stanley T. Sutphin, *Options in Contemporary Theology* (Washington, D.C.: University Press of America, 1977), pp. 69–102.

[365] E. R. Baltazar, "Teilhard de Chardin: A Philosophy of Procession," in *New Theology No. 2,* ed. Martin E. Marty and Dean G. Peerman (New York: Macmillan, 1965), pp. 134–50; Jürgen Moltmann, *The Theology of Hope* (New York: Harper, 1967).

[366] Harry K. Wells, *Process and Unreality* (New York: King's Crown, 1950). Whitehead's seminal work was titled, *Process and Reality.*

[367] Bertrand Russell, *A History of Western Philosophy* (New York: Simon and Schuster, 1945), pp. 731–46.

[368] Alan Gragg, *Charles Hartshorne* (Waco, Tex.: Word, 1973), p. 55.

[369] At McMaster University, Canada, I debated the Bishop a year before his death; my presentation at that debate appears as the title essay in my *Suicide of Christian Theology* (op. cit. in n. 183 above), pp. 17–46; cf. in the same volume my analysis of the Bishop's theology and ethics, pp. 47–61, and, on pp. 231–32, my review of his book *What Is This Treasure.*

[370] James A. Pike, *Beyond the Law* (Garden City, N.Y.: Doubleday, 1963), p. xii.

[371] Ibid., pp. 14–15.

[372] Joseph Fletcher, *Situation Ethics* (Philadelphia: Westminster, 1966) and *Moral Responsibility* (Philadelphia: Westminster, 1967).

[373] I have referred earlier to the fallacious notion that the end justifies the means—a supposition that Fletcherian situationism shares with Marxism-Leninism; see nn. 165 and 308, and corresponding text passages.

[374] Fletcher and Montgomery, *Situation Ethics—True or False* (op. cit. in n. 308 above).

[375] "Joseph Fletcher, the theologian whose advocacy of 'situation ethics' created a stir among Christians some years ago, is even more explicit in saying that decisions to treat disabled infants should be based on estimates of their future quality of life. There is, he says, no point in prolonging the life of an infant who will end up spending all his or her days in an institutional 'warehouse' for the mentally or physically handicapped"—Peter Singer, review of *Selective Nontreatment of Handicapped Newborns. Moral Dilemmas in Neonatal Medicine* by Robert F. Weir, *Los Angeles Daily Journal,* 19 October 1984, p. 16.

[376] It should not be necessary to point up the radical contrast between the classical Reformation lesser-of-evils ethical principle and situationism. The latter operates (or thinks it operates) with no principles at all, love being a motive and not a principle, so there is never a question of conflicting absolutes. One cannot have conflicting absolutes if there are no absolutes (or even if there is but a single absolute)! Reformation ethics, however, so firmly holds to absolute principles that it is regretfully willing to admit that they may come into genuine conflict in a sinful world. Choosing the lesser of evils never exonerates the sinner from judgment—unlike Fletcherian "love," which, together with the notion that the end justifies the means, serves as a device to get the sinner off scot-free. Cf. above, n. 347.

[377] Maritain, op. cit. (in n. 229 above), pp. 67–68. His last book, *The Peasant of the Garonne,* trans. Michael Cuddihy and Elizabeth Hughes (New York: Macmillan, 1969) contains a devastating indictment of liberal theology.

[378] Wolfgang Huber and Heinz Eduard Tödt, *Menschenrechte—Perspecktiven einer menschlichen Welt* (Stuttgart: Kreuz Verlag, 1977), pp. 64–73.

[379] Lienhard, "Protestantism and Human Rights" (op. cit. in n. 8 above), pp. 30–31.

[380] For motif-analysis of theological positions, see Montgomery, "Evangelical Unity and Contemporary Ecumenicity" (dealing with Eastern Orthodoxy, Roman Catholicism, and Evangelicalism), in his *Ecumenicity, Evangelicals, and Rome* (op. cit. in n. 342 above), pp. 13–44.

[381] See the references in nn. 76 and 77 above.

[382] *RES Testimony on Human Rights* (op. cit. in n. 78 above), pp. 73–74.

[383] See above, text corresponding to nn. 143–45 and 236–40, for the problems with natural law thinking.

[384] Peter Putnam, "A Critique of Liberation Theology," unpublished M.A. thesis, Simon Greenleaf School of Law, 1984. Cf. Montgomery, *Ecumenicity, Evangelicals, and Rome* (op. cit. in n. 342 above), pp. 73–107.

[385] Cassin, "Religions et droits de l'homme" (op. cit. in n. 221 above), p. 101. Cf. O. Frederick Nolde, *Free and Equal: Human Rights in Ecumenical Perspective* (Geneva: World Council of Churches, 1968), with introduction by Charles H. Malik.

[386] Lienhard, "Protestantism and Human Rights" (op. cit. in n. 8 above), p. 24. On Luther and human rights, see the references in n. 231 above.

[387] Montgomery, *Law & Gospel* (op. cit. in n. 247 above), pp. 5–10. See also Montgomery, *Crisis in Lutheran Theology* (op. cit. in n. 306 above), *passim,* and *In Defense of Martin Luther* (op. cit. in n. 276 above), *passim.*

[388] See Paul Althaus, *The Ethics of Martin Luther,* trans. Robert C. Schultz (Philadelphia: Fortress, 1972), pp. 43–82, 143–54; William H. Lazareth, "Luther's 'Two Kingdoms' Ethic Reconsidered," in *Christian Social Ethics in a Changing World,* ed. John C. Bennett (New York: Association, 1966); and William H. Lazareth, "Luther on Civil Righteousness and Natural Law," in *The Church, Mysticism, Sanctification and the Natural in Luther's Thought,* ed. Ivar Asheim (Philadelphia: Fortress, 1967).

[389] Carl E. Braaten, "Toward an Ecumenical Theology of Human Rights," in *How Christian Are Human Rights?* ed. Lorenz (op. cit. in n. 78 above), p. 48. See also Jorg Baur, et al., *Zum Thema Menschenrechte* (Stuttgart: Calwer, 1977).

[390] See, e.g., *RES Testimony on Human Rights* (op. cit. in n. 78 above), pp. 40–43.

[391] Althaus, op. cit. (in n. 388 above), pp. 79–80.

[392] George W. Forell, *Faith Active in Love: An Investigation of the Principles Underlying Luther's Social Ethics* (Minneapolis: Augsburg, 1959).

[393] Cf. John Warwick Montgomery, "Millennium," *International Standard Bible Encyclopedia,* rev. ed., vol. 3 (Grand Rapids: Eerdmans, 1985); and Montgomery, "The Millennium," in *Dreams, Visions and Oracles,* ed. Carl E. Amerding and W. Ward Gasque (Grand Rapids: Baker, 1977), pp. 175–85.

[394] Werner Elert, *The Christian Ethos,* trans. Carl J. Schindler (Philadelphia: Muhlenberg, 1957).

[395] Luther, *Weimer Ausgabe* 11, 259, 8ff.

[396] Lienhard, "Luther and Human Rights," in *A Lutheran Reader on Human Rights*, ed. Lissner and Sovik (op. cit. in n. 231 above), p. 70.

[397] Luther's distinction between foregoing one's own rights and defending the rights of others ties to his harmonization of the Sermon on the Mount with such passages as 1 Timothy 5:8, requiring the believer to care for others. Luther saw that in the Sermon on the Mount Jesus was not setting forth a plan to perfect society (as certain Calvinists and many religious liberals would later claim), but was showing each person, as a single individual, how far short he falls when measured by God's ideal standards—and therefore how much he needs the salvation Jesus came to earth to provide. The moment other persons besides the individual believer enter the picture, the Christian must take their interests into account (and not, for example, give away his purse to the thief, so as to reduce his own children to starvation).

[398] Gordon Spykman, "Toward a Biblical View of 'Human Rights,'" *RES Theological Forum* 7:1 (December 1979): 1–2, 10–11. Space forbids us from extending this discussion of the Calvinist theme of "offices" into the complexities of Dooyeweerdian "sphere sovereignty" (cf. Marshall and Vanderkloet, *Foundations of Human Rights* [op. cit. in n. 80 above], pp. 14–15). Doubtless we would all agree theologically with Vanderkloet when he asserts, "The state must respect the independence, internal order and affairs of the family, the school, the business enterprise, the church, and the labour union, etc." But such "respect" can only be achieved if Christians can produce and justify a reliable revelation from God defining the proper boundaries and interrelationships of these spheres of life. Unhappily, Dooyeweerd's philosophy falls down at precisely this point: it suffers from (a) epistemological presuppositionalism, and (b) a critical stance vis-à-vis the verbal trustworthiness of biblical revelation; see Montgomery, *Faith Founded on Fact* (op. cit. in n. 137 above), pp. 69, 116–17, 159–60; and Montgomery, *Where Is History Going?* (op. cit. in n. 233 above), pp. 156–57.

[399] Karl Barth, "The Christian Community and the Civil Community," in his *Community, State, and Church: Three Essays,* ed. Will Herberg (Garden City, N.Y.: Doubleday, Anchor Books, 1960), especially sec. 33, pp. 186–87; and Karl Barth, *Church Dogmatics,* vol. 4/2, ed. G. W. Bromiley and T. F. Torrance (Edinburgh: T. & T. Clark, 1958), pp. 719–26. Lutherans, unlike Calvinists, maintain that there is no normative order of church government (either Presbyterian or Episcopal) set forth in Scripture; in the Lutheran view, therefore, the Calvinist position dangerously confuses Law and Gospel. Of course Lutherans agree with Barth that ethically the church should be a light to the secular world.

[400] Jürgen Moltmann, "A Definitive Study Paper," in *Christian Declaration on Human Rights,* ed. Miller (op. cit. in n. 78 above), p. 131. See also Moltmann's "Original Study Paper: A Theological Basis of Human Rights and of the Liberation of Human Beings," ibid., especially pp. 31–32.

401 Jürgen Moltmann, "Christian Faith and Human Rights," in *How Christian Are Human Rights?* ed. Lorenz (op. cit. in n. 78 above), p. 21. Moltmann's essay was originally published in *Understanding Human Rights,* ed. Alan Falconer (Dublin: Irish School of Ecumenics, 1980).

402 *RES Theological Forum* 7:1 (December 1979): 12.

403 Scheuner, op. cit. (in n. 334 above), p. 392.

404 See above, the citations in n. 243.

405 *RES Testimony on Human Rights* (op. cit. in n. 78 above), p. 25.

406 Pagels, op. cit. (in n. 193 above), p. 4.

407 H. D. McDonald, *The Christian View of Man* (London: Marshall, Morgan & Scott, 1981), p. 2.

408 Donald M. MacKay, *Human Science and Human Dignity* (London: Hodder and Stoughton, 1979), pp. 114–15. Cf. Pico of Mirandola's "Oration on the Dignity of Man"; and John Warwick Montgomery, "Eros and Agape in Pico of Mirandola," in his *The Suicide of Christian Theology* (op. cit. in n. 183 above), pp. 404–22.

409 Lienhard, "Protestantism and Human Rights" (op. cit. in n. 8 above), p. 32.

410 R. C. Sproul, *In Search of Dignity* (Ventura, Calif.: Regal, 1983), pp. 98–99.

411 See above, chap. 3, text at nn. 111–19.

412 Herbert T. Krimmel and Martin J. Foley, "Abortion and Human Life: A Christian Perspective," *Simon Greenleaf Law Review* 5 (1985–86). Cf. also the citations in n. 56 above.

413 Tooley, op. cit. (in n. 116 above), p. 421.

414 Epistle 262.1. On the Orthodox Eastern church and human rights, see Stanley S. Harakas, "Human Rights: An Eastern Orthodox Perspective," *Journal of Ecumenical Studies* 19:3 (Summer 1982): 13–24; Constantin Voicu, "Romanian Orthodox Theology and Human Rights," in *How Christian Are Human Rights?* ed. Lorenz (op. cit. in n. 78 above), pp. 67–73; and *RES Testimony on Human Rights* (op. cit. in n. 78 above), pp. 36–39. Eastern Orthodoxy's Caesaropapism has, over long centuries, blunted a prophetic witness, resulting in ideological accommodation to whatever government is in power and a quietism vis-à-vis human rights. Theologically, a contributing factor is surely Orthodoxy's biblically doubtful Holy Spirit mysticism: see Montgomery, "Evangelical Unity and Contemporary Ecumenicity" (op. cit. in n. 380 above), especially pp. 25–32.

415 McDonald, op. cit. (in n. 407 above), pp. 42–43. On p. 37 McDonald observes that the Genesis account of creation gives "singular honour to both man and woman alike, suggesting that at the deeper level of mutual confrontation as equals with each other and before God they attain their chiefest good and highest glory."

416 See chap. 2, text at n. 30.

417 See the text corresponding to n. 55.

418 Christopher J. H. Wright, *Human Rights: A Study in Biblical Themes* (Bramcote, Notts, England: Grove Books, 1979), pp. 11–12.

419 Théo Tschuy, "L'action protestante dans la mise en oeuvre des droits de l'homme," in *Christianisme et droits de l'homme,* ed. Hirsch (op. cit. in n. 8 above), p. 223.

420 Ibid.

421 Cf. Maria Borucka-Arctowa, "The Conception of Legal Consciousness As a New Approach to the Problems of Natural Law," in *Contemporary Conceptions of Law,* ed. Adam Łopatka (Warsaw: Polish Academy of Sciences/Institute of State and Law, 1979), especially pp. 156–57, 166–67.

422 Wright, op. cit. (in note 417 above), pp. 13–16.

423 Ibid.

424 See above, the conclusion of chap. 5 (the text at n. 240).

425 Henri Bergson, *The Two Sources of Morality and Religion,* trans. R. Ashley Audra and Cloudesley Brereton (Garden City, N.Y.: Doubleday, Anchor Books, 1956), p. 282.

426 See above, chap. 2, the text at n. 81.

427 See above, chap. 4, *passim,* and the chart on p. 183.

428 See chap. 5, text corresponding to n. 197.

429 Herbert McClosky and Alida Brill, *Dimensions of Tolerance: What Americans Believe about Civil Liberties* (New York: Russell Sage Foundation/Basic Books, 1983); reviewed by Stanford constitutional law professor Paul Brest in *The Los Angeles Daily Journal,* 13 January 1984, p. 14.

430 E.g., John McLachlan, *Human Rights in Retrospect and Reality: The Essex Hall Lecture for 1968* (London: Lindsey Press, 1968), especially pp. 20–21.

431 Barth, "The Christian Community and the Civil Community" (op. cit. in n. 399 above), sec. 15, p. 172.

432 De Pury, op. cit. (in n. 355 above), pp. 261–62.

433 Coste, op. cit. (in n. 76 above), p. 79.

434 Lienhard, "Protestantism and Human Rights" (op. cit. in n. 8 above), p. 33. Lienhard here summarizes Huber and Tödt, op. cit. (in note 378 above).

435 Scheuner, op. cit. (in n. 334 above), p. 380.

436 Sydney Hall Evans, "Christianity and Human Rights," in *An Introduction to the Study of Human Rights,* ed. Sir Francis Vallat (London: Europa Publications, 1971), p. 15. ("The series of lectures was largely inspired by the purposes of the International Institute of Human Rights [René Cassin Foundation] established at Strasbourg in 1969.")

437 Peter Saladin, "Christianity and Human Rights: A Jurist's Reflections," in *How Christian Are Human Rights?* ed. Lorenz (op. cit. in n. 78 above), pp. 29–30.

438 First Corinthians 3:11.

439 The quotations concerning René Cassin are taken from Marc Agi, *René Cassin, fantassin des droits de l'homme* (Paris: Plon, 1979), pp. 284–85.

440 Ibid., pp. 294–97; see also Cassin's essay as cited in n. 23 above.

For Further Reading

HUMAN RIGHTS PROTECTIONS TODAY

Hannum, Hurst (ed.). **Guide to International Human Rights Practice.** London: Macmillan, 1984.

Similar in coverage and recency to Meron's volumes but less detailed. The ideal vade mecum *for the legal practitioner and serious human rights activist.*

International Institute of Human Rights. **Résumés (*Recueils*) des Cours.** Strasbourg, France: Institut International des Droits de l'Homme. Vol. I (1970) to date.

The annual summary of lectures presented in the summer study sessions at the most prestigious center of human rights teaching in the world. Roughly half of the summaries are in English, half in French. They are prepared by the distinguished guest lecturers themselves and provide the very best means of keeping current on what is happening in this developing field.

Meron, Theodor (ed.). **Human Rights in International Law: Legal and Policy Issues.** Oxford: Clarendon, 1984. 2 vols.

The very best and most up-to-date academic survey of the entire field of the international and comparative law of human rights, with excellent bibliographies and teaching suggestions. Includes chapters on domestic legal protections in the United States, humanitarian law, and the contributions of nongovernmental organizations.

Sieghart, Paul. **The Lawful Rights of Mankind: An Introduction to the International Legal Code of Human Rights.** Oxford: Oxford University Press, 1985.

A well-written survey, whose thesis is that international law now provides a "code" of human rights. Little attention to the underlying philosophical issues, but a polished introduction to the development of existing legal protections.

PHILOSOPHICAL PROBLEMS

Dworkin, Ronald. **Taking Rights Seriously.** London: Duckworth, 1977.

H. L. A. Hart's successor as professor of jurisprudence at Oxford sets forth, in this influential book of essays, a philosophy of law and a theory of human rights developed both as an extension of and as a corrective to the basic themes of legal realism/legal positivism.

Finnis, John. **Natural Law and Natural Rights.** Oxford: Clarendon, 1980.

The most impressive contemporary philosophical effort to rehabilitate natural law theory.

Gewirth, Alan, **Human Rights: Essays on Justification and Applications.** Chicago: University of Chicago Press, 1982.

Gewirth has developed (like Rawls, on a neo-Kantian base) "one of the most sophisticated and powerful contemporary theories of human rights"—Human Rights Quarterly.

McDougal, Myres S., Lasswell, Harold D., and Chen, Lung-chu. **Human Rights and World Public Order: The Basic Policies of an International Law of Human Dignity.** New Haven, Conn.: Yale University Press, 1980.

The bible of "policy-orientated" human rights theory. Provides helpful insights and vast quantities of empirical and bibliographical data useful even to those who disagree with the authors' central philosophical thesis.

Montgomery, John Warwick. "The Marxist Approach to Human Rights: Analysis & Critique." **Simon Greenleaf Law Review**, 3 (1983–84).

A book-length evaluation of the Marxist world-view, its philosophy of law, and its theory of human rights—with a transcendental corrective. The author's thesis for the degree of M.Phil. in Law at the University of Essex, England.

Rawls, John. **A Theory of Justice.** Oxford: Oxford University Press, 1973.

By all odds the single most influential statement of moral philosophy and social ethics in our time.

Rosenbaum, Alan S. (ed.). **The Philosophy of Human Rights: International Perspectives.** Westport, Conn.: Greenwood, 1980.

A useful collection of essays reflecting a variety of philosophical and religious viewpoints. The editor's introductory survey of human rights in the history of ideas is particularly valuable.

Shestack, Jerome J. "The Jurisprudence of Human Rights" in Theodor Meron (ed.)., **Human Rights in International Law: Legal and Policy Issues.** Oxford: Clarendon, 1984. Vol. 1, pp. 69–113.

Indispensable overview of the issues, competing viewpoints, and literature.

White, Alan R. **Rights.** Oxford: Clarendon, 1984.

The clearest thinking to date on the meaning *of the concept of rights. Does not treat the more difficult question of the* justification *of rights.*

Wittgenstein, Ludwig. "A Lecture on Ethics." **Philosophical Review**, 74 (January 1965).

Classic, posthumously published statement of the impossibility of establishing absolute values nontranscendentally; by the greatest name in the twentieth-century analytical philosophy movement.

THE CHRISTIAN SOLUTION

Friedrich, Carl J. **Transcendent Justice: The Religious Dimension of Constitutionalism.** Durham, N.C.: Duke University Press, 1964.

Friedrich holds dual appointments as Eaton professor of the science of government at Harvard and professor of political science at Heidelberg; he is the author of such standard works as The Philosophy of Law in Historical Perspective. *He argues in* Transcendent Justice *that constitutionalism came into being in the West in order "to protect the* self *in its dignity and worth" and that this preoccupation with the paramount worth of persons sprang not from pagan antiquity but from Christian beliefs.*

Lienhard, Marc. "Protestantism and Human Rights." **Human Rights Teaching** [UNESCO]. 2:1 (1981).

This issue of Human Rights Teaching *features a series of articles on the "Place of Human Rights in Different Religious Perspectives," of which Lienhard's contribution is by far the strongest. Lienhard is François Wendel's successor as professor of church history at the Protestant Theological Faculty of the University of Strasbourg. Lienhard's treatment of Luther on human rights should not be missed:* "Luther et les droits de l'homme," Revue d'Histoire et de Philosophie Religieuses *54:1 (1974): 17–29 English translation in* A Lutheran Reader on Human Rights, *ed. Jørgen Lissner and Arne Sovik:* LWF Report *1–2 [September 1978]: 66–80); see also Lienhard's* Luther: Witness to Jesus Christ, *trans. E. H. Robertson (Minneapolis: Augsburg, 1982).*

Miller, Allen O. (ed.) **A Christian Declaration on Human Rights: Theological Studies of the World Alliance of Reformed Churches.** Grand Rapids: Eerdmans, 1977.

Uneven in theological quality, ranging from orthodox in the tradition of the Reformers (Daniel Vidal's essay) to liberal-secular (Jürgen Moltmann's "original" and "definitive" study papers). Emphasis on human rights in terms of such themes as "liberation" and "indigenous theology."

Montgomery, John Warwick. **The Law Above the Law: Why the Law Needs Biblical Foundations/How Legal Thought Supports Christian Truth.** Including Greenleaf's "Testimony of the Evangelists." Minneapolis: Bethany, 1975.

______. **Law & Gospel: A Study in Jurisprudence.** Oak Park, Ill.: Christian Legal Society, 1978.

———. **The Shaping of America: A True Description of the American Character, both Good and Bad, and the Possibilities of Recovering a National Vision Before the People Perish.** Minneapolis: Bethany, 1976.

——— (ed.). **Jurisprudence: A Book of Readings.** Strasbourg, France: International Scholarly Publisher, 1980. (Available in the United States from Simon Greenleaf School of Law, Anaheim, California.)

RES Testimony on Human Rights. Grand Rapids: Reformed Ecumenical Synod, 1983.

The most ambitious attempt to arrive at a theology of human rights from a generally biblical viewpoint yet produced within (broad-church) Evangelicalism. The doctrinal perspective is Calvinist-Reformed.

The Simon Greenleaf Law Review. A Scholarly Forum of Opinion Interrelating Law, Theology & Human Rights. Anaheim, California, and Strasbourg, France: The Simon Greenleaf School of Law. Vol. 1 (1981–82) to date.

Index of Persons

Index of Subjects